Politics, Participation, and Poverty
Development Through Self-Help in Kenya

DATE DUE

Westview Special Studies

The concept of Westview Special Studies is a response to the continuing crisis in academic and informational publishing. Library budgets are being diverted from the purchase of books and used for data banks, computers, micromedia, and other methods of information retrieval. Interlibrary loan structures further reduce the edition sizes required to satisfy the needs of the scholarly community. Economic pressures on university presses and the few private scholarly publishing companies have greatly limited the capacity of the industry to properly serve the academic and research communities. As a result, many manuscripts dealing with important subjects, often representing the highest level of scholarship, are no longer economically viable publishing projects--or, if accepted for publication, are typically subject to lead times ranging from one to three years.

Westview Special Studies are our practical solution to the problem. As always, the selection criteria include the importance of the subject, the work's contribution to scholarship, its insight, originality of thought, and excellence of exposition. We accept manuscripts in camera-ready form, typed, set, or word processed according to specifications laid out in our comprehensive manual, which contains straightforward instructions and sample pages. The responsibility for editing and proofreading lies with the author or sponsoring institution, but our editorial staff is always available to answer questions and provide guidance.

The result is a book printed on acid-free paper and bound in sturdy, library-quality soft covers. We manufacture these books ourselves using equipment that does not require a lengthy make-ready process and that allows us to publish first editions of 300 to 1000 copies and to reprint even smaller quantities as needed. Thus, we can produce Special Studies quickly and can keep even very specialized books in print as long as there is a demand for them.

About the Book and Author

Focusing on the distribution of benefits in relation to class, ethnicity, and gender, this book explores the methods by which the rural poor can organize themselves to participate in economic and social development and examines the roles that self-help organizations play in the political economy of Kenya. Dr. Thomas looks at the competition for power and scarce resources, the impact on emerging patterns of stratification, and the ideological role of self-help in state formation.

Self-help has become an integral part of Kenya's political and economic life. From the politician's point of view, success in electoral politics is linked to project effectiveness in the home district. For the community, a premium is placed on organizational capacity since those with initiative can gain access to resources available primarily through the political process. By placing the responsibility for initiating development on the community, self-help projects have become a buffer between the central government and the demands of a sensitized rural public. Dr. Thomas looks at how self-help has served special political interests, has been used to legitimize and justify the political and economic systems of post-colonial Kenya, and has blurred class differences while permitting great inequitites. Assessing the capacity of this development approach to lead to structural change, Dr. Thomas asks if Kenya's self-help program has led to a more equitable distribution of benefits or if it only encourages and strengthens existing regional and class differences.

Barbara P. Thomas is assistant professor and director of the Teaching Program in International Development and Social Change at Clark University. She spent ten years living in various countries in Africa and Asia, including three years in Kenya.

Politics, Participation, and Poverty
Development Through Self-Help in Kenya

Barbara P. Thomas

Westview Press / Boulder and London

Westview Special Studies in Social, Political, and Economic Development

Published in 1985 in the United States of America by Westview
Press, Inc.; Frederick A. Praeger, Publisher; 5500 Central Avenue,
Boulder, Colorado 80301

Library of Congress Cataloging in Publication Data
Includes bibliographical references and index.
    1. Community development--Kenya. 2. Self-help groups--Kenya.
3. Kenya--Economic conditions--1963- . 4. Kenya--Politics and
government--1978-   . I. Title.
HN793.Z9C674 1985   307'.14'096762   85-10492
ISBN 0-8133-7068-X

Composition for this book was provided by the author
Printed and bound in the United States of America

10 9 8 7 6 5 4 3 2

To my mother, Virginia, who has always been an inspiration and support in my academic endeavors, as well as a lively companion whether on an elephant in Jaipur, on a steamer navigating the Buri Ganga, on safari in Masai Mara, or on her own back porch in Washington, D.C.

Contents

Tables

Figures and Maps

Preface

How can the rural poor organize themselves to participate in economic and social development? This book examines the roles of self-help organizations and community projects in the political economy of Kenya. Locally organized, cooperative action on community projects, known as Harambee in Kenya, has become an integral part of Kenya's political and economic life. From the politician's point of view, success in electoral politics is linked to project effectiveness in the home district. For the community, a premium is placed on organizational capacity since those communities which exercise self-help initiative can gain access to resources available primarily through the political process.

This study looks at the competition through self-help for power and scarce resources, at the effect of group activity on household economic behavior, and at the contribution of these organizations to building rural infrastructure. It focuses on the impact of self-help on emerging patterns of stratification and on the ideological role of self-help in state formation. It addresses whether Harambee as an approach to development can lead to structural change and to a more equitable distribution of national resources, or if it simply encourages and strengthens existing regional, class, ethnic or gender differences.

As a student of politics, I have long been interested in the dynamics of political and economic change, particularly in the Third World. My first foray into this arena was a senior honor's thesis at Bryn Mawr College in which I investigated politics in three Indian states, Kerala, West Bengal and Andhra Pradesh. Shortly thereafter living in Bangladesh, Sri Lanka, and in the Philippines provided me with an opportunity to explore at the grass-roots level some of the issues and concepts first encountered in the college classroom. Subsequent graduate work in comparative politics at Brandeis University led to a more specific focus on rural development, peasant or small farmer organiza-

tion, women's socio-economic roles, and the relationship between the state and local communities. Three
years' residence in Kenya, from 1976 to 1979, during
which I was associated with the Institute for Development Studies at the University of Nairobi, offered me
an opportunity to explore some of these issues in an
African setting.

Although the specific characteristics of rural
Kenya are vastly different from those of Bangladesh,
India or Sri Lanka, fundamental human needs and concerns are shared across continents. In rural Kenya, as
in rural Bangladesh or Sri Lanka, people are concerned
about improving their agricultural production, finding
new economic opportunities, securing health and education, meeting their basic requirements for food, clothing and shelter, and assuring a safe and prosperous
future for their children. Yet in Kenya, as in many
countries throughout the world, rural poverty persists
and rural people have great difficulty gaining access
to the nation's resources and sharing in its wealth.
This book examines one approach whereby rural communities in Kenya organize themselves to meet some of their
needs and to address some of their problems. What can
be learned from this effort to bring about rural change
in Kenya? What in their experience might be relevant
to other nations where rural communities seek both to
improve their well being and to increase their share of
national resources?

I begin with a discussion of some of the key characteristics of peasant and elite behavior, present the
Kenyan self-help model, and establish a framework for
considering Harambee in Kenya. I then consider a model
of political behavior in Kenya and place Harambee within the framework of that model. The latter part of the
book looks at the specific findings of the research
from the six communities investigated, and draws on
district level and national data as well. In particular, I address questions pertaining to self-help's impact on the development of rural infrastructure, on
equity issues both within local communities and between
communities, and on local participation. The study relates findings at the local-level to the broad issues
involved: the place of self-help in the context of
Kenyan politics, its relation to both national and
local socio-economic objectives, and its utility both
as an approach to development and as a form of organization enabling the rural poor to share in the benefits of development. Finally, the book reflects on
some of the insights offered by Kenya's experience with
decentralized self-help development efforts, and some
of the lessons which might be relevant to other countries.

Barbara P. Thomas

Acknowledgments

Many friends and colleagues have generously offered support and advice to me during the course of this project. I am grateful to all of them. I am appreciative of the Kenyans whose lively interest, friendliness, and keen observations made this project an enjoyable experience. In particular, Esther Keli, Benson Kibutu, Enid Miriti and Rose Muguchu, offered valuable assistance. My student research assistants in each district worked carefully and conscientiously, and the residents of each of the locations in which we investigated Harambee efforts were not only hospitable, but were also willing to share their knowledge and their viewpoints.

In addition, colleagues at the Institute for Development Studies in Nairobi, at Brandeis University, and at Clark University have shared my interest in local development efforts. I appreciate the support, suggestions and insights of many, including Leonard Berry, David Brokensha, Richard Ford, Judith Geist, Frank Holmquist, Edmond Keller, Ruth Morgenthau and Norman Uphoff. I am grateful to Clark University for a grant from the Mellon Fund to assist with manuscript preparation and to Karen Shepardson for her excellent assistance finalizing the manuscript for publication. To my children, Gwen, Patricia, and Stephen, go my thanks for weathering the demands of field trip and typewriter, and to my husband, John, my deepest thanks for the inspiration he has provided and the invaluable insights he has shared not only in regard to this project, but in many other ways as well, over the years.

B.P.T.

I
Organizing the
Rural Disadvantaged

> We must organize ourselves for self-help projects.
> We must look ahead and think about our future.
>   Assistant Chief
>   Soin Location

CRITICAL ISSUES

How can the rural poor organize themselves to participate in economic and social development and to
assure themselves an equitable share of its benefits?
This question addresses one of the most intractable
problems of modern times: the persistence of widespread rural poverty throughout much of the Third
World. The World Development Report, 1980 of the World
Bank states that more than 780 million people in developing countries live in absolute poverty. Of these
three-fourths are in the rural areas of Africa, Asia
and Latin America.[1] Moreover, The World Development
Report, 1983 indicates that the per capita income of
low-income countries in Africa is likely to be lower by
the end of the 1980's than it was in 1960, and The
World Development, 1984 suggests that in sub-Saharan
Africa the number of people living in poverty at the
end of the century is likely to increase by nearly 70
per cent over 1980 figures.[2]

In Rural Poverty

What underlies this rural poverty? Efforts to
find the answers are legion. Some analysts have con-
cluded that the causes are structural and originate in
the dependency relationships of many Third World
nations with developed countries and the consequent
draining of resources to more affluent nations. They
focus on international terms of trade, debt servicing,
capital flows, trade and protectionism, interest rates,
and energy costs.

2

Others have suggested that there has been an investment bias toward industrial growth and urban areas, despite the high proportion of the population involved in agriculture and resident in the rural areas. One analyst, Michael Lipton, suggests that in many countries agriculture has received much less investment than is warranted by its share of the national product and employment or by considerations of equality, and he concludes that neglect of the rural sector has perpetuated the poverty of many nations.[3]

Some have noted the difficulties in improving conditions for the rural poor given their limited resources and narrow economic base. Others have pointed out that rural development requires organizations as well as resources and that it is necessary to begin by building strong organizational structures. Some analysts have voiced concern about the mode of seeking development - national plans and centrally administered projects. Still others have emphasized political will, vested interests, and behavior of the elite as major causes of rural poverty. Whatever the cause or mix of causes, the inadequacies of many policies and programs for generating rural growth and development are apparent. Many economies have barely kept up with their rapid population growth. In some instances, large sums of money spent on rural development projects have yielded little improvement in welfare and productivity to the people who should have benefitted from them. Problems encountered in fostering economic and social change have often seemed insurmountable and progress in rural development minimal.

These difficulties have generated widespread concern about stagnation or deteriorating conditions in many areas around the world as well as interest in new approaches for fostering rural development. This interest has been directed toward decentralized development planning, toward local participation in planning and implementation, and toward the use of local institutions and organizations for development purposes. It is currently reflected in the focus of United Nations' organizations and donor agencies on extension services, bank credit and loans for small farmers, and improved marketing structures. Third World governments are modifying national plans to incorporate procedures for fostering rural participation in development planning and implementation, and donor agencies are establishing criteria for insuring local-level participation in their development programs.

In Organizing the Rural Poor

Although scholars may differ in regard to the underlying causes of development or underdevelopment,

most agree that development efforts to date have not
achieved notable success. The emphasis on large-scale
projects, centralized plans, and top-heavy bureaucracies has failed to improve the levels of productivity
and the quality of life for vast numbers of rural people. Other approaches and new initiatives are necessary. Among these is a fresh look at local-level organizations. Can local-level organizations contribute
to the development process? If so, in what ways? What
functions do they serve? What kinds of issues arise in
the process of using local organizations to foster development?

Some scholars have emphasized the central role of
local organizations. Hunter and Jiggins state that,
"The area of local participation and local decision is
the most critical in the whole development process."[4]
Analysts from Development Alternatives, a research and
consulting firm in Washington, D.C., have advised that
the keys to project success are small farmer involvement and resource commitment, which are most actively
generated through local organizations and groups.[5]

Local organizations may be defined as voluntary
associations or institutionalized groups in which membership is based on common interest and is attained
simply by joining.[6] There are many types, among them
cooperatives, credit societies, neighborhood or community development associations, water-sharing associations, or women's groups. They are accountable primarily to their members and work largely by consensus and
persuasion.

These local organizations can serve a variety of
functions. Four are particularly important in the context of development efforts. First, they are information channels or conduits, directing information, concerns, and opinions from individuals to the appropriate
authorities. The reverse flow is also important.
Organizations can effectively convey ideas and information from the government or other agencies to the individual household. As Uphoff points out, they help meet
the challenge of linking development efforts at
"higher" levels to the needs and capabilities of individuals and households.[7]

Second, local organizations can help mobilize resources for development purposes. These resources may
be in the form of labor, cash, or material, and they
may constitute a significant impetus to development
efforts. Without organizations these resources would
remain idle and unused.

Third, local organizations can mobilize their membership for collective action. This is usually in the
form of group activity in order to achieve a public
good and carries with it a range of concerns about the
illogic of collective action, the incentives for individuals to be "free riders" and the difficulties organ-

izations face in obtaining fair contributions from all
those who benefit from their goods and services. These
problems are noted particularly in situations in which
organizations are attempting to provide rural infrastructure and amenities.

Fourth, organizations can change power and resource allocations. As Chen has pointed out, there is
a fundamental relationship between the power structure
and the distribution of resources.[8] She suggests that
the rural poor do not participate effectively in shaping their environment because they are powerless.
Through organized, collective efforts, the rural poor
can begin to redress the disparities in power and in
the distribution of resources.

A number of issues arise in regard to local-level
organizations. These include issues of local control,
of commitment, of accountability, and of credibility.
They include questions pertaining to support systems,
to linkages with other organizations both horizontally
and vertically, and to the relative merits of traditional organizations or "modern" ones. They include
structural issues concerning the purpose, composition
and leadership of specific organizations.[9] If local
organizations constitute a critical ingredient in the
development process, it is necessary to build their
capacity to anticipate and influence change, solve
problems, implement decisions and act effectively within their environment. Thus, an underlying objective in
an analysis of the role of local-level organizations in
the development process, is to determine ways to
strengthen them.

In Understanding the Actors

Recent studies of peasant behavior offer useful
insights for interpreting local-level development in
Kenya.[10] Some examine the development of capitalism,
the commercialization of agrarian relations, the growth
of a centralizing state, and the response of peasants
to external forces impinging upon traditional village
life.[11] They suggest that traditional behavior has
been transformed by outside intrusions, most particularly in the form of external wage labor, commodity
marketing mechanisms, and involvement with cash. Some
observe that these changes are harmful to peasants, and
they stress issues of peasant insecurity and survival.
Others suggest that, in an environment characterized by
both competition and cooperation, peasants find ways to
benefit from these changes and pursue their own interests vigorously.[12]

Still other scholars suggest that the influence of
the market has been overemphasized in the African context.[13] They suggest that prevailing theories account

inadequately for peasant modes of production based on an "economy of affinity" in which familial and other communal ties are the basis for the organization of activities, decisionmaking and resource transfers. Peasant autonomy, rather than control by external institutions of market and state, is hindering rural change.

Understanding the impact of Western imperialism and capitalism on Kenya is critical. It is also important to consider conditions existing within Kenyan societies before their contact with the West. These conditions may be physical or environmental, they may be socio-political or economic. For example, Kenyan tribes responded to the arrival of settlers, in part, according to the existing economic system. The most important factor of production was land, the quality of which affected both the intensity of the colonial thrust and the response of the indigenous residents. Persons occupying highly productive land reacted differently from those occupying marginal or unproductive lands.

Population/land ratios also affected tribal response to the impact of colonialism. Among the Kikuyu in Central Kenya there was considerable population pressure which pre-dated the arrival of foreign settlers. Settler colonialism greatly aggravated this situation but did not initiate the adverse land/man relationship. Among the Kipsigis in Western Kenya, the land/man ratios were not a problem, and the Kipsigis were able to accommodate colonialism far more easily than were the Kikuyus.

Little work has been done on rural voluntary associations and the roles they play in providing the structures for adaptation to a cash economy and to a centralized state system.[14] Some analysts have suggested that the process of social mobilization and the increasing outward orientation of a village diminish the residents' involvement in traditional rural institutions and local-level self-help groups.[15] Evidence from Kenya suggests that it is important to look at indicators other than outward orientation to determine involvement in traditional institutions. These may include levels of communal solidarity and the nature and level of resources available to a community. Among the Kikuyu, the largest ethnic group in Kenya, for example, there is a high level of outward orientation, and there is a high level of involvement in self-help groups.

Scott suggests that rural voluntary associations are a response to "subsistence problems when other courses fail."[16] In Kenya this is not necessarily the case. Such groups are, in many areas, long-standing ways of organizing the factors of production and are utilized over time, regardless of the acuteness of subsistence needs. They allow people to seize hold of new

opportunities in ways which may be impossible or difficult for a farmer to do alone. In some instances, they
may be "re-active" institutions with a protective,
risk-diminishing function. In others, they may have
new functions related to opportunities offered in an
expanding socio-economic situation. They may also
simultaneously serve both functions. For example, they
may be attempting to deal with imperfect market structures in enterprising or imaginative ways.

Analysis of rural organizations in Kenya must consider the long-term structural conditions which have
led to their formation and evaluate their adaptability
in meeting new needs. It does not assume that they are
transitory phenomena which will disappear under the
impact of development. Such analysis must examine a
variety of issues concerning voluntary associations
including their relationship to an emerging class
structure, their roles as adaptive mechanisms and their
usefulness for reaffirming ethnic, village, or community concerns.

Drawing on economically derived models of socio-
economic change, many analysts observe the potential
for peasants, particularly landless peasants, to share
common interests and a common role in the organization
of the means of production at the bottom of the socio-
economic structure. They suggest that, to varying degrees depending on specific circumstances, peasants are
developing class consciousness through conflicts with
superior and more powerful classes over the distribution of economic rewards.

We would argue that in Kenya a class analysis must
be supplemented by consideration of other variables.
At the present time small farmers do not perceive themselves as members of a single class, nor do they perceive their interests as bound to a given class.
Ethnicity is of central importance. It interacts with
other interests in critical ways, often overshadowing
and dominating the nascent class concerns. Another important category in the Kenyan context is gender. Sex-
determined occupational structures cut across class and
family interests. In addition, the multiplicity of
roles, functions and loyalties engaged in by a typical
extended family complicates analysis. The diversifica-
tion of interests and of sources of income eludes the
simplicity of class analysis and necessitates inclusion
of other variables in the model of socio-economic
change. Class, ethnicity, regionalism, sex-
differentiated roles and a multiplicity of family functions must be unraveled in an effort to interpret and
understand the behavior of small farmers in Kenya.

THE KENYA MODEL: SELF-HELP AT THE GRASS ROOTS

A Definition

    This study examines one approach to organizing the rural poor in the context of local-level development in Kenya.   It focuses on self-help community projects and autonomous self-help organizations which are a tradition in parts of Kenya and are being encouraged and supported by the government.   The study is based on field research conducted in Kenya in 1978 and 1979.

    In Kenya, local self-help development efforts – Harambee – have been operating concurrently with centrally planned and implemented development programs since independence in 1963.   Harambee is the Swahili term for   "Let's pull together."   Harambee self-help consists of community members working collectively toward a common goal. Harambee takes two forms.   There are specific community-based development projects for which the community will mobilize on a short-term basis, and there are ongoing local self-help groups. The cooperative work on communal projects begins with a community initiative, often fostered by local Government officers, to meet a recognized local need by selecting, planning and implementing a community project or improvement.   Self-help emphasizes small-scale community concerns such as schools, health clinics, wells, cattle dips, community halls, roads, bridges, culverts, village polytechnics or fish ponds.   This form of community self-help is call "mobilized" because members of a community living within a fixed geographical boundary are "mobilized" to assist with the selected project.[17]   Such Harambee self-help involves local organization and leadership for making decisions, generating resources, and mobilizing community members in constructing or carrying out projects.

    This study also examines self-help groups which have been designated "autonomous" as opposed to "mobilized."   These groups are voluntary associations focused on one or more shared interests and possessing a voluntary membership ranging from ten to more than 200 persons.   Membership is usually defined by locality, sex, religious affiliation, ethnic group or clan.   These groups engage in a wide variety of activities characteristic of both support groups and income-sharing or income-generating associations.   They may be involved in providing agricultural assistance to members of the group, in poultry or pig raising, in loan sharing or in a variety of other activities and community services. Members are free to come and go as long as any commitments made upon becoming a member are honored.   Although these groups have a long tradition in some parts of Kenya, the Government has adopted a policy of encouraging their formation, and they are now spreading to areas where formalized groups have been uncommon.

There are indigenous values and customary social ties and obligations which legitimize community activity and which account, in part, for the unusual esprit which the Harambee effort has been able to arouse in Kenya. Among many of Kenya's ethnic groups, a tradition of mutual assistance and cooperative effort has existed on two levels. Small groups comprised of several families have helped each other on the land and with domestic tasks. Broad neighborhood, clan or community groups have organized themselves for projects or services of benefit to the community at large.

It was former President Kenyatta who, in the first months of independence, conceptually linked the traditional, village-level principles of Harambee with the broad national requirements for cooperative endeavor on the part of all citizens of the new nation. He first articulated the concept in May, 1963, when he used Harambee as a rallying cry for all Kenyans to work together as an independent people. Since that time the concept of Harambee, of all people working together to build a strong and prosperous Kenya, has become an important development theme and has emerged as the foremost symbol of national integration. It has also become an important part of Kenya's politics since independence. As rural communities have struggled to provide services and facilities, national and local elites have become deeply involved in Harambee self-help development efforts, catapulting Harambee to the center of the political process.

Varying Viewpoints on Harambee

Many Kenyans believe that Harambee self-help has contributed significantly to national development.[18] Their evaluations are based on what they perceive to be its achievements in enhancing productivity and rural welfare, as well as its contributions to national cohesion and rural solidarity. They believe that Harambee, an approach to development grounded in traditional social ties, obligations and commitments, has become a major vehicle for fostering national modernizing objectives at the local level. On the other hand, some question the usefulness of this approach, pointing out the problems which arise with locally-initiated projects and voicing concern that Harambee projects become political "footballs," tossed about in the changing winds of electoral politics and rising - or falling - political fortunes.

There has been a limited amount of research conducted on Harambee self-help in Kenya, and it has resulted in several differing interpretations of the nature and importance of this kind of development ef-

fort.   Analysts who   have focused   on Harambee can   be
divided into four categories. First, there are several
theorists who have attempted to link the Harambee movement with broad theoretical question concerning voluntarism and collective goods as well as historical
patterns of development and socio-economic change.[19]
Second, there are those who have investigated Harambee
specifically for its origins and role within the Kenyan
context.   This is the largest group of analysts.
Third, several analysts have chosen to concentrate on
specific types of Harambee projects such as secondary
schools or institutes of technology and to evaluate
these projects for their impact on development and on
various aspects of Kenyan society.[20]   Finally, several
analysts have investigated Harambee as a mode of development in order to assess this approach for policy purposes at the national level.   None of these analyses
investigates the Harambee approach within the context
of particular communities in order to assess its impact
over time upon the local residents.   Nor do they link
Harambee to the broad issues of equity, participation
and decentralization in order to test the validity of
current assumptions about rural development and local
organization.   Nevertheless, they do offer insights
into the nature of Harambee and evaluate performance of
specific kinds of projects.
     Of particular interest for this study are anal-
yses of the origins and role of Harambee within the
Kenyan context and analyses of Harambee as a mode of
development.   A review of these interpretations
provides a useful perspective for analyzing and interpreting data on self-help at the local level.   Among
analysts of Harambee who have examined its political,
social and ideological origins and implications is
Philip Mbithi.   He has been interested in problems of
rural stress and rural disintegration, particularly
under the impact of colonialism and modernization, and
he has emphasized the importance of Harambee in fostering social cohesion and solidarity.   Mbithi suggests
that the basic organizational principle behind self-
help activity is the traditionally sanctioned, informal, cooperative work group structure.[21]   "Tradition,"
says Mbithi, "forms the most important basis for the
legitimate use of power in a rural Kenyan setting."[22]
     Mbithi characterizes self-help groups as solidar-
ity groups permitting a local response to problems,
deprivations and frustrations while at the same time
showing individual commitment to national development
and fostering a sense of national solidarity.   Mbithi
perceives self-help as a useful tool of government
policy for invigorating, mobilizing and uniting rural
peoples.   He also sees it as a grass-roots movement, a
"collective self-reliant development effort born of the
frustration of the poor, marginal, non-elite popula-

tions," hence a common man's endeavor.[23] Evidence from
this study supports a perspective on Harambee which
differs from Mbithi's.   Specifically, this evidence
suggests that much Harambee activity derives from
inter-elite competition both at the national and local
level, as well as from the need for local leaders and
government officials to "produce" results. Rural residents have indeed responded, but the activists in the
locations studied have not usually been poor and marginal citizens as Mbithi suggests.

     In contrast to Mbithi's emphasis on Harambee's
roots in traditional forms of association, Ng'ethe suggests that there are many important differences between
the current practice of Harambee self-help and what
have been traditional methods of mutual support.[24]
While Mbithi explores traditional practices among the
Kamba, Ng'ethe examines mutual support systems among
the Kikuyu.   Differences among the traditions of the
two groups may, of course, account for the varying perspectives of the two analysts. The Kamba are known for
their strong tradition of communal work groups called
Mwethya.   Ng'ethe states that the organizational base
for self-help among the Kikuyu in the pre-colonial
period was the clan, and that the principles of reciprocity and voluntarism were followed closely.   Traditionally, contributions were made in the form of collective labor, but the gains were individual.   Hence,
it was possible to insure that everyone who contributed
could benefit.

     At the present time, Harambee's national character
and its extension well beyond the immediate neighborhood, age or clan group make it quite a different
activity from the traditional methods of support.
Moreover, government involvement in self-help, suggests
Ng'ethe, has transformed it, involving both direction
and sanctions which traditional forms did not require.
Ng'ethe's observations lead him to a class analysis of
Harambee. He states,

> Harambee serves the ideological purpose of mysti-
> fying the inequalities between the   various socie-
> tal   strata by making it appear legitimate to
> accumulate so long as one is doing one's duty by
> 'participating' in development through contribu-
> tions outside one's home area.   In other words,
> the idea of Harambee serves the political inter-
> ests of a particular stratum in the political
> system, and it should be possible to identify the
> particular stratum and the interests which Haram-
> bee serves.[25]

Ng'ethe perceives Harambee as part of an exploitative
system in which inequalities are being perpetuated and
justified.   The perspective offered in this study sees

the role of elites as somewhat more differentiated than
Ng'ethe's theories suggest. It assumes that ethnicity,
as well as class, is an important factor in an interpretation of Harambee in Kenya.

Like Ng'ethe, Mutiso is interested in elites and
elite behavior; however, he frames his theory in terms
of center-periphery relationships.26 He perceives the
mobilization of rural people through Harambee in the
context of colonization, the imposition of western
values and the formation of a westernized elite. He
observes a social cleavage between the westernized
values of this emerging elite and the indigenous values
and patterns of behavior held by the majority of the
population. Mutiso sees the periphery as alienated
from the economic, social and political changes taking
place at the center, and he perceives Harambee as a way
to organize rural people around a new political base
and indigenous values. Mutiso's analysis is ideologic-
ally and value oriented.

Holmquist's observations are similar to some of
those of Mutiso, but without the ideological component.
Holmquist argues that self-help is a "pre-emptive strategy" by which rural people attempt to bring pressure
to bear on the government to provide assistance to projects which are local choices and local priorities.27
He perceives a continuing conflict between the objectives and strategies of policy makers and those of
local groups. He also observes a strong measure of
rural initiative and the emergence of local-level
political leadership. His emphasis is on the conflict
arising between centrally planned and directed development schemes and those emerging at the local level. He
does not focus on the competition among communities for
scarce resources. Thus, there is a center-periphery
orientation without the ideological characteristics
which are central to Mutiso's arguments.

Hill, working among the Kamba in Kitui, agrees
with Mbithi's analysis, stating that,

> Self-help is grounded firmly in existing social
> ties, rights and duties which are permanent beyond
> any particular projects and beyond individual
> interests and even life-spans. It is based on
> 'community' in contrast to 'association.'28

Hill maintains that the roots of self-help are in the
village-level traditional social groupings even if
these have become obscured by external administrative
controls and decision-making through committee structures. Without the cultural pre-conditions, Hill be-
lieves, self-help would have been extremely disorgan-
ized and would have lacked the dynamic quality which
has characterized it in Kenya.

Hill, Mbithi and others have observed that ethnic

cohesiveness and strong traditional social groupings underlie the self-help endeavor in Kenya. Yet one may also observe different levels of self-help activity among ethnic groups which show similar levels of cohesiveness, sense of identity and solidarity. Therefore, other determinants of self-help must be examined. Such variations may be shaped, for example, by the external pressures felt by the community, and the severity of the struggle for land and other goods and services within the community. To illustrate, the Kalenjin peoples have a strong tradition of active exchanges of communal labor and other services. They have, as well, a strong sense of identity, yet they have lagged behind the Kambas or the Kikuyus in terms of self-help activism in the post-independence period. This may be attributed, in part, to the greater geographic distances between the Kalenjins and the colonial center than that of the Kambas or Kikuyus. It may also be attributed to more favorable land/man ratios than either of the other two ethnic groups enjoys and to a lower level of pressure for various opportunities, benefits and services.

Thus, the impact of colonialism and the development of an urban commercial center in Nairobi may have had an impact on the nature and levels of self-help experienced by the various ethnic groups. Such an assumption relates to Mutiso's theories concerning a center-periphery analysis of Harambee, but the argument is different. It regards Harambee not as an indigenous reaction in opposition to modern values, but as an outgrowth of various pressures to achieve certain benefits of modernity. It focuses not on the ideological and value aspects of this impact but upon the economic and political conditions which have shaped the responses of different ethnic groups to the influence of colonialism, independence and modernization.

Political interpretations of Harambee self-help since independence are important. Barkan suggests that the impetus for Harambee in the early years of independence was more political than economic.[29] Public expectations for the benefits of independence were high in 1963. Official encouragement of local-level self-help development was a way to reduce the level of demands upon the Central Government and to permit the central administration to proceed with national planning relatively free of concerns from below. Such an approach to rural development permitted a new and beleaguered Government some breathing-space for policy formulation. Another interpretation would suggest that a focus on local self-help was a critical step in permitting a national elite to consolidate power at the center.

A second group of analysts has been particularly interested in the policy implications of Harambee self-

help as a mode of development. A major survey of four-
teen rural areas in Kenya, conducted in 1968 by the
Social Science Division of the University of Nairobi's
Institute for Development Studies examined overall
strategies for rural change in Kenya.[30] These analysts
stress the tremendous potential of self-help groups.
Their central recommendation on self help asserts,

> It is extremely difficult to devise a means to
> supply professional expertise for local project
> activities, but this need ought to be faced ... We
> cannot afford to waste such a potentially valuable
> resource as self-help, nor can we expect to rec-
> tify the situation [problems specified] without
> spending money on recruiting the necessary addi-
> tional staff to exploit it successfully.[31]

Winans and Haugerud have raised several policy-
oriented questions concerning self-help in Kenya.[32]
Their analysis suggests that over time Harambee might
contribute to a regional equalization in development,
particularly through a balancing of educational opportunities.[33] Data collected for this study of self-help
suggests that this is not the case.
Mbithi and Rasmusson, in the only book devoted to
a study of Harambee, suggest that Harambee mobilizes
hitherto inflexible resources and fills developmental
gaps in terms of project choice and project scale.[34]
They recommend three forms of support which the Government of Kenya can provide to Harambee self-help:
financial support; cadre support through staff and
leadership training; and regulatory practices which
will minimize some of the problems encountered by this
approach to development.

A COMPARATIVE ANALYSIS OF SELF-HELP

Key Questions

Harambee in Kenya is clearly shaped by various
structural conditions found in the environment, resource base, political system, social composition,
economy, and Kenya's position in the international
state system. At the same time, a behavioral approach
using a conflict model in which there are shifting patterns of consensus and competition offers insights.
According to such an interpretation of social change,
the dynamic operating within a broad structural context
is a struggle of individuals, groups and classes for
advantage in economic and power relationships. Such a
model can be useful in exploring Harambee. In Kenya
one must search for a subtle mix of cooperation and
conflict crossing ethnic, class, gender and geo-

political lines as groups compete for power and re-sources under conditions of scarcity.

Four central questions guide this study:

1) What is the role of Harambee self-help in the Kenyan political process? What has been its function in both national and local politics and how has the political process shaped self help?

2) What has been the impact of Harambee on local development? How do we assess Harambee's effect on rural infrastructure, on local equity concerns and on levels of participation at the local level?

3) How does Harambee self-help link national with locally defined social and economic objectives?

4) Given Harambee's political and ideological functions as well as its role in local socio-economic change, how do we assess its effectiveness as a mode of development?

Self-help as an approach to local-level develop-ment is commended in the 1979-1983 National Plan as "useful for building rural infrastructure, for creating solidarity, and for achieving more equitable distribu-tion of incomes."[35] The Plan observes that Harambee is based on a sense of mutual social responsibility deriv-ing from the African family tradition and is useful for building rural communities in Kenya.[36] The 1984-88 Development Plan also emphasizes the importance of mobilizing local resources for development through self-help. To date, however, there has been no attempt to gather empirical data in order to assess the actual impact of Harambee self-help on rural communities.[37]

This study investigates Harambee self-help in depth in six communities in Kenya. In doing so, it tests some of the Plans' fundamental assumptions about the value of Harambee. It examines the performance of Harambee according to three criteria:

1) rural infrastructure: What is the contribution to Harambee to building rural infrastructure and what are the consequences for rural productivity and social welfare?

2) equity: What is the contribution of Harambee to achieving greater equity for all peoples in Kenya, including that between socio-economic groups within a community, that between communities on a geographic, regional or ethnic basis, and that between rural and urban areas?

3) participation: Has Harambee contributed to broadening participation in the development process in terms of expanded opportunities for decision-making, implementation, enjoyment of benefits and evaluation of project and programs?

Methodology

 The method of analysis incorporates both a transnational and an intra-societal focus. An historical
interpretation of the context in which Harambee has developed requires an understanding of colonial political
structures, the introduction of cash crops, and the influence of missions on local-level organizational
activity. Transnational influences have helped shape
the present-day forms of Harambee and continue to influence local development efforts in a variety of ways
including the prices of energy imports or agricultural
exports and strategies of international aid organizations. Intra-societal concerns such as elite behavior,
leadership patterns, individual values and group behavior are also important in this analysis.
 Data was collected during 1978 and 1979. Six
locations (an administrative unit) in three districts
were selected for an in-depth longitudinal consideration of local development efforts through Harambee, as
well as a cross-sectional evaluation of specific types
of projects commonly found at the local level. Districts were selected on the basis of contrasting
approaches and performances in regard to Harambee projects, according to the statistical data suggested at
the district level and published by the Ministry of
Housing and Social Services. Two locations within each
district were chosen on the basis of contrasting characteristics of land potential, land use, population
density and general levels of well being. Locations
included in the study are Kyeni and Nthawa in Embu District of Eastern Province, Kisiara and Soin in Kericho
District of Rift Valley Province, and Weithaga and
Mbiri in Murang'a District of Central Province (See Map
1).
 According to the 1972 rankings used in the selection of districts, out of forty districts, Kericho and
Murang'a ranked second and third in terms of levels of
contributions to self-help, and twelfth and tenth, re-
spectively, in terms of number of projects completed.[38]
Kericho has had more than half of its project value in
economic projects; whereas Muranga's has emphasized
educational projects. In 1972 Embu ranked much lower
in terms of value of contributions and number of projects per district. This district was selected for the
insights a contrasting situation and variable success
with self-help might offer.
 Districts were not selected on the basis of a random sample, and they do not represent a cross-section
of Kenya's districts. It would not be possible to
achieve this with only three districts in a land of
Kenya's diversity. The districts were chosen on the
basis of differing focuses and differing levels of performance in Harambee development efforts. Similarly,

16

Map 1.1

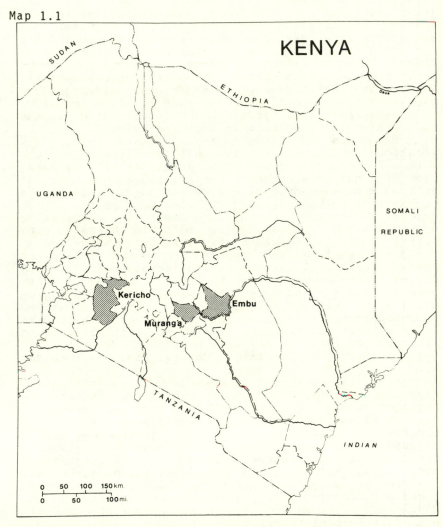

Source: Survey of Kenya, based on or extrapolated from topographical series on East Africa, 1:250,000. Sheets used include Kisumu, Chuka, Nyeri (Nairobi: Government of Kenya, 1971).

the locations do not represent a cross-section of a
random sample of Kenya's locations. They do not include pastoralists or large commercial farmers. They
are, however, typical of a large group of communities
in Kenya. They are representative of the smallholder
farm population where the emphasis is on agriculture,
sometimes in cash crops and always in food crops. In
two of the locations, the people were traditionally
pastoralists. They have, today, a strong emphasis on
livestock and still retain some inclination to move
with their livestock according to the requirements for
pasture and water. Approximately 85 percent of Kenya's
population is rural, and the vast majority of rural
residents are smallholders who are farming or squat-
ters/near landless who derive much of their income from
casual farm or non-farm labor. Hence, the locations
selected are typical of much of rural Kenya.

The field work conducted in the six locations includes four methods for collecting data. First, research assistants administered questionnaires to 500
local residents. The questionnaires focused on a) participation of respondents in Harambee projects both as
contributor (cash, labor, materials or committee
involvement) and as beneficiary; b) attitudes toward
various local development issues; and c) personal background of the respondent. Sampling procedures were
based on stratification of the population to be interviewed. The number of questionnaires administered in
each sublocation was based on the proportion of population in the sublocation, according to the 1969 census
data and subsequent population projections. Within the
sublocations there was then a subsequent stratification
according to age and sex ratios.

Second, information was collected in interviews
and meetings with more than 130 project committees and
self-help groups concerning their work, the performance
of the project, and the role of the project within the
location.

Third, interviews were conducted with a variety of
local teachers, ministers and other community leaders,
as well as district, locational and sublocational officials to ascertain their views about local development
concerns and self-help activities, and to obtain specific information about economic and social change within
their area.

Fourth, statistical information concerning the six
locations was collected from quarterly reports, monthly
reports and annual reports found in the District Community Development Offices. Information was collected
whenever possible for the years 1971-1978. Most of the
districts do not have complete records of activity in
the locations for that period. However, cross-checking
data from a variety of sources made it possible to develop a picture of self-help activities within each of

the locations for the period specified.

In Kenya there are two kinds of information which are difficult to obtain through a survey questionnaire. They are questions related to income and to personal family relationships. The survey avoided questions on these two subjects. Although information concerning household incomes would have been useful, it is unlikely that respondents would have given accurate answers to anyone they did not know personally. Therefore, several proxy measures for income levels were used to establish relative socio-economic positions within a community. These included size of landholding and status of ownership, employment, quality of housing and presence of various household amenities. A composite score was developed and respondents were ranked accordingly.

The research assistants administering the questionnaire were supervised closely, and we are confident that questionnaires were not falsified. What is, of course, more difficult to ascertain is the degree to which respondents were candid. While the questionnaires yielded a great deal of information about local-level participation in Harmabee projects and about attitudes toward development, they did not provide insights into the friction and conflicts within communities over selection, funding and implementation of projects. Meetings with the project committees and self-help groups yielded much useful information but little that was controversial about self-help projects. Private conversations with residents of the six communities offered the key insights concerning community differences and conflicts over self-help.

To supplement the field work and to provide the necessary historical perspective, several other forms of research were conducted, primarily in Nairobi. These included extensive research at the Archives using public documents related to the history of the districts under investigation and to relevant national policies. Of particular importance were the District Annual Reports, the Handing Over Reports from one District Commissioner to another, and the Political Record Books of each district included in the study. These were on microfilm at the National Archives of the Government of Kenya.

In addition, a small number of anthropological studies provided detailed analyses of the traditional social patterns of the ethnic groups found in the three districts. Of these, the Kikuyu are most widely researched; there are several excellent studies of the Kipsigis, and there is relatively little available on the Embu and Mbeere peoples. These works provide insights into the role of cooperative efforts in the traditional societies under investigation, the effects of settler colonialism, the impact of the British colonial

administration, and the growth of a market economy as
they relate to the questions under consideration. Although analysis focuses primarily on empirical data in
the post-independence period, interpretation of that
data depends in part upon the historical materials and
the evidence they present.

Finally, current public documents have provided
useful information. The District Development Plans,
the National Five-Year Plans, the Ministry of Local
Government reports on the three Districts, quarterly
reports on self-help written by the district staff members of the Ministry of Housing and Social Services,
the data on self-help collected by the Community Development Division of the Ministry of Housing and Social
Services have all been used. The national and district
level data on self-help covers the years from 1967-
1978.

NOTES

1. The World Bank, World Development Report, 1980
(New York: Oxford University Press, 1980), p. 33.
2. The World Bank, World Development Report, 1983
(New York: Oxford University Press, 1980), p. 2, and
The World Development Report, 1984 (New York: Oxford
University Press, 1984), p. 83.
3. Michael Lipton, Why Poor People Stay Poor:
Urban Bias in World Development (London: Temple Smith,
1977).
4. G. Hunter and J. Jiggins, Farmer and Community
Groups, Agricultural Administration Unit: Local Diag-
nosis, Farmer Groupings and Coordination of Services
Network; Paper IV, Overseas Development Institute, Lon-
don, 1976, p. 15.
5. Development Alternatives, Inc., Strategies for
Small Farmer Development: An Empirical Study of Rural
Development Projects, an Executive Summary. A report
prepared for AID under contract no. AID/CM/ta-c-73-41,
May, 1975, p. 32.
6. See Kenneth Little, West African Urbanization:
A Study of Voluntary Associations in Social Change
(Cambridge: Cambridge University Press, 1965, p. 1 and
Malcolm Walker and Jim Hanson, "The Voluntary Associations of Villalta: Failure with a Purpose," Human
Organization, vol. 37, no. 1, 1978.
7. Norman Uphoff, Analyzing Options for Local In-
stitutional Development, a report prepared by the Rural
Development Committee, Cornell University, for the
Office of Rural and Institutional Development, Bureau
of Science and Technology, U.S. Agency for International Development, May, 1984, p. 19.
8. M. Chen, "Organizing the Poor in Bangladesh:
Evolution of an Approach to Rural Development," Paper

prepared for the Rural Development Seminar, Harvard
Institute of International Development, Cambridge,
Mass., March, 1981, p. 13.

9. The most comprehensive work on rural organizations in the development process has been undertaken by
Cornell University's Rural Development Committee which
has published several monograph series pertaining to
rural local organization, local government, and specific local development issues.

10. Many analysts offer definitions of the word
"peasant", all of which are slight variations on a
theme. Of greatest importance in all definitions is
the centrality of land and agriculture. Most see peasants as involved in both cash and market relations.
Politically they are subordinate in a hierarchical,
relatively centralized state. Culturally, they are
part of a society which has a literate tradition and
systematic religious and political thought. The definitions are clearly derived from European experience,
and to a lesser extent from Latin American experience.
They do not transfer readily to East Africa. See
Migdal (1974), Geertz (1971) and Wolf (1966).

11. For example, Joel S. Migdal, Peasants, Politics and Revolution (Princeton: Princeton University
Press, 1974); and James C. Scott, The Moral Economy of
the Peasant (New Haven: Yale University Press, 1976).

12. Samuel L. Popkin, The Rational Peasant (Berkeley: University of California Press, 1979).

13. Goran Hyden, Beyond Ujamaa in Tanzania,
Underdevelopment and an Uncaptured Peasantry (London:
Heinemann Educational Books, 1980) and Jan Rudengren,
Peasants by Preference, Socio-Economic and Environmen-
tal Aspects of Rural Development in Tanzania (Stock-
holm: Economic Research Institute, 1981).

14. The two exceptions to this statement are cooperatives, which have a large literature, and rotating
credit associations on which there has been some research. See Geertz, "The Rotating Credit Association:
A 'Middle Rung' in Development," Economic Developmental
Change, XIV, no. 3, 1966. See also John Hamer, "Voluntary Associations as Structures of Change Among the
Sidamo of Southwestern Ethiopia," Anthropological Quarterly, Vol. 40, no. 2, 1967, p. 73.

15. See Karl Deutsch, "Social Mobilization and
Political Development," in Harry Eckstein and David
Apter, Comparative Politics (New York: The Free Press,
1963), and Migdal, op. cit.

16. Scott, op. cit., p. 206.

17. This distinction is borrowed from Huntington
and Nelson's No Easy Choice (Cambridge: Harvard University Press, 1976). It is a distinction which they
use in their discussion of different forms of participation in developing societies, and seems particularly
useful as an organizing scheme for local-level partici-

pation in present-day Kenya. Huntington and Nelson did
not use these terms in a specifically African context.
    18. See Philip Mbithi, Rural Sociology and Rural
Development (Nairobi: East African Literature Bureau,
1974), for example. This view was shared by the District Commissioners in all three districts where research was undertaken, as well as by most local-level
leaders. Rural citizens tend to view Harambee projects
within their own areas favorably, as data in Chapters
VI and VII indicate.
    19. See B.R. Bolnick, "Comparative Harambee:
History and Theory of Voluntary Collective Behavior,"
Institute for Development Studies, University of Nairobi, Working Paper #139, 1974, pp. 6 and 11. Frank W.
Holmquist, "Towards a Political Theory of Rural Self-
Help Development in Africa," Rural Africana, no. 18,
1972.
    20. See J.E. Anderson, "The Harambee Schools:
The Impact of Self-Help," in Richard Jolly (ed.), Edu-
cation in Africa (Nairobi: East African Publishing
House, 1969); Martin Hill, "Self-Help in Education and
Development: A Social Anthropological Study in Kitui,
Kenya," Unpublished paper, Bureau of Education Re-
search, University of Nairobi, 1974; Edmond J. Keller,
"Harambee! Educational Policy, Inequality and the
Political Economy of Rural Community Self-Help in
Kenya," Journal of African Studies, vol. 4, no. 1,
1977; and E.M. Godfrey and G.C.M. Mutiso, "The Insti-
tutes of Technology," Canadian Journal of African
Studies, vol. 8, no. 1, 1974.
    21. Philip M. Mbithi, Rural Sociology and Rural
Development (Nairobi: East African Literature Bureau,
1974), p. 176.
    22. Ibid., p. 181.
    23. Phillip M. Mbithi and Rasmus Rasmusson, Self-
Reliance in Kenya, The Case of Harambee (Uppsala:
Scandinavian Institute of African Studies, 1977), p.
33.
    24. Njuguna Ng'ethe, "Harambee and Rural Develop-
ment in Kenya, Towards a Political/Administrative Re-
Interpretation," Institute for Development Studies,
University of Nairobi, Working Paper #302, 1977, p. 18.
    25. Ibid., p. 2.
    26. G.C.M. Mutiso, "Harambee and Employment," Un-
published paper for the Kenya Employment Mission to the
ILO, 1972.
    27. Frank Holmquist, "Implementing Rural Develop-
ment Projects," in Goran Hyden, Robert Jackson and John
Okumu (eds.), Development Administration, The Kenyan
Experience (Nairobi: Oxford University Press, 1970),
p. 222.
    28. Martin Hill, "Self-Help in Education and
Development: A Social Anthropological Study in Kitui,
Kenya," Unpublished paper, Bureau of Educational Re-

22

search, University of Nairobi, 1974, p. 27.

29. Joel Barkan, Frank Holmquist, David Gachuki, Shem Migot-Adholla, "Is Small Beautiful? The Organizational Conditions for Effective Small-Scale Self-Help Development Projects in Rural Kenya," paper presented at the African Studies Association, November 2, 1979; also conversations with Edgar Winans, 1978.

30. J. Heyer, D. Ireri and J. Moris, Rural Development in Kenya (Nairobi: East African Publishing House, 1971).

31. Ibid., p. 39.

32. Edgar V. Winans and Angelique Haugerud, "Rural Self-Help in Kenya: The Harambee Movement," Human Organization, November. 1976, p. 15.

33. Ibid., p. 24.

34. Mbithi and Rasmusson, op. cit., p. 164.

35. Government of Kenya Development Plan, 1979-1983, Parts I and II (Nairobi: Government Printer, 1979), pp. 18, 40 and 42.

36. Ibid.

37. Specific types of projects have been assessed for their impact - secondary schools for example - but there have not been any community studies which consider the effectiveness of the self-help approach to development within a given community.

38. Community Development Division, Ministry of Cooperatives and Social Services/Ministry of Housing and Social Services, A Statistical Analysis of Self-Help Projects (1967-1971), cyclostyled report, Nairobi, 1972.

II
A Framework for Examining
Self-Help: National, Historical,
and Community Perspectives

> I remember our first community self-help effort in
> 1950 - a bridge over a river which... had claimed
> several lives. I had to encourage people to coop-
> erate. Now they do so willingly.
>   Assistant Chief
>   Kisiara Location

THE NATIONAL CONTEXT

Long a "most favored nation" of western scholars
eager to find a congenial environment in which to conduct their research, Kenya has usually been described
as economically prosperous, politically stable, culturally and ethnically diverse, and endowed with a most
attractive population and landscape. Given the declining per capita GNP and the political transformation by
coup that characterize many African nations, Kenya
seems to deserve the glowing observation. The August
1982 coup attempt reminds us, however, that Kenya, too,
must be analyzed judiciously. The nation does indeed
have some serious problems arising from fundamental
contradictions and dilemmas in national political and
economic life. These problems are found in acute class
and ethnic rivalries for national resources, in an increasingly straitened middle class, in a bloated
bureaucracy, in declining international terms of trade,
and in a political and economic vulnerability that
shapes relations with several other nations.
Kenya's geographic as well as human diversity,
however, will not be disputed. With a total area of
224,960 square miles, the nation possesses six distinct
ecological zones including desert, high altitude moor-
lands, rain forests, fertile highlands, and a tropical
coastal strip. There are four major concentrations of
population: the coast, the highlands east of the Rift
Valley, western Kenya near Lake Victoria, and central
Kenya to the west of the Rift Valley. According to the
1979 census, Kenya had a population of 15,322,000, an

increase of approximately 50 percent over its population in 1969 when the last census was taken.[1]   In 1983
it had 17,470,000 inhabitants, and Kenya's population
is projected to be 34 million by the year 2000.   The
population is growing at a rate of 3.5 percent a year;
approximately 50 percent is under 15 years of age.[2]

Linguistically this population is divided into
Bantu, Nilotic, Nilo-Hamitic, and Hamitic-speaking
groups.   The Bantu peoples constitute about 65 percent
of Kenya's population and include, among others, the
Kikuyu, Embu, Meru, Kamba, Mbeere, Abaluhya and Kisii
ethnic groups.   The Nilotic-speaking peoples, 14 percent of the population, are represented primarily by
the Luo in Western Kenya.   The Nilo-Hamitic speaking
peoples are traditionally pastoral and constitute about
16 percent of the population.   They include more than
14 ethnic groups, among them the the Kipsigis, who
occupy Kericho District.   Finally, the Hamitic-speaking
peoples, found in the northern portions of Eastern and
Northeastern Provinces, constitute roughly 4 percent of
the population and are represented by the Galla and
Somali sub-groups.   The four largest ethnic groups are,
in descending order, the Kikuyu, Luo, Abaluhya, and
Kamba.   The Kikuyu, who occupy the Central Province
heartland and have dominated economic and political
life since independence, constitute approximately 15
percent of the total population.

Educationally, Kenya has made enormous progress
since independence.   The National Literacy Survey
undertaken in 1976 indicated that approximately 46 percent of the age group over 15 is literate.   These figures vary by province from 60 percent in Central Province to 25 percent in Coast Province with the remaining
provinces being much nearer the national average.
Overall the male literacy rate is 65 percent while that
of females is only 30 percent.

In 1974, educational fees were abolished for Standards I to IV, the equivalent of U.S. first through
fourth grades.   At that time enrollments increased by
51 percent.   By 1980 free education was extended to all
the Standards in primary school.   Primary school en-
rollment is now more than 85 percent of the total estimated six to twelve age group in the population.[3]   Secondary school enrollments have increased from 30,000 at
the time of independence in 1963 to over 350,000 in
1978.

Kenya is currently facing a variety of economic
problems, many of which are related to international
factors - worldwide inflation, increasing energy costs,
a decline in the value of several of her export crops,
and balance of payments.   Since 1981, the government
has had to use valuable foreign exchange to import
agricultural produce, especially maize, a crop in which
the country had been self sufficient.   Between 1964 and

1981 Kenya's overall rate of growth averaged 5.2 percent and the nation managed to stay somewhat ahead of the 3.6 percent average annual population increase. The 1984-1988 Development Plan sets a target of 4.9 percent GDP growth annually, despite GDP growth rate of approximately 3.3 percent in 1982 and in 1983.[4]

With 85 percent of the Kenyan population living in the rural areas and dependent for the most part upon agricultural pursuits, the rural areas form the backbone of the Kenyan economy. Agriculture is clearly the nation's most important sector. Maize is the leading food crop and is widely cultivated by smallholders who produce over 90 percent of the crop and sell what is not needed for family consumption. Wheat, millet and sorghum are also important food crops. Over the last ten years the volume of production has risen appreciably in only two commodities, sugar and tea.

The crops which are most important for export purposes are coffee, tea, sisal and pyrethrum. Most coffee is grown in Central and Eastern Provinces. Approximately 90 percent of the coffee produced in Kenya is for export. Kenya benefited from the large rise in the value of marketed coffee as well as from a record crop in the mid-1970s. The coffee boom, however, peaked in 1977 and 1978 and has now subsided, though coffee remains Kenya's largest export earner. Despite the vulnerability of coffee exports to international price fluctuations and the constraints of the International Coffee Agreement, the major task is to increase yields on areas currently under cultivation. Analysis has suggested that yields could increase by 80 percent with higher applications of chemicals and labor.[5]

Tea is second to coffee as an export crop. The areas of the country suitable for tea growing are, however, much more limited than for coffee as the crop needs high and well distributed rainfall. The main locations for tea growing are Kericho, Nandi, and Sotik, west of the Rift Valley, and portions of Meru and Embu Districts east of the Rift. Kenya's sugar yields are among the highest in the world, and its production costs are 20 percent below the long-term world price, but Kenya cannot expand its exports of sugar without increasing its processing capacity.[6]

Kenya's rural population, agricultural sector and the constraints of the international political economy are inextricably linked in a number of complicated challenges. Among these are the need to address income distribution and equity issues, to stem rural-urban migration, to improve agricultural production, and to generate employment opportunities in the rural areas. They involve examination of export policies and commodity price policies. If increased food exports result in higher domestic food prices, as has occurred in the recent past, there is a direct conflict between the interests of the rural producers and the urban consumers. Moreover, Government marketing boards and parastatals have assumed responsibility for the marketing of major agricultural commodities, not necessarily to the advantage of the rural smallholding producer.

And who are these Kenyan smallholders? According to the Integrated Rural Surveys, 1976-1979, 69 percent of the total population or 13.8 million people live on small farms of less than 20 acres (8 hectares). There are 2.6 million smallholdings in rural Kenya.[7]

The total area of land under smallholder agriculture is approximately 3.5 million hectares or 8.65 million acres (one hectare equals 2.47 acres). Among smallholders the median holding size is within a range of 1.0 - 2.0 hectares. The mean holding size is 2.33 hectares or 5.8 acres. Table 2.1 shows the percentage distribution of holdings by size of holding.[8]

Table 2.1
Percentage distribution of holdings by size of holding

Hectares	Percentage of Holdings
0.5	14
0.5 - 1.0	17
1.0 - 2.0	27
2.0 - 3.0	15
3.0 - 4.0	9
4.0 - 5.0	7
5.0 - 8.0	7
8.0 +	3

The data indicate that the median annual average household income is in the range of Kenya shillings 2000 to 3000 ($250 to $375). Table 2.2 shows the percentage distribution of holdings by income group.[9]

Extrapolating from these figures and using data from the Integrated Rural Survey of 1974-1975, as well as criteria established by the World Bank, approximately 52 percent of the Kenyan smallholders live near or under an absolute poverty line. Table 2.3 shows the distribution by province of holdings which would fall under a poverty line.[10] These figures indicate that rural poverty is more widespread in Western Province than in the other provinces and least widespread in Central Province, though it is indeed present in that province since 46 percent of its households have family incomes of less than Kenya shillings 3000.

Table 2.2
Percentage distribution of holdings by income group

Kenya Shillings	Percentage of Holdings
0	6
0 - 999	11
1000 - 1999	21
2000 - 2999	14
3000 - 3999	12
4000 - 5999	14
6000 - 7999	9
8000 +	13

Table 2.3
Provincial distribution of household incomes under Kshs. 3000

Province	Percentage of Household Incomes Under Kshs. 3000
Central	46
Coast	53
Eastern	53
Nyanza	55
Rift Valley	50
Western	71

Kenya is currently implementing its fifth national development plan. This plan, 1984-1988, emphasizes the need to mobilize domestic resources for development purposes. In fact, the plan states emphatically, "Unless domestic resources, including earnings of foreign exchange, can be marshalled to support a larger part of the cost of development, the pace of development must slow."[11] Recognizing that collective efforts have played a major role in providing health and education facilities, community centers, access to water, cattle dips, minor irrigation schemes, and other improvements in infrastructure, the Government has indicated it will "focus its efforts on establishing a favorable setting within which Kenyans can help themselves through their self-help and other private sector activities."[12] Moreover, the Government has shifted the primary responsibility for planning and implementing rural

development from the headquarters of ministries to the
districts. The Plan specifies that this new district-
based development policy is intended to facilitate
local initiatives through self-help development activities.[13]

What has been the magnitude of Harambee's contribution to development? Views vary. Several analysts
estimate that Harambee activities constitute about 30
percent of all capital formation in the rural areas.[14]
Mbithi and Rasmusson believe that the economic significance of Harambee is crucial. Their data indicates
that between 1967 and 1973, Harambee contributed 11.4
percent of the overall national development expenditure.[15] The Government Plan for 1979-1983 estimates
that the value of Harambee projects will be about 10
percent of total national development expenditure.[16]

Official figures for the people's contribution,
that is, private, non-governmental, non-organizational
contributions, to Harambee projects between 1967 and
1978 indicate that approximately 48,138,000 Kenya
pounds (in 1979, Ksh. 20 equals KL 1; KL 1 equals U.S.
$2.66) have been raised through cash, labor and mate-
rial contributions to Harambee projects over a twelve
year period.[17] In dollars this is approximately
$128,047,000, an average annual figure of $10,670,000
which, at the 1969 census figures for population comes
to approximately $1.00 per person per year. It would
be unrealistic, however, to assume that this sum has
been contributed to rural capital formation in Kenya.
This, of course, is not the case. Some projects are
abandoned after funds have been collected or labor or
materials contributed, and these contributions are then
wasted. In other instances there may be misuse of
funds or inefficient use of contributions.

During this same period of time, according to Government statistics, more than 58,987 projects were completed.[18] This figure does not include projects which
are carried forward year by year and which people complete in a piecemeal manner. For example, it would not
include a church until the last windows were in place.
It would, however, include school classrooms which may
be undertaken as a single project, a single completed
classroom constituting a completed project. Many projects are carried forward for several years and are
registered thus in the self-help statistics. Figures
for 1978, found in Table 2.4, are illustrative. Completed projects for that year constitute 12 percent of
the total projects carried forward from 1977 or begun
in 1978. Those abandoned in 1978 constitute 3 percent
of the total.

Table 2.5 shows the magnitude of the people's contribution to self-help projects. It is evident that
over the twelve year period the sum contributed annually has risen more or less steadily from more than KL

Table 2.4
All-Kenya Harambee projects for 1978

```
Projects carried forward from 1977 . . . . 8517
Projects started in 1978 . . . . . . . . . 3155
Projects completed in 1978 . . . . . . . . 1401
Projects abandoned in 1978 . . . . . . . .  455
Projects carried forward to 1979 . . . . . 9816
```

Source: Ministry of Housing and Social Services, Department of Social Services, Community Development
Division, Research and Evaluation Unit, data sheets for
1978. Unpublished documents.

Table 2.5
People's contribution to Harambee projects including
cash, labor, and materials in KL '000

Year	People's Total Contribution	% Cash	% Labor	% Materials
1967	1,825	36	32	32
1968	2,522	33	25	42
1969	2,004	45	25	30
1970	2,022	41	34	25
1971	2,207	49	30	21
1972	2,707	49	31	20
1973	3,976	62	26	12
1974	4,621	63	21	16
1975	4,222	61	15	24
1976	5,631	58	21	21
1977	7,644	64	16	20
1978	8,757	63	17	20

Source: Ministry of Housing and Social Services, Department of Social Services, Community Development
Division, Self-Help Statistics, volumes 1974-1978.
Ministry of Housing and Social Services/Ministry of
Cooperatives and Social Services, A Statistical Analysis on Self-Help Projects, 1967-1971, 1972. (Cyclostyled report). Report of a University of Nairobi
Team, Toward Strategies for Intensified Social Development, mimeographed report, December, 1977, for the purpose of preparation of the Fourth Development Plan.

one million to over KL eight million in 1978.   At the
same time the distribution among cash, labor and material contributions has shifted substantially. In 1967,
contributions were divided almost equally among the
three modes of assisting projects.   Over the twelve
years, the level of cash contributions has risen to
just over 60 percent of the total, whereas labor and
material contributions have each dropped to 20 percent
or just below.   The implications of these findings are
numerous, and some of them will be discussed in later
chapters.   They suggest not only that the Kenyan economy has become more monetized in the past twelve
years - which is clearly the case - but they also suggest observations about shifting size and type of projects, large outside donors, and regional clustering.

     While the monetary value of Harambee project con-
tributions has been increasing, the number of projects
completed per year has been decreasing.   Table 2.6
shows the changes over the twelve year period in number
of projects completed.   The Government began to keep
records on Harambee in 1964.   These records show that
the number of projects completed peaked in 1967
and has been dropping ever since.   Although the official statistics indicate that 26,267 projects were com-

Table 2.6
Harambee projects completed between 1967 and 1978

Year	Number Completed
1967	26,267
1968	20,521
1969	1,490
1970	1,826
1971	1,841
1972	1,800
1973	1,704
1974	1,982
1975	1,799
1976	1,705
1977	1,671
1978	1,401

Source: Ministry of Housing and Social Services, De-
partment of Social Services, Community Development
Division, Self-Help Statistics, volumes 1974-1978; and
Ministry of Housing and Social Services/Ministry of
Cooperatives and Social Services, A Statistical Anal-
ysis of Self-Help Projects, 1967-1971, 1972. (Cyclo-
styled report); Edgar V. Winans and Angelique Haugerud,
"Rural Self-Help in Kenya: The Harambee Movement,"
Human Organization, November, 1976.

pleted in 1967, at an average of 657 projects per district completed in that year alone, these figures lack
credibility.   Strict record keeping, careful assessments of projects actually completed, and the introduction in the early 1970s of registration of new projects
for purposes of collecting funds have caused a significant   reduction in the number of completed projects
recorded.   This reduction may also be attributed to a
gradual increase in the size, scope and complexity of
projects being introduced.   The water project which
involves more than one sublocation or location, the
secondary school with boarding facilities, the maternity ward or institute of technology constitute examples
of complicated projects which may require considerable
time, effort and money for a community to complete.
       On a   national level the mix of projects selected
has stayed relatively constant.   Table 2.7 shows that,
for the most part, education-related projects have constituted over half the completed projects in any given
year.   Health projects have slowly decreased as a percentage of the total.   Water projects have hovered at
about five percent of the total projects completed and
economically-related projects such as cattle dips or
soil conservation measures have varied from 14 to 28
percent of the total.   Over time, social welfare projects are increasing.   These include churches, youth

Table 2.7
Changes in project choice 1967-1978 (Figures show
project category as a percentage of total completed
by year)

Year	Education	Health	Water	Economic	Social Welfare
1967	57	11	4	19	8
1968	55	11	5	22	7
1969	58	11	5	24	2
1970	56	8	6	27	2
1971	53	6	9	27	5
1972	54	6	7	22	11
1973	52	2	3	28	15
1974	55	3	5	17	20
1975	57	3	4	20	16
1976	44	3	7	21	25
1977	50	4	5	23	18
1978	55	2	1	14	28

Source: Ministry of Housing and Social Services, Self-
Help Statistics for 1974-1978, cyclostyled reports.
Winans and Haugerud, op. cit., Table 9.

centers, sports grounds and amenities such as water tanks or latrines for public buildings.

The distribution of contributions to various types of projects has remained relatively constant in recent years. Table 2.8 shows that education projects have absorbed more than 60 percent of people's contributions. The magnitude of citizen involvement in building secondary schools is documented in the Economic Survey for 1979. Examining the 1974 through 1978 planning period, the Survey states that the proportion of students in unaided (Harambee) secondary schools has increased from 48 percent in 1974 to 65 percent in 1978. The number of pupils enrolled in Form 1 in Government support schools increased by 9 percent between 1974 and 1978, whereas the increase in registrations in Form 1 in Harambee schools during that same time period was 97 percent.[19] These figures attest to the widespread popular support which Harambee secondary education has received in Kenya.

Table 2.8
National statistics showing the percentage of the value of people's contributions allocated to different project categories

Year	Education	Health	Water	Economic	Social Welfare
1967	58	11	4	18	9
1968	55	11	5	22	7
1969	58	11	5	21	5
1970	56	8	6	15	15
1971	52	6	9	15	18
1972	54	6	7	19	14
1973	53	4	5	15	23
1974	71	4	5	10	10
1975	63	4	6	10	17
1976	62	5	11	10	12
1977	64	4	9	10	13
1978	62	4	5	13	16

Source: Ministry of Housing and Social Services, Self-Help Statistics for the years 1974-1978.

Referring again to Table 8, economic and social welfare projects have each absorbed 10 to 23 percent of the value of people's contributions, and health and water projects have, for the most part, utilized less than 10 percent of the contributions. In part, however, these disparities relate to a Government policy

for providing matching grants for some types of economically productive projects, such as cattle dips, whereas a secondary school, as well as all primary school
facilities, will usually be built exclusively from
local contributions.

What is the relative magnitude of contributions
from the public as opposed to other donors, including
the Central Government, private voluntary agencies,
local authorities such as County Councils, or foreign
aid donors? Statistics show that the contribution of
"other donors" varies from 6 percent of the total value
of self-help projects in 1967, 1968, 1969 and 1974 to
15 percent in 1971.[20] That is, the contributions to
self-help projects which come in the form of cash,
labor and material contributions from the people themselves constitute from 85 percent to 94 percent of the
value of self-help during each of the twelve years
under consideration. Thus, although outside funding
may be important in serving as a catalyst for raising
funds or as a topping-up device for assuring completion
of a project, it does not provide the main impetus for
self-help projects. This impetus derives partially
from the politics of independence and partially from a
variety of long-term conditions - environmental, historical and social - which facilitate self-help and
which account for the interest in self-help activities
generated by various rural communities.

AN HISTORICAL PERSPECTIVE ON SELF-HELP IN EMBU,
KERICHO, AND MURANG'A DISTRICTS

Scholars have explored Harmabee's derivation from
pre-colonial, indigenous social ties and institutions.[21] What they have not emphasized is that, in
some ways, Harambee owes its particular, contemporary
forms to ecological conditions and to the socio-
economic and political characteristics of the colonial
period as well as to the structures of tribal society.
The variations in Harambee self-help in Embu, Kericho
and Murang'a District suggest that geographical features of the land, the nature of the climate, and the
resource base affect the ways people organize themselves for political and social action. Evidence from
these three districts also illustrates the varying impact of colonial institutions on the development of
local-level self-help organization. At times under the
aegis of the Colonial Government and its allies, and at
other times in direct opposition to these institutions,
Harambee community organization for self-help emerged
in these districts.

Political, social and ecological conditions shape
the use of self-help in the three districts under
study. The four major ethnic groups in these districts

have experienced widely differing ecological circumstances. They have also enjoyed varying pre-colonial structures with differences in land use and governance to be found between those with a pastoral inclination (Kipsigis and Mbeere) and those with an agricultural background (Kikuyu and Embu). Colonialism affected these areas in ways which varied not only according to the existing tribal structures and the ecological conditions, but also according to the proximity and strength of the settler community and according to the links established between the rural community and the Government in Nairobi.

Here we examine, in particular, the colonial period as it affected the growth of local-level self-help organizations. In all three districts there were four major colonial influences. First, all moved slowly and inexorably toward involvement in the cash economy. This process occurred because cash and therefore wage labor were needed to pay taxes and because of the increasing availability of goods and services for which cash was necessary. For a variety of reasons the Kikuyus moved the most rapidly; the Mbeere and Kipsigis are still only partially involved.

Second, the introduction of individual ownership of land was a distinct break from tribal systems of land tenure and land use patterns. While individual land ownership developed rapidly among the Kikuyu because of pre-existing land use patterns, and slowly among the Mbeere where it is still evolving, it has dramatically changed the rural areas, attitudes toward land, and those social and political institutions which grew out of communal land use arrangements.

Third, the introduction of formal education has had an important impact in all three districts. During the colonial period this impact was most dramatic among the Kikuyu. Now it would be difficult to distinguish among at least three of the four ethnic groups - the Embu, Kikuyu and Kipsigis - in the level of educational interest.

Fourth, the Colonial Government's deliberate efforts to supplant tribal governing institutions affected all four ethnic groups significantly. This policy created cleavages within the Kikuyu community which have lasted into the post-independence period. Among the Kipsigis it involved a lengthy effort to create a local authority responsive both to the Colonial Government and to the people, and having, as well, an indigenous validity.

These four areas of colonial impact resulted in a variety of secondary changes which in themselves sent a rippling effect throughout the four communities. For example, changing forms of land tenure have meant that there is growing differentiation between rich and poor. Under a system of individual freehold title, the cush-

ioning effect of clan or communal land ownership is
reduced. The problems of landlessness have become increasingly acute. The need for cash, combined with
pressures on the land and increasing landlessness, have
meant that people leave home seeking employment elsewhere, perhaps in Nairobi or Mombasa, often setting up
a semi-permanent residence near their place of employment. This rural-urban migration has affected local
development through Harambee self-help because wage
earners living outside their home areas send contributions for projects back to their natal communities.

The departure of young people to towns and cities
has activated a growing rift between the young and the
old. Elders no longer have the same control over young
people, particularly if they are employed elsewhere.
Likewise the new forms of education have aggravated
generational divisions and distrust. As political and
social institutions have changed, there have been, in
some areas, considerable uncertainty and unease.
Again, this was more acute during the colonial period
among the Kikuyu than among the other three ethnic
groups. Mbeere stands at the opposite pole with a much
slower rate of change.

The remainder of the section does not constitute
an historical survey of these three districts. Rather,
it is a selective and interpretive comparison of conditions which have led to local-level development through
Harambee self-help efforts. It clarifies some of the
variations in the self-help approach to development
within these communities.

Geography and Pre-Colonial Socio-Political
Structures

There is a link between the geographical and ecological environment and the socio-political structures
which emerge within any community. Anthropologists
have attributed certain characteristics of Kikuyu
social structures to the dominant geographical features
of their landscape.[22] Steep ridges divided by rivers
and streams arising from the Nyandarua (Aberdere) Moun-
tains and Mount Kenya have accentuated Kikuyu lineage
or descent groups, which form an important link among
individuals. Communication moves along the crests of
the ridges, and habitation, as well as cultivation, has
taken place at the tops and along the steep sides in a
pattern of individual homesteads.

Over time ridges were occupied by specific families and clans.[23] These ridges fostered closely-knit
communities and, according to Muriuki, often bred a
"pronounced localism and particularism."[24] Thus, the
kinship loyalties based on the mbari or sub-clan were
encouraged by the topography. Today one can observe

the strong identification Kikuyus feel for their own village or mbari area. Data collected for this study suggests that geography helps explain the high level of Kikuyu involvement with Harambee self-help development projects within their home communities.

Much of the land which the Embu inhabit is topographically similar to that of the Kikuyus, and like the Kikuyus, the Embu have tended to settle in patterns of family and clan along ridges. Here, too, this form of settlement has contributed to local-level solidarity. Data from Kyeni Location suggest that these strong local loyalities are related to high levels of Harambee self-help development activity.

Perhaps the most important characteristic of pre-colonial social structures, one noted by several anthropologists,[25] is the strong sense of solidarity within kinship groups. In addition, this may have a spatial dimension, which, as indicated, is a strong component of Kikuyu and Embu solidarity. Lineage and local communities are central to Kikuyu and Embu social and political life. Cutting across these kinship and territorial loyalties, in pre-colonial times, was the mariika system or age-sets, whereby boys and girls at adolescence were organized into corporate groups based on age and initiation rites. The dominant characteristics emerging in Kikuyu pre-colonial social and political structures were the sense of communal solidarity, a high level of territorial insularity and loyalty, the subordinate position of women, and the egalitarian structures existing among men for both military and political functions and among women for agricultural and domestic purposes. These characteristics are important determinants of the nature and role of contemporary organization and institution-building among the Kikuyus at the local level. They are central, for example, to the formation of the strong Harambee women's groups characteristic of the Kikuyu areas. Pre-colonial political and social structures among the Embu are similar in a variety of ways to those of the Kikuyu. Although titles and names vary, the pattern included a patriarchal family, village or ridge councils, clan councils, councils of warriors and councils of elders.

Among the Mbeere, settlements are dispersed and customarily only a few homes of close relatives are likely to be located near one another. Movement from one area to another occurs often because of infertile land, the need for grazing space, and the frequency of drought and famine. While loyalty to a particular locale may not exist among the Mbeere, clan loyalties are important. Even now, clan structures are stronger among the Mbeere than among the other three ethnic groups. Mwaniki observes that, "The clan authority is still very strong. For instance, a clan's member cannot sue another one in a modern court of law wihtout authority of the clan council."[26] The necessity for frequent moves, imposed by a harsh environment, has led to social institutions which are flexible and trans-portable. The contemporary focus of self-help on building rural infrastructure of a permanent nature, and on groups existing over time in one locale does not coincide with fundamental ecological requirements and Mbeere time-honored responses.

The Kipsigis, occupying a land quite generously endowed, and enjoying comfortable man-land ratios, have been affected still differently by their environment. Primarily pastoralists who also practiced some shifting cultivation, their traditional social structure at the local-level was relatively fluid. Unlike the mbari of the Kikuyu which originally developed along fairly tight lineage lines, the kokwet or village community of the Kipsigis traditionally has contained people from different lineages, clans, and age sets.[27] Membership in the kokwet was flexible and the sizes of these com-munities varied considerably. In large measure this flexibility was based on sound agricultural practice in which land was allowed to lie fallow for periods of time, and people moved both for purposes of cultivating new land and for finding new grazing areas.

Like the Kikuyu, the Kipsigis tribal organizations had no centralized binding political authority. Among the Kipsigis, the most important level of government was the local level where traditionally political and judicial functions were carried out for the community. Normal political functions were thus decentralized, and the community was structured in a loose and flexible manner without rigid membership requirements and with infrequent recourse to higher authority.[28] These are characteristics which are important to consideration of contemporary institutional and organizational change. The flexible and pragmatic manner with which the Kipsigis have carried out certain types of Harambee projects at the village level may be traced in part to these early patterns of local-level decision-making.

Thus, local-level social structures relevant to the emergence of Harambee have developed in response to environmental conditions. These include strong local affiliations among the Kikuyu and Embu, strong clan loyalties and comparative dispersal and frequency of movement among the Mbeere, and patterns of movement combined with a flexible social structure at the local level among the Kipsigis. These characteristics affect current local institutional development, organizational capacity, and participation within these communities.

Colonialism: Land and Agricultural Policies

Doubtless, the most pervasive and far-reaching influence of colonialism in the rural areas of Kenya was the introduction of Western forms of individual ownership with regard to the land. Relentlessly, the British Colonial Government pursued the policy that rural Kenya's prosperity depended upon sound agricultural practices and that the implementation of such practices depended upon individual land ownership. This was closely linked with the government's concept of community development and notions of the appropriate use of communal labor for the development and improvement of rural infrastructure. These approaches have affected the form of Harambee self-help in local-level development efforts.

From the early years, the Colonial Government alienated land to the European settlers and various foreign-owned companies. Such land was considered "owned" by the settlers and companies. Other land was "owned" by a particular tribe as a "native reserve." Still other land was considered "owned" or held by the Crown. For example, in Murang'a (formerly called Fort Hall District), according to the District Commissioner's Handing Over Report of 1926, land was divided as follows:

```
European Land . . . . . . . . 500 square miles
Native Reserves . . . . . . . 580 square miles
Forest Reserves (Crown Land). 130 square miles
```

The European Land supported a total European population of 385 persons deriving their living primarily from sisal and coffee. The Native Reserves supported a total population of 143,924, also primarily in agriculture.[29]

Among both the Kikuyu and the Kipsigis, the land designated for European settlement was continually a matter of dispute. For the Kikuyus, however, the alienation of land seriously aggravated what was already a growing problem concerning the ratio of population to cultivable land. From the latter part of the 19th century, population pressures, increasing fragmentation of the land, and growing number of landless or near landless began to characterize the Kikuyu areas. Encircled as they were by the White Highlands, with outlets for increased use of land or migration cut off, pressures and tensions within the community built to high levels.

Throughout the 1920s, the use of settler lands by squatters and settler requirements for labor somewhat alleviated these pressures. The depression of the 1930s, however, with wage cuts, unemployment, and a diminishing squatter system, increased the pressure on the crowded Kikuyu reserves where the mbari holdings were being subdivided into miniscule, frequently badly eroded holdings. The breakdown of the indigenous system of land tenure, the increasing number of landless, the rapid deterioration of the intensively cultivated land in the reserve, and the juxtaposition of large tracts of alienated settler land were central to a Kikuyu-Colonial Government confrontation in the 1950s. This took the form of guerrilla insurgency known as Mau Mau and the resulting Emergency in which the colonial government attempted to suppress the independence struggle.

In 1952 and 1953, during the Emergency, the Government passed a Forfeiture of Lands Act which provided for the confiscation of land individually owned by "terrorists." Ultimately, the Government confiscated mbari lands of "terrorists" as well. By 1956, 868 people from Murang'a District had had their land taken away and set aside for public purposes such as markets and schools.[30] Forfeiture was closely followed by a villagization policy in which the entire Kikuyu and Embu tribes were put into fortified villages with varying degrees of punishment or privilege according to the amount of aid that particular group had offered to the "terrorists."

A massive land consolidation program followed this procedure. Fragmented holdings were consolidated into single units with subsequent registration of these units under freehold title. The program was originally directed primarily toward the Kikuyu, but it eventually included the Embu and Meru peoples as well.

As Sorrenson points out, the Government's justification for consolidation was primarily political rather than economic:

> Thus land consolidation was to complete the work of the Emergency: to stabilize a conservative middle class, based on the loyalists; and, as confiscated land was to be thrown into the common land pool during consolidation, it was also to confirm the landlessness of the rebels.[31]

There were also economic reasons for land consolidation although they may appear to have been secondary. Many officials, particularly District Agricultural Officers, had expressed alarm over the deteriorating condition of Kikuyu lands and genuinely believed that consolidation was a critical step in bringing sound agricultural practices and improved conservation and fertility to Kikuyu lands.

In Embu, as among the Kikuyu, those who had a substantial claim to mbari land could benefit by the formalization of a freehold title, whereas those whose claim was tenuous stood to lose by the destruction of

the various informal rights and benefits offered to any
member of the community insofar as use of the land was
concerned. Land consolidation and demarcation in Embu
was complicated by the fact that numerous Kikuyu <u>ahoi</u>
(landless) had settled in Embu District, occupied the
land as tenants, and had to give it up as consolidation
progressed. Ultimately, however, the process of land
consolidation was accomplished with far greater ease
than among the Kikuyu and in Embu District, except for
Mbeere, it was nearly completed by 1961.

In Nthawa the process of land adjudication did not
begin until 1970, and it is continuing at the present
time. Brokensha and Glazier point out that,

> Until recently, cash crops were few, education was
> not advanced, and communications were poor: the
> result is that there has been, until recently,
> little emphasis on individual land rights, the
> traditional system of land tenure persisting.
> Mbeere land tenure must be considered in the con-
> text of patrilineal kinship, emphasizing seniority
> based on age, and the organization of clans into
> maximal lineages and minimal lineages with their
> constituent agnatic cores, localized in home-
> steads.[32]

Brokensha has independently described some of the out-
comes of the process of land adjudication. They include a growing class of landless people, increasing
stratification, a heightened suspicion and hostility
and an increasing number of outsiders who have bought
land in Mbeere.[33]

Among the Kipsigis there were mixed reactions to
the question of land consolidation and individual tenure. Some feared that this was going to be imposed on
the tribe unfairly because of the unstable political
conditions among the Kikuyu. Others viewed the introduction of freehold title as a benefit. As Manners has
pointed out, there were crucial changes in the Kipsigis
culture between World War I and World War II.[34] The
introduction of cash crops provided the motivation for
some Kipsigis to expand their cultivated holdings.
Throughout the 1940s, the Kipsigis continued to cultivate in increasingly large holdings. Further, they began to enclose these holdings and to create paddocks in
those areas which were not under cultivation, an
important step in the direction of individual land tenure.[35] As the more modernized Kipsigis cultivated
larger and larger areas, with no built-in indigenous
constraints, the amount of general grazing area was reduced. This situation was made worse by the fact that
much of the best grazing land was alienated to the
Europeans. C.M. Dobbs writes, as early as 1920,

The Lumbwa (Kipsigis) have far more cultivable land per head than any other tribe, but all their grazing land has been taken away and given to European farmers and they practically have to become serfs to get grass for their cattle.[36]

By 1950, the District Commissioner in Kericho reported that in Buret Location individual land tenure was becoming recognized in lieu of the old system of communal grazing.[37] Clearly, the traditional system of land use among the Kipsigis, under the impact of the introduction of cash crops, the orientation toward a cash economy, and the alienation of lands to settlers, was undergoing radical changes. These changes were likely to lead to the growth of a wealthy class cultivating large tracts of land on the one hand, with a landless class on the other.

By the mid-1950s, the Colonial Government was developing some concern about the growth of this landless class.[38] Its concern was shared by many Kipsigis, primarily from the perspective of future generations rather than acute current need. There was, at that time, throughout much of the Kipsigis Reserve, virtually de facto individual tenure. However, because of the reasonably low population to land ratios in the cultivable areas, there was not yet a problem of land fragmentation. In the late 1950s, the Government invited the Kipsigis to form a committee to investigate the question of customary law and land tenure and to work out guidelines on tenure and inheritance for the Government's use in forming policy. The Government intended to move slowly, and, using the findings of the committee, started land registration on a voluntary basis in 1960.

Thus, the existence of alienated lands, strict limitations on tribal reserve areas, the introduction of a cash economy, and the development of cash crops resulted in a drastic transformation of land tenure and cultivation patterns in the areas under discussion, with the exception of Mbeere. These tenure and cultivation patterns were formalized by the colonial policy of establishing freeholding land rights. Among the Kikuyu, this policy aggravated what was already becoming a system of individual land ownership under conditions of high population pressure. To a somewhat lesser extent this was also true for the Embu. Among the Kipsigis, individual land ownership transformed an egalitarian and laissez-faire system into one in which wide disparities of land ownership and wealth were possible. Among the Mbeere, who are just now experiencing the first major impact of these factors - cash cropping, a cash economy, land adjudication and land consolidation - initial findings suggest disparities

and stratification are developing and distrust and dis-
harmony are part of the transition process.[39]

Colonialism: Impact on Local Institutions

The most important objectives of the Colonial Government were to establish a system of control which
would enable it to maintain law and order, to collect
taxes, and to make settler farming profitable. In the
process of trying to achieve these objectives, the
Colonial Government virtually dismantled the traditional system of governance. At times the Government utilized tribal structures to deal with specific issues or
problems, but over time, it gradually usurped the
powers of indigenous institutions and created new institutions which it dominated.

In an effort to reach down to the village level,
the Government established Location Advisory Committees
in 1931.   These committees were to advise chiefs on
various matters related to the welfare of the location.
In 1932, Agricultural Committees were formed at the
divisional level, and considerable progress was made in
providing agricultural services. By the mid-1940s, the
District Commissioner in Murang'a was questioning
whether the Kikuyu people had been given sufficient
opportunity to shape their own destiny.[40] He suggested
that the system of local government, including both the
Local Native Council and the chiefs, was often out of
touch with the views held by the community. He advo-
cated some form of local government at the location
level, recommending a freely elected council of 35 to
40 members with every village having one or more representatives depending on its size.   The purpose of such
a group, in his view, would be to discuss issues, solicit views of the populace and relay information up-
wards.

In 1946, Location Councils were formally created
as a second tier of government in the areas of certain
Local Native Councils, including Murang'a and Embu.
These Location Councils were comprised of one member
from each sublocation, and they were responsible for
advising on such matters as granting permits for growing wattle, granting licenses for shops and trucks, or
designating sites for new roads.   They tended to include not only village representatives, but a cross
section of professional interests such as teachers and
traders. As would be anticipated, some chiefs used the
Location Councils effectively; others found them
threatening. One important function which the Location
Councils acquired was approval and processing of nomin-
ations for the Local Native Council. This consisted of
one elected member for each location, plus a group of
nominated members. Each Location Council reduced the

nominees to two or three who were then put before the
male electorate for public vote. Slowly the Location
Councils developed interest in the right to raise revenue. This included interest in collecting money for
water supplies, for educational purposes and for care
of cattle. Such rights were not granted, however, until the mid-1950s.

One Colonial Government activity which has influenced the use of Harambee self-help as an approach to
local development was the creation of local-level committees. These committees were task-oriented. That
is, they were established to deal with a specific problem or need. They had objectives, and they had to establish ways to meet them. Often these objectives were
specifically related to agricultural policy and rural
development. Thus, there grew, from the 1920s, a network of adults in the rural areas whose responsibility
it was to work cooperatively with others in organizing
their community for specific development-oriented
tasks. This sort of experience is a predecessor of the
project-oriented focus of the post-independence Harambee self-help efforts.

The impact of this network of committees varied
from locality to locality. For example, in Kericho
District, the Local Native Council and the colonial
administration worked out an effective system of dam
construction and road construction and maintenance
using a combination of communal labor for the lighter
clearing and maintenance, and digging/grading equipment
for the heavy work. In the 1940s Locational Agricultural Committees were functioning effectively among the
Kipsigis. The Locational Soil Conservation Committees
were so active and persuasive that an aerial survey
conducted in 1949 showed only two farms in the entire
district which were not implementing soil conservation
measures. The District Commissioner at that time acknowledged that this "remarkable progress is not due to
the Government. The credit for it belongs to the
Kipsigis."[41] Other officials noted that the Kipsigis
had become very conscious of soil conservation; the
people were exceedingly cooperative and the district
was an "excellent example of what could be accomplished
when a people made up their minds to practice sound
agricultural land preservation methods."[42] Through
such committees, the Kipsigis planned and implemented
policies for themselves and developed administrative
and political skills at the village level. In general,
relations between the Government, the Kipsigis Local
Native Council, and various committees were harmonious,
and work was carried out effectively and sensitively.

Among the Kikuyus, soil conservation and road
building through communal labor became volatile issues
from the 1930s through the 1950s. The Colonial Government required extensive bench terracing and road build-

ing throughout the Kikuyu reserve, even attempting, though unsuccessfully, at one point to demand from each adult ten days of unpaid communal labor a month on anti-soil erosion works.[43] In the post-World War II years, the Colonial Government forced such a frenzied pace of communal labor that hostility and alienation with regard to this kind of work was widespread. With the declaration of the Emergency at the end of 1952, communal labor became a major governmental weapon for dealing with insurgency, rebellion and general recalcitrance. A bulletin went out from Murang'a District Headquarters authorizing communal labor four days a week from 8:00 a.m. to 2:00 p.m. during which time all shops would be closed.[44] Attendance was to be taken and penalties for failing to contribute included fines and detention. Two days a week were to be devoted to agriculture-related labor and two days to other types such as road building. It was not until 1957 that the Provincial Commissioner's office reduced the maximum period for which communal services could be demanded to 60 days per year, in spite of urging from the District Commissioner of Murang'a to permit four mornings per week in order to complete the planting of hedges and the construction of access roads.[45] Thus, it is not surprising that negative attitudes toward communal road maintenance and soil conservation emerged among the Kikuyu during the colonial period and still exist. Today there are not many Harambee projects related to roads or soil conservation in Kikuyu areas.

Throughout the colonial period, one problem in particular characterized the affairs of local governance. This was the increasing hiatus in authority structures. Slowly the indigenous authorities lost their effectiveness as they lost control over land, over warfare, over the maintenance of law and peace, and over the nature of their society. Schools, missions, a settler-oriented, cash economy, and government introduced an outside world with new modes of access through education and wage employment. Propelled by a variety of economic and social circumstances, many young people oriented themselves rapidly toward this modern life style, a life style for which their elders had little enthusiasm and over which they had virtually no control. At the same time, many of the chiefs were regarded by their respective communities not as leaders but merely as arms of the government. Time and again in their Handing Over Reports, Annual Reports and the Political Record Books, throughout four decades, the 1920s through the 1950s, District Commissioners observed this breakdown in authority at the local level. As one stated, "The greatest difficulty and bar to progress, however, is the increasing inability of elders and indigenous authorities, as well as Government servants, to control the young men."[46] This problem

- a changing younger generation, often dissatisfied and
sometimes confused, accompanied by the deterioration of
indigenous authorities and the inadequacy of new ones -
characterized local communities during the colonial
period.

Colonialism: The Impact on Education

Under missionary guidance, many local communities
organized to contribute materials and labor to the construction of mission schools. However, in Kikuyu
areas, political and religious conflicts precipitated
the formation of new community self-help organizations
related to education and catapulted them to the center
of national political life. The conflict between the
Kikuyus and the Church of Scotland focused on the issue
of female circumcision. This had long been practiced
by the Kikuyus; missionaries from the Church of Scotland forbid its practice among their congregation. In
the late 1920s, when this conflict surfaced, many
Kikuyu adherents broke away from the Church of Scotland
and organized themselves into the Kikuyu Independent
Schools Association (KISA) financing and constructing
their own schools. By 1936, there were nine Kikuyu independent schools, founded by the KISA, functioning in
Murang'a District alone.
Throughout the 1940s, the Kikuyus expended much
effort on their independent schools. One Murang'a District Commissioner noted in 1946 that "A large number
of school buildings in stone have been put up by the
people without any aid from the Local Native Council or
Government, and the elementary schools are maintained
by them."[47]   By 1947, many students were qualified for
admission to government junior secondary schools.
There were insufficient places for these students and
almost every location started a fund for building a
junior secondary school within the location. By 1949,
there were over 170 primary schools in the district,
and new primary schools were continuing to spring up.[48]
Meanwhile, the desire for junior secondary schools continued to be very keen, and there was increasing interest in technical education. Shortly before Independence
every primary school in Murang'a District was granted
permission to collect money for building new classrooms
in order for each to be able to provide seven years of
education. The District Commissioner stressed at that
time that it was the job of each school committee to
erect and maintain school buildings and to provide permanent school equipment.[49]
As in Murang'a, local school committees in Embu
actively tried to raise funds for classrooms and furniture, and communal labor was an important part of the
building program. In general, mission education in

Embu was inferior to that of Murang'a. In 1937 there was no school which went beyond third grade. Only in 1947 was construction on a secondary school started.

In 1928 there was 27 mission schools and one Government school in Kericho District. (By contrast, in Murang'a there were 82 schools operating at that time and serving a population approximately half that of Kericho District.) Interest in education increased slowly among the Kipsigis. A District Commissioner observed in 1935, "The Kipsigis are beginning to be interested in education, but have little enthusiasm for mission teaching."[50] It was not until 1946 that the Kericho Local Native Council voted to implement its first educational cess, and it was not until 1953 that the Government actually posted an Education Officer in Kericho. The arrival of this officer coincided with, and perhaps helped to generate, an increased interest in education on the part of the Kipsigis. In the mid-1950s there was much progress in constructing primary schools of permanent materials within the district through voluntary collections of funds from local people. In fact, the primary school building program was handled entirely from local resources.

Thus, well before independence communities were involved in trying to improve educational facilities and opportunities through self-help efforts. In Mbeere these efforts were negligible; among the Kikuyu, they were prodigious. Among the Embu and Kipsigis, there was a steadily growing interest in community action to improve the quality of educational resources.

Colonialism and the Development of African Political Organizations

Throughout most of the colonial period, the Embu, Kipsigis and Mbeere peoples were generally apolitical, at least insofar as the Colonial Government was concerned. The indigenous forms of participation in groups and councils according to prescriptive characteristics of age and sex did not lend themselves to activism in regard to the new government. Few were educated; they had no vote and no formal access to the political system. Furthermore, funds were limited, and for the Kipsigis and Mbeere, Nairobi was remote. A quiet, though not always passive acceptance was the mode of response in most cases. As one District Commissioner stated, "For their taxes, the Kipsigis expect little and obtain less."[51] The mood was quiescent; the organizational/political response to Government policies was minimal until independence was fairly close at hand.

This was not so for the Kikuyus. In the Kikuyu areas the dual agricultural economy of settlers and reserve was of paramount importance. The settlement of the Kikuyu Highlands has been characterized as a "sudden invasion."[52] This settlement began in earnest in 1903 in the Thika area where sisal and coffee became the major crops. To prevent competition from the Kikuyu farmers and to assure a supply of labor for the settler farms, the Government forbid the Kikuyus to cultivate sisal and coffee. The settlers put constant pressure on the Government to get labor for them; the Government facilitated the process but did not actually supply labor for the farms. There was, in general, continuing friction and disagreement among Government, settlers and Kikuyus over labor policies. Pressures of hut and poll tax payments, as well as new opportunities for spending money on goods and services, provided incentives for Kikuyus to enter the cash economy. Unable to grow cash crops, they had to obtain cash by working as laborers on settler farms.

Among the Kikuyus political activism started shortly after World War I. In the Kiambu area where much land had been alienated to the settlers, the Kikuyu Association and the East Africa Association first arose. Support for them rapidly spread to the Murang'a and Nyeri sections of the Kikuyu Reserve. In several instances the claims and concerns of these groups were assisted and supported by various missionaries. Of particular concern, in addition to the land issues, was the kipande system of "native" registration, designed to facilitate the provision of labor for settler farms and the collection of hut and poll taxes.

By the mid-1920s, the moderate approach to political change, such as that embodied in the Kikuyu Association, was overtaken by a more militant approach represented by the Kikuyu Central Association. The KCA reached prominence in the confrontation with the Church of Scotland between 1928 and 1931. Dating from this period were the Kikuyu Karing'a Schools, localized in the southern and western part of Kiambu District, and the Kikuyu Independent Schools Association (KISA), mentioned earlier, which attained the status of a pan-Kikuyu organization with educational objectives. Also dating from this period were two independent African Churches, the African Independent Pentecostal (AIPC) and the African Orthodox Church, both of which had African clergy and leadership. KISA and AIPC were linked together.

An activist Kikuyu Central Association continued throughout the 1930s, particularly in response to the Kenya Land Commission appointed by the Government in 1932. This Commission had confirmed the relationship between communalism and land, legalizing the existing frontiers of Kenya's indigenous communities with minimal compensation and cutting of all existing claims and rights of Africans. In 1940, at the beginning of World

War II, prominent leaders of the Kikuyu Central Association were detained, and the KCA thereafter existed primarily in committee form at the local level.

World War II accelerated African Kenyan nationalism. Many Kikuyus, as well as people from other ethnic groups, served in the army in other countries, lived for the first time in multi-racial situations on an equal basis, and had an opportunity to gain an outside perspective on colonialism in Kenya. Returning soldiers brought new attitudes to their communities, as well as increased political awareness. This latter was observed by a District Commissioner in Embu who noted a "marked increase in the tendency to join political associations on the part of Embu people in 1946."[53] Shortly after the war, the Kenya Africa Union (KAU) was formed, and Jomo Kenyatta became its President in 1947. In the next six years the Kikuyu and their allies tried to bring other ethnic groups into alliance under the mantle of the Kenya African Union. However, Kikuyu frustrations were more acute and their aspirations for independence more keen than those of others, and other ethnic groups were only marginally involved in the national movement. Growing Kikuyu militancy led finally to the declaration of a State of Emergency by the Government in October, 1952, to the detainment of Kenyatta and other leaders, and to the outbreak of widespread rebellion in the Kikuyu areas.

During that period, an intricate network of leadership and organization grew among the politically-conscious Kikuyu. Rosberg stresses the importance of this network which functioned despite acute differences among the Kikuyus in economic well-being, degree of political militance, religious allegiance, factional loyalties, and increasing numbers of litigations over land.[54] In spite of these different perspectives, the Kikuyus were united by over-riding concerns about the land and increasing dedication to nationalism and independence. The Kikuyu network to which Rosberg refers was in operation a full two years before the outbreak of the Emergency. The proscribed KCA and KAU had operated committees throughout the Kikuyu areas in which each location had its own committee with representatives from the sublocations. Affiliated with the secret "parliament" of KAU and KCA were the Kikuyu Independent Schools Association, the Karing'a Schools and the Kikuyu Land Board Association.

Thus, a high level of social mobilization and political organization existed among the Kikuyu people during the colonial years. They spearheaded the independence movement, while trying, not very successfully, to incorporate other ethnic groups into their efforts. For them, the issues were most acute and the tensions most severe; their feelings were not shared with the same intensity by other ethnic groups. Among the Embu,

Mbeere and Kipsigis political activity was limited. A Kipsigis Political Association was formed in 1937, and ten years later a Kipsigis Tribal Association was formed, but these were desultory organizations. For the most part, the Kipsigis cooperated quite fully with the Colonial Government and were considered by it an exemplary people.

In Embu there were several branches of the Kikuyu Central Association as early as 1930. In the mid-1940s a KAU branch was established in Embu. The District Commissioner characterized its leadership as "intelligent, energetic and keen to cooperate with the Government and the Local Native Council."[55] At the official level, cooperation rather than confrontation was the pattern in Embu. The Embu District Association, formed in 1956, presented a modest and non-controversial set of aims at that time. In 1961, the District Commissioner spoke with great respect of the Embu Member of the Legislative Council, indicating that he was a man who had established good working relations with the Government.[56]

By contrast at the same time, Murang'a was welcoming back detainees who had been key figures during the Emergency. Simultaneously, two organizations considered illegal by the Government were in the process of forming in Murang'a: the KANU Youth Wing and the Kenya Land Freedom Army. Clearly the orientation toward politics and the interest in organization for political purposes were far greater among the Kikuyus than among the Kipsigis, Embu or Mbeere peoples.

In the post-Independence era, the organizational skills of the Kikuyu have manifested themselves not only in politics but also in their efforts to develop their own communities through Harambee. Other ethnic groups demonstrated organizational skills at the local level during the colonial period. In particular, the Kipsigis had effective Agricultural Committees and Soil Conservation Committees. It was the Kikuyus, however, who combined political awareness and savvy with organizational skills and community action, and it is this combination which is central to local-level development through self-help. In the historical confrontation between the Kikuyus and the Colonial Government/settlers are some of the seeds of effective Kikuyu mobilization for self-help. Thus the Kikuyu "head start" arises not only in the organizational structures fostered by the geography, and not only in pre-colonial group solidarities, but also in the socio-economic and political confrontations of the colonial era.

Out of the blend of ecological circumstances, precolonial tribal structures, and changes precipitated by the impact of a settler economy and colonial government, have evolved institutions which today are grappling with various forms of change at the local level.

Harambee self-help, as an approach to rural development, is among them.

A PORTRAIT OF SIX COMMUNITIES

People don't "live" in Districts. They "live" in communities with commitment, ties, affiliations and loyalties to friends, relatives, institutions, and organizations at the local level. The broad historical brush strokes through which we have considered patterns of change in Embu, Murang'a and Kericho must be transformed into the more detailed observation of the political anthropologist seeking to understand the critical socio-economic and political configurations within the six localities selected for the field study. Understanding these local level relationships within the context of historical patterns of change should help illuminate the roles of local organizations. The remainder of the book draws on data gathered in these six locations.

Kyeni and Nthawa: Two locations in Embu District

On a clear day, heading northeast out of Nairobi, one can glimpse Mount Kenya nearly all the way to Embu town. The road to Embu passes the Blue Post Hotel, at one time a favorite gathering place for Thika settlers, and the Del Monte pineapple plantation. It meanders across the hills of Kiambu's prospering Kikuyu coffee farmers and into the flatlands of the Mwea rice cultivation scheme. Matatus, pick-up trucks converted into oversized taxis, can reach Embu in about two hours. There, the Provincial Headquarters and District Headquarters, set behind masses of bougainvillea, make Embu town the administrative center for both Eastern Province and Embu District.

Kyeni is another twenty miles up the road past the market town of Runyenjes. (See page 51 for a map showing the six locations.) Two-thirds of this wedge-shaped location contain medium and high potential land cut into numerous ridges, well-watered by streams arising on the slopes of Mount Kenya, prime land for the tea growers of Rukuriri Sublocation or the coffee growers of Mufu and Kathari. The remaining third of the location trails off to the southeast into a dry, hot region of Karurumo Sublocation where the popular Karurumo Village Polytechnic is located. Cash crops are not found in this section of the location, and the area is sparsely populated in comparison with the more northern parts of Kyeni.

Over 31,000 of Embu's population of 262,000 people live in Kyeni Location at a population density nearly

51

Map 2.1

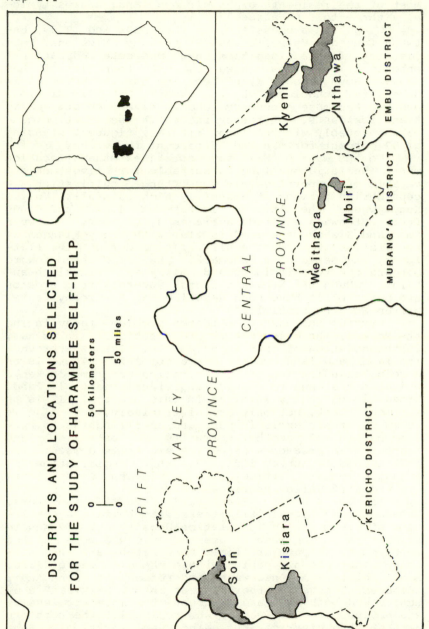

Source: Survey of Kenya, National Atlas of Kenya (Nairobi: Government of Kenya, 1970), p. 53.

3 1/2 greater than that of the rest of the district.[57]
Most of the residents own their own land, farms typically three to five acres.[58]
    Caught in a crossfire, in the 1920s and 1930s, be-
tween feuding Catholic and Protestant Missions, Embu
District for a long time had mediocre educational
opportunities. Now, however, the town itself has
Kangaru Boys School; Kyeni Location has the Kyeni Girls
Secondary School run by the Kyeni Catholic Mission,
and two Harambee secondary schools have been started by
Kyeni residents. Literacy rates in the location com-
pare favorably with national literacy figures, standing
at 87 percent for men and 76 percent for women.
    To the east of Embu town stretches Nthawa Location
where semiarid bushland is suitable for livestock and
capable of supporting only subsistence cultivation except during periods of unusually high rainfall. Unlike
Kenyi where the altitude is between 4,500 and 6,000
feet, Nthawa's altitude averages 3,000 feet. Between
Embu and Siakago the land is flat with only Kiangombe,
the distinctive granite hill rising out of the flatlands, to serve as a landmark. Beyond Siakago toward
Gangara the terrain is rugged, hilly and starkly beautiful. Much of Nthawa suffers severely from erosion
and parts of it have been described as "a rocky waste,
barren and inaccessible."[59]
    Perhaps the most complicated problem today facing
the Mbeere, the major ethnic group resident in Nthawa,
is the question of land adjudication. Issues surrounding land and land ownership are complex. There is an
ongoing adjudication and registration program in Kenya
which is designed to provide individual rights in land.
Nthawa is currently involved in this process. It is an
enormous task, not only administratively, but also in
terms of ethnic exclusiveness and unwillingness to permit people of another community to establish land
rights in an area considered its exclusive domain. The
1977 Economic Survey indicates that registration and
adjudication are particularly slow in the Coast, Eastern and Rift Valley Provinces.[60]
    In contrast to Kyeni's 99 square kilometers,
Nthawa has 370 square kilometers with half the population of Kyeni and a population density of 42 square
kilometers. The Mbeere are a people who cope with a
land and a climate at times both harsh and inhospit-
able. They are now coping with a changing way of life.
Some deplore the new ways and refuse to send their
children to school; others lament their "backward" community and both envy and distrust the more progressive
and prosperous Embu people who reside in the northern
part of the district, including Kyeni Location. Some
are eager to bring change to their communities. A
leader in Gitiburi Sublocation said proudly, "In 1970
we had only two boys who had attended secondary school;

now there are six."[61]   One observer   cast light on the
changes among   the Mbeere   when he stated,   "The Mbeere
are   poised between   weakened   traditional institutions
and sanctions on one hand, and imperfectly grasped modernization on the other."[62]

Weithaga and Mbiri: Two Locations in Murang'a District

   Weithaga's steep ridges are covered with extensive
terraced cultivation and the countryside is green and
lovely.   Farms are small, similar in size to those of
Kenyi, with well cared for coffee trees, banana trees
and patches of maize. The visitor in 1978 and 1979 observes many signs of Weithaga's recent coffee prosperity. A lot of building is underway. Families are constructing "permanent homes" of stone and iron sheet
roofs, rather than the customary mud, wattle and
thatch, and in many gardens there are truck loads of
stone deposited and ready for construction to begin.
New or improved public buildings are in evidence as
well: a stone church is going up on a hillside in
Mukangu Sublocation, another in Wanjengi and still
others in Gatheru and Kianderi Sublocations, as well as
new primary school classrooms and secondary schools.
   An area which has had mission schools since early
in the 20th century, Weithaga has nearly 100 percent
literacy among adult males and 77 percent among females.[63]   One sees clusters of neatly uniformed children going to and from the Harambee day secondary
schools which are becoming increasingly popular in
Weithaga.
   As in Weighaga, the people of Mbiri are Kikuyu,
but the area they occupy is quite different. Their
land is flat and the weather is relatively dry and hot.
Where 32,350 people occupy the 50 square kilometers of
Weithaga, 19,410 live in Mbiri's 48 square kilometers.[64]   The Kikuyu of Mbiri feel frustrated by the
prosperity of others not far away, and have long felt
that they are being left behind in the development
process. To the south, the Kikiyu of Kiambu occupy the
third most prosperous district, and to the north and
west of them, Kikuyus of the rest of Murang'a and of
Nyeri District have shared in the benefits brought to
Central Province's smallholder coffee farmers in the
mid-1970s coffee boom.   While the men of Weithaga manage their small coffee farms, the men of Mbiri are frequently looking in Nairobi for whatever work they can
find, or laboring in the quarries which are providing
the stones for houses in the more prosperous sections
of the district. In Mbiri one finds many female headed
households, a rare circumstance in Weithaga.   In Mbiri

many families face hardships; dissatisfaction is widespread; and morale is low.

Kisiara and Soin: Two locations in Kericho
District

The journey from Nairobi to Kisumu, located on
Lake Victoria, takes one through Kericho District, the
heart of tea growing in Kenya. There are nearly 13,800
smallholder tea farmers cultivating a total of 6,255
hectares or roughly one acre of tea per farm in that
district.[65] Kisiara is located among the rolling green
hills of Kericho's tea country.   With 50,800 people,
primarily Kipsigis, it is the most populous location
under investigation.   Landholdings are larger in
Kisiara than in the four locations previously discussed, and nearly half the households have between 10
and 20 acres of land, frequently with grown sons
assisting an elderly father in whose name the land is
held.   Maize is the leading food crop in Kenya, and it
is widely cultivated by Kisiara's smallholders. A typical farm family will grow both tea and maize and keep
cattle for milk production as well.

Kisiara is beginning to experience the problems of
educated but unemployed sons and daughters.   For the
typical Kipsigis, Nairobi is somewhat far away and too
alien for casual efforts to seek employment.   Not much
development has occurred in Kericho town since independence, and, consequently, the opportunities near
home are limited.

Where land in Kisiara was selling in 1979 for Ksh.
10,000 ($1,333) an acre, in Soin, to the north in
Kericho District, the price of land was Ksh. 2,000
($267) an acre.[66] Soin is a relatively poor and very
stony area of primarily high rainfall savannah, just
now beginning to feel some limited measure of prosperity through the introduction of sugar cane as a cash
crop.   In 1979, the Government announced that a sugar
factory would be constructed in Kapsarok, a sublocation
of Soin, a decision received with great enthusiasm by
Soin farmers. Not all of Soin Location residents, however, are in a position to grow sugar cane.   In Koitaburot Sublocation, for example, some people live in a
remote area backing up to the Nandi Escarpment and to
Mount Tinderet which rises dramatically to over 8,000
feet.   The eastern end of this sublocation is accessi-
ble only by foot and possessions must be carried on
back or head or put on a donkey.

In Soin the literacy rates are below the national
average - 44 percent for men and 26 percent for
women.[67] Women seemed less well informed and less
active in matters outside the home than did women in
the other locations visited.   Men, on the other hand,

often showed a lively interest not only in their own
community but in other parts of Kenya.

The six locations reflect some of the diversity
which is characteristic of Kenya. Three are high
potential areas - Kyeni, Weithaga and Kisiara - and
three have a poor resource base - Mbiri, Nthawa and
Soin. Table 2.9 provides some comparative data which
points out the similarities and differences among the
locations selected for the study. In this table, and
in others to follow, locations are arranged from left
to right along a continuum indicating the least prosperous and least developed (Soin and Nthawa) to the
most prosperous and most developed (Kyeni and Weithaga). The ordering of the locations along a continuum is based on a careful ranking of each location in
the following categories: 1) percentage of subsistence
households interviewed; 2) levels of male employment
(casual and regular); 3) presence of cash crops; 4)
standard of housing; 5) nature of household furnishings; 6) land ownership; 7) levels of education among
men; 8) levels of education among women.

Information on the above points was collected
through the survey questionnaire. Locations were then
ranked on each item, and a composite score for each
location was used to determine its relative position
among the locations under investigation. Information
gathered in these locations constitutes the basis for
observations about the role of Harambee self-help in
Kenyas' political economy and in its development
process.

NOTES

1. The Weekly Review, (Nairobi: Stellascope
Limited) November 30, 1979. This issue contains pre-
liminary findings of the census conducted in August,
1979.
2. Government of Kenya, Development Plan for the
Period 1979-1983 (Nairobi: Government Printer, 1979),
Part I, p. 61; and the Government of Kenya, Ministry of
Finance and Planning, Central Bureau of Statistics,
Social Perspectives, vol. 2, no. 1, March, 1977, p. 2.
3. Government of Kenya, Development Plan for the
Period 1979-1983 (Nairobi: Government Printer, 1979),
Part I, p. 152.
4. Government of Kenya, Ministry of Finance and
Planning, Development Plan for the Period 1984-88
(Nairobi: Government Printing Office, 1984) pp. 68-69.
5. Michael Schluter, "Constraints of Kenya's Food
and Beverage Exports," IFPRI Abstract, (Washington,
D.C.: International Food Policy Research Institute,
#44, April, 1984), p. 3.
6. Michael Schulter, "Constraints on Kenya's Food

and Beverage Exports," IFPRI Abstract, #44, (Washington, D.C.: International Food Policy Research Institute, April, 1984), p. 2.

7. Government of Kenya, Integrated Rural Surveys, 1976-1979, Basic Report, Ministry of Economic Planning and Development, Central Bureau of Statistics (Nairobi: Government Printers, 1982) pp. 17, 42 and 93.

8. Government of Kenya, Ministry of Finance and Planning, Central Bureau of Statistics, Social Perspectives, vol. 2, no. 1, March, 1977. Data for Tables 1 and 2 is from page 7.

9. Ibid.

10. Government of Kenya, Ministry of Finance and Planning, Central Bureau of Statistics, Integrated Rural Survey, 1974-1975 (Nairobi: Government Printer, March, 1977). Data for Table 3 are adapted from pp. 43 and 51.

11. Government of Kenya, National Development Plan 1984-88 op. cit., p. 40.

12. Ibid, p. 53.

13. Ibid, p. 95.

14. Ng'ethe, op. cit., quoting Voice of Kenya, January, 1977. Also Mbithi and Rasmusson, op. cit., p. 13.

15. Mbithi and Rasmusson, op. cit., quoting the Development Plans, 1970-1974 and 1974-1978, and the Statistical Abstract, 1973.

16. Government of Kenya, Development Plan, 1979-1983, Part I, p. 185.

17. Ministry of Housing and Social Services, Department of Social Services, Community Development Division, Self-Help Statistics, volumes 1974-1978; Ministry of Housing and Social Services/Ministry of Cooperatives and Social Services, A Statistical Analysis on Self-Help Projects, 1967-1971, 1972. (Cyclostyled report.); Report of a University of Nairobi Team, Toward Strategies for Intensified Social Development, mimeographed report, December, 1977, for the purpose of preparation of the 4th Development Plan.

18. This figure includes very large figures for 1967 and 1968 for completed projects. It seems unlikely that the figures for these two years are correct.

19. Government of Kenya, Ministry of Economic Planning and Community Affairs, Central Bureau of Statistics, Economic Survey, 1979, p. 175.

20. Ministry of Housing and Social Services, Self-Help Statistics, op. cit., and Ministry of Housing and Social Services/ Ministry of Cooperatives and Social Services, A Statistical Analysis on Self-Help Projects, 1967-1971, 1972.

21. See Mbithi and Rasmusson, op. cit., or Martin Hill, op. cit.

22. See Godfrey Muriuki, A History of the Kikuyu, 1500-1900 (London: Oxford University Press, 1974).

See also, J.M. Fisher, <u>Reports on the Kikuyu</u> (Nairobi: Government of Kenya Archives, 1952); Jomo Kenyatta, <u>Facing Mt. Kenya</u> (New York: Random House, 1965); and H.E. Lambert, <u>Kikuyu Social and Political Institutions</u> (London: Oxford University Press, 1956).

23. According to Kikuyu legend, as described by Jomo Kenyatta in <u>Facing Mt. Kenya</u>, there are nine families which were the founders of the Kikuyu <u>meherega</u> or clans. These clans constituted patrilineal, exogamous structures within the Kikuyu community, Kenyatta, <u>op. cit.</u>, p. 7-10. Among the Mbeere there are 50 patrilineal, exogamous clans with various subdivisions or moieties. Brokensha and Glazier, "Land Reform Among the Mbeere of Central Kenya," <u>Africa</u>, vol. 43, no. 3, July, 1973.

24. Muriuki, <u>op. cit.</u>, p. 116.

25. For studies of the Embu and Mbeere see David Brokensha and Jack Glazier, "Land Reform Among the Mbeere of Central Kenya," <u>Africa</u>, vol. 43, no. 3, July, 1973; David Brokensha and E.H.N. Njeru, "Some Consequences of Land Adjudication in Mbeere Division, Embu," Working Paper #320, Institute for Development Studies, University of Nairobi, September, 1977; and H.S.K. Mwaniki, <u>The Living History of Embu and Mbeere</u> (Nairobi: East African Literature Bureau, 1973).

For studies of the Kipsigis, see Robert A. Manners, "The Kipsigis of Kenya: Culture Change in a 'Model East African Tribe'," in Julian H. Steward's Three African Tribes in Transition, vol. 1 of <u>Contemporary Change in Traditional Societies</u>, University of Illinois Press, 1967; Henry A. Mwanzi, <u>A History of the Kipsigis</u> (Nairobi: East African Literature Bureau, 1961); and J.G. Peristiany, <u>The Social Institutions of the Kipsigis</u> (London: George Routledge and Sons, 1939). See also Footnote no. 2 above.

26. Mwaniki, <u>op. cit.</u>, p. 57.

27. Manners, <u>op. cit.</u>, p. 244; See also the Colonial, <u>Reports Kericho Political Record Book, 1927</u>.

28. Notes by I.Q. Orchardson, <u>Kericho Political Record Book, 1927</u>.

29. Colonial Reports, <u>Fort Hall (Nurang'a) Handing Over Report, 1926</u>. Government of Kenya Archives, microfilm.

30. Geoff Lamb, <u>Peasant Politics</u> (Dorset: Davison Publishing Limited, 1974), p. 11.

31. M.P.K. Sorrenson, <u>Land Reform in the Kikuyu Country</u> (Nairobi: Oxford University Press, 1967), p. 118.

32. D. Brokensha and J. Glazier, "Land Reform Among the Mbeere of Central Kenya," <u>Africa</u>, vol. 43, no. 3, July, 1973.

33. Brokensha and Njeru, <u>op. cit.</u>, seminar presentation of IDS Working Paper #320, University of Nairobi, September 6, 1977.

34. Manners, op. cit., p. 281.
35. Colonial Reports, Kericho Annual Report, 1947. Government of Kenya Archives, microfilm.
36. Colonial Reports, C.M. Dobbs, Political Record Book, Kericho, 1920. Government of Kenya Archives, microfilm.
37. Colonial Reports, Kericho Annual Report, 1950. Government of Kenya Archives, microfilm.
38. Kericho District, Annual Reports, 1955 & 1956. Also the Agricultural Gazetteer, 1956.
39. See Brokensha and Njeru, op. cit.
40. Colonial Reports, Murang'a Annual Report, 1944. Government of Kenya Archives, microfilm.
41. Colonial Reports, Kericho District, Annual Report, 1949. Government of Kenya Archives, microfilm.
42. Colonial Reports, Kericho District, Annual Report, 1946 and Annual Report, 1947. Government of Kenya Archives, microfilm.
43. Colonial Reports, Murang'a Annual Report, 1943. Government of Kenya Archives, microfilm.
44. Office of the District Commissioner, Fort Hall (Ref. No. Lab 27/1/15. November, 1953), Communal Labour File, 1946-1957. DC/MUR/318/14. Government of Kenya Archives.
45. Emergency Regulation from the Provincial Commissioner's Office regarding communal services, January, 1957; Communal Labour File and letter from the District Commissioner, Fort Hall, June 10, 1957. Communal Labour Files, DC/MUR/318/14. Government of Kenya Archives.
46. Colonial Reports, Embu Annual Report, 1947. Government of Kenya Archives, microfilm.
47. Colonial Reports, Murang'a Annual Report, 1946. Government of Kenya Archives, microfilm.
48. Colonial Reports, Murang'a Annual Report, 1949. Government of Kenya Archives, microfilm. In the late 1940s there were approximately 170 primary schools among the Kikuyu of Murang'a; 150 in Embu District, primarily among the Embu, and 80 in Kericho District. See Colonial Reports for Embu Annual Report, 1951, Kericho Annual Report, 1949, and Murang'a Annual Report, 1949. Government of Kenya Archives, microfilm.
49. Colonial Reports, Murang'a Annual Report, 1962. Government of Kenya Archives, microfilm.
50. Colonial Reports, Kericho District Commissioner, Handing Over Report, 1935. Government of Kenya Archives, microfilm.
51. Colonial Reports, Kericho Annual Report, 1923. Government of Kenya Archives, microfilm.
52. Colonial Reports, Murang'a Political Record Book History of Fort Hall, 1898-1944. Government of Kenya Archives, microfilm.
53. Colonial Reports, Embu Annual Report, 1946. Government of Kenya Archives, microfilm.

54. Carl Rosberg and John Nottingham, The Myth of Mau Mau: Nationalism in Kenya (Palo Alto: Stanford University, Hoover Institution press, 1966), p. 242.

55. Colonial Reports, Embu Annual Report, 1947. Government of Kenya Archives, microfilm.

56. Colonial Reports, Embu Annual Report, 1961. Government of Kenya Archives, microfilm.

57. The Weekly Review, (Nairobi: Stellascope Limited), November 30, 1979. This issue contains preliminary findings of the census conducted in August, 1979. Full census information has not yet been processed and released by the Central Bureau of Statistics. Population figures for the locations are based on 1974 figures from the District Development Plans, as a percentage of the whole district, and extrapolated on the basis of the 1979 census figures for the districts involved.

58. The survey questionnaire asked for information on land ownership and size of holding. These figures are based on respondent answers.

59. Colin Maher, Soil Erosion and Land Utilization in the Embu Reserve, Part I, April, 1938. Government of Kenya Archives, Unpublished report, p. 34.

60. Government of Kenya, Ministry of Finance and Planning, Central Bureau of Statistics, Economic Survey, 1977, pp. 99-100.

61. Mr. G.W. Mwangario, Chairman of the School Committee, Gitiburi School, Nthawa Location, April, 1978.

62. D.O. Naysime, Final Report on the Mbeere SRDP, May, 1977, in the SRDP files, Siakago, Nthawa Location.

63. The survey questionnaire asked for information on literacy and levels of education, and these figures are based on the answers of respondents.

64. Population figures are based on 1974 figures in the District Plan, which gives population data by location, extrapolated on the basis of the 1979 preliminary figures for district populations.

65. Government of Kenya, Kericho District Development Plan, 1974-1978, January, 1978, p. 3.

66. Wilson Siongok, Location Community Development Assistant, in conversation, May, 1979 and Charles Sang, LCDA, June, 1979.

67. The survey questionnaire contained questions related to literacy in all the locations.

Table 2.9
Basic data on the locations selected for research on Harambee self-help

	Soin	Nthawa	Mbiri	Kisiara	Kyeni	Weithaga
Area in sq. km.	227	370	48	223	99	50
Population*	12,700	15,720	19,410	50,800	31,440	32,350
Average population density (sq. Km.)	56	42	404	228	318	647
District	Kericho	Embu	Murang'a	Kericho	Embu	Murang'a
Distance from Nairobi (km.)	300	190	87	280	160	110
Province	Rift Valley	Eastern	Central	Rift Valley	Eastern	Central
Major ethnic group	Kipsigis	Mbeere	Kikuyu	Kipsigis	Embu	Kikuyu
% of households owning land**	76	87	85	62	95	61
Subsistence households (%)	20	29	23	8	1	4
% households with male employment, casual or regular	15	48	74	26	38	62

	Poorest/least developed					Wealthiest/most developed
Male literacy (%)	44	60	74	76	87	97
Female literacy (%)	22	39	50	54	76	77
Cash crop (established)				tea, maize	coffee, tea	coffee
Cash crop (beginning)	sugar cane	cotton, tobacco	coffee			

Locations: Poorest/least developed --- Wealthiest/most developed.

* Population figures are based on district figures from the 1979 census. The location figures are extrapolated on the basis of percentages of the population of the district resident in that location according to the 1969 census.

** These figures, and those in the columns to follow, are based on a random-sample survey questionnaire administered to residents of the locations. Such information is not available in Government records below the district level.

III
The Role of Self-Help
in the Political Process

> Always there is evidence of politics. It seems to
> take a politician to get a project going and to
> bring it to the attention of the appropriate offi-
> cials.
>
> Respondent
> Mbiri Location

At Independence, Harambee became a rallying cry
throughout the country declaring to one and all that
Kenya was independent and self-reliant and that her
people would work together for common objectives. More
than twenty years later, Harambee, as an approach to
local rural development, is an integral part of Kenya's
political life. It is influenced by, and in turn
affects, the structure, style and process of Kenyan
politics. This chapter examines the links between
Harambee, as a mode of local-level development, and
national politics in Kenya. It presents a model for
interpreting Kenyan politics and explores the relationship between this model of political behavior and
Harambee self-help. It examines the role of national-
level elites in Harambee, and it explores the role of
local elites in development through self-help.

A MODEL OF CONTEMPORARY POLITICAL BEHAVIOR IN KENYA

Like many nations, Kenya has a modern bureaucracy,
a Parliamentary system of Government, and a nationwide
political party, the Kenya Africa National Union
(KANU). These have functioned continuously and effectively since Kenya's independence, and Kenya has received much praise for the stability and permanence of
her institutions. It is necessary, however, to go beyond a formal, legal interpretation of Kenyan institutions to understand how Kenya's political system works.
A model which is useful in interpreting this system draws on Weber's interpretations of patrimonialism

in combination with more recent theoretical explorations of clientelism and elite behavior.[1] Patrimonialism is derived from traditional, patriarchal domination. The central features of a patrimonial system are traditional status and authority, and the personal loyalty of staff, retainers, subjects or followers. As a model, patrimonialism is useful for analysis of politics in Kenya because it clarifies and provides possible explanations for relationships and informal power structures. It offers insights into the political processes of Kenya's first years under the leadership of former President Jomo Kenyatta and aids in the understanding of a continuing style of politics widespread in Kenya today.

This model is even more useful if combined with a theory of elite behavior such as that offered by Gerald Heeger in The Politics of Underdevelopment.[2] Much political analysis of developing countries has focused on institutional development, assessments of party structures, the growth of governing institutions, and organizational change. Heeger, however, focuses attention on elite behavior as the critical ingredient in the politics of developing nations. He is concerned less with organized groups and institutions than with the politics of faction, coalition, maneuver and personalism. He suggests that politics in the Third World revolves around the political functioning of the elites, elite interactions with one another, and the effect of such interactions on non-elites. He states,

> Power and support tend to be localized, and political institutions and organizations are characterized by coalitions of semi-autonomous elites and groups at the local, regional and national levels. The political process, as a result, is defined by the efforts of the elites to coalesce with one another in order to establish national institutions in the center of the new society, by attempts to enlist societal support and elites outside that center, by group and elite responses to policies and politics in the center, and by efforts of center elites to accommodate such responses when they are dissident.[3]

A model drawing on concepts of patrimonialism and analysis of elite behavior according to Heeger's approach suggests that there are patterns of elite coalitions revolving around a patrimonial leader or leaders, determining their loyalties on the basis of confidence in personal leadership and on the rewards and benefits which will result from a particular association. This is not simply the dyadic relationship described in much of the literature on patron-client relationships, in which each link is a separate personal tie between patron and client.[4] The model is characterized by congeries and factions with linkages to the larger system through the patrimonial leader.

The means for forming these linkages are numerous. Patronage and the rewards of office are, of course, central. Personal charisma and common ideological concerns are also important. This is reciprocal obligation, but it may not be of a strictly personal nature. It may involve access to resources at the center and delivery of benefits, resources and services to followers, while support, usually political, moves upward to the benefactor. Followers may be at the periphery, literally part of a rural constituency, or they may be members of elite factions engaged in an unending process of merging, separating and shifting coalitions around the center.

Patrimony building, constructing a network of elites and linking different groups of elites behind a given leader are all characteristic of this model. Within this structure there may be, and often are, highly personal, informal agreements between leader and follower or patron and client, in which there is private, though not public, accountability. These personal sets of obligations lead to what some analysts have called clientelist states in which "bonds of reciprocal obligation align dependent subordinates with individual political or administrative leaders in more or less cohesive informal structure."[5] Hence, clientelist politics can co-exist with "modern" political parties and governing bureaucracies, serving as the dominant organizational mode within these structures.

To what ends has this political structure functioned in Kenya? First, it has permitted the cultivation of power bases on the part of politicians at various levels of the system. For many national figures the system has provided a constituency from which to develop national status and power, linking them to the sublocation through key people at the local level.

Second, Jomo Kenyatta's long tenure as President, and his secure position as "Father of his Country" permitted the consolidation of power at the center in much the way that has been described: patrimony building, organizing factions, building networks. In addition, this consolidation of power has an ethnic dimension. Given the role of the Kikuyus in the independence struggle and their centrality as inheritors of power at Independence, consolidation of power at the center has, in some measure, meant consolidation of power for the Kikuyus.

Third, Kenya has elected to pursue a strategy of maximizing economic growth, and is only now beginning to look closely at some of the equity issues which arise in pursuit of such a policy. The political structure has not only permitted, but has encouraged,

elites to seek personal prosperity and to regard the
growth of individual wealth as a national good. Fourth,
remarkable stability has, to date, been the outcome of
this political structure. Various ethnic groups, factions, parties and cliques have maneuvered around a
strong center, and the results have been an uncommonly
stable political system, despite the coup attempt of
August, 1982.

What is the role of Harambee self-help in shaping,
preserving and fostering this system? What are the
political dimensions of Harambee? Harambee cannot be
examined simply in a developmental context or along
lines of economic cost/benefit analysis. Rather, it
must be examined within the larger framework of power
relationships and the political process.

FUNCTIONS OF SELF-HELP: LINKING POLITICS TO
ECONOMIC AND SOCIAL SPHERES

One of the most important functions served by
Harambee is that of reconciling the values of the
pre-colonial political and social systems with those of
a modern economy based on individual enterprise.
Ciparisse points out, "There is a major conflict between social structure and value system of clan and the
spirit of individual enterprise that develops within
the context of a modern economy."[6] Sharing of wealth,
which was practiced throughout much of pre-colonial
Kenya, produces a fairly equitable distribution of income but discourages economic growth and development by
diminishing incentives for individuals to increase
their own incomes. Harambee is a bridge which permits
the individual to accumulate wealth, a non-traditional
form of behavior, and to share it with his community in
a way which is not customary, provision of development-
related public goods, but which is socially acceptable
and which benefits the individual contributor as well
as other members of his community. That is, Harambee
capitalizes on the old value of wealth-sharing but with
new objectives. It thus permits a pragmatic adaptation
of pre-colonial tribal customs to modern objectives and
needs.

Evidence suggests that development through Harambee self-help works best in those places where there is
already widespread interest in rural development. That
is, it has been most successful where people are already drawn into the modernization process, as opposed
to situations in which people are not yet involved. It
is not easily forced upon a community by an enthusiastic administration, for it does not, in such a situation, serve the value/ideological or the socio-
economic needs of the community. Thus, Harambee justifies in familiar, customary terms what the economic

system requires. Harambee means "Let's pull together," and Kenyans have interpreted this phrase in terms of unified efforts to build up their nation. In a more abstract sense, the term Harambee unites the past and the present, the old and the new in a politically and socially acceptable concept. In a blend of indigenous values, new ways of earning and sharing wealth, new patterns of upward mobility, new concepts of welfare and opportunity, and political structures forged in the post-independence era, the significance of Harambee can be found.

Second, within the framework of Kenya's economic system, Harambee is an important mechanism for the transfer of resources from center to periphery. It serves as a legitimate means for private income to be channeled into public use in the outlying areas. Government funds, foreign aid or aid from non-governmental organizations also reach the rural areas through Harambee projects, but this assistance could easily be channeled though other means. Harambee offers an opportunity for individual incomes as well to benefit a rural public. In fact, it is based upon the assumption that everyone who can will try to contribute what he is able to the development of community projects in his home area.

Whether or not Harambee is a fair means of transferring resources is another question. Clearly, the existence of this mode of development is being used to justify inequities in incomes. The Kenyan Government officially justifies its economic growth strategy and the resulting inequities in income level on the basis of Harambee's potential for directing individual profit to public, social purposes. It states in the 1979-1983 Plan,

> The Harambee movement and the extended family system are important means by which, after tax, incomes are further redistributed from the wealthier to the poorer sections of the nation. Direct transfer payments from those employed in urban areas to family members in rural areas is a source of substantial funds for rural development and the alleviation of poverty. Harambee efforts provide an array of social, educational, and economic facilities whose services are available to the poor ... These efforts will continue to receive support and guidance from the Government as an essential ingredient of incomes policy and rural development.[7]

Third, the Harambee approach to local development has permitted the Government to focus on national priorities by placing responsibility for initiatives with the local community. Not only has this approach

been an important method for generating local resources, but it also has taken the pressure off the
Government for building local rural infrastructure and
has enabled it to consolidate power at the center.
Some have argued that the approach has been costly for
the Government because it has not been able to control
project type adequately and has been expected to take
over the recurring costs of some projects. The statistics presented in Chapter II provide ample evidence
that the Government contribution to Harambee projects
has been a small part of the resources generated.
Nevertheless, by focusing on national priorities and
moving selectively in the rural areas, the Central Government has been able to consolidate its strength. It
has further enhanced power at the center by strengthening the capabilities of the Ministries at the district
level and by severely curtailing the responsibilities
of district local government through the County Councils.[8]

Finally, the existence of Harambee has permitted a
marriage between the desire of elites for a strong
power base in the rural areas, and the desire of local
communities to promote and secure their own interests.
Much of the Harambee self-help effort can be interpreted as action to extend mobility opportunities and
to expand a given group's share of available resources.
In this context, the emergence of a strong Harambee
development effort appears to be related to a growing
awareness by rural Kenyans of the ways in which an
independent Kenya is allocating resources, benefits and
privileges. While such an interpretation may sound
somewhat abstract and removed from reality, in fact, it
quickly translates itself into particulars relevant to
every household: a new school for the children, a dip
for the cattle, health care, feeder road into the village, a water supply. Public awareness was built up
during the independence struggle. In addition, widespread opportunities to listen to the radio, as well as
numerous public meetings, led by political and administrative leaders to discuss public issues, have led to
an expanding public consciousness. The notion of helping yourself, and using every possible means to obtain
outside assistance as well, has taken root in fertile
ground.

At the same time, competition among elites, elite
efforts to organize bases of support in the rural
areas, and the reciprocal relationships between
national-level elites and local elites forge a link between Harambee's political role and its developmental
role and between the structural limitations on Harambee
and questions of individual choice, motivation and behavior. If behavioral and structural approaches can be
said to stand at opposite ends of a continuum,[9] they
come into contact in a consideration of the roles of

both local and national elites in the politics of
development through self-help.

SELF-HELP AND POLITICAL STRUCTURES

Party Politics

Party politics and the electoral process underlie
the struggle to shape Harambee development efforts.
The Kenya Africa National Union (KANU) has an administrative structure down to the locational level and in
some instances to the sublocational level. District
branches of KANU are influential organizations with the
participation and loyalty of many leading persons in
the community. The Members of Parliament in particular
are active in organizing the activities of KANU in
their districts. Members and those who oppose them at
election time seek the loyalty of their constituency in
a variety of ways. Among the most important is demon-
strating their ability to aid their people through fostering Harambee projects. Candidates seek to prove
their loyalty to their constituency through organizing
development projects, contributions to projects, and
indications that, if elected, they would be able to
provide largesse of various sorts for their people.
Commenting on the pending 1979 elections, an editorial
in The Daily Nation pointed out, "Careful scrutiny of
the way in which some people dish out Harambee funds
and areas they choose to display their philanthropy
will show clearly which people are interested in which
constituencies."10
Thus, Harambee is closely linked with the electoral political process, and its momentum accelerates
as party politics and elections are increasingly close
at hand. It is instructive to look at the political
competition in Mbiri constituency for the Member of
Parliament's seat in 1979, for it illustrates very
clearly the role of Harambee in politics.
Until November, 1979, Dr. J.G. Kiano had been the
incumbent from Mbiri constituency and Minister for
Water Development. He was first elected to Parliament
in 1958, and since 1964, he had represented the Mbiri
constituency which includes both Weithaga and Mbiri
Locations. He had served as Minister in four different
ministries during that time, and was with the Ministry
of Water Development for the three years preceding his
defeat. He is a powerful figure in Kenyan politics and
despite his defeat, probably ranks among a handful of
Kenyans who are highly influential politically. He was
challenged by Mr. K.B. Matiba, a prominent businessman
and former Executive Director of a major corporation,
Kenya Breweries. Matiba won the election.
The duel was waged with Harambee projects. It had

several dimensions. At fundraising occasions, there was direct competition with Mssrs. Kiano and Matiba both occupying the speakers' platform and vying with one another for top position in bringing in the most funds for the project from themselves, their friends and associates. In a special, pre-election edition of The Weekly Review, Peter Kareithi and Hilary Ng'weno estimated that "between July, 1974 and January, 1979, Matiba had contributed over Shs. 1.5 million ($200,000) to development projects in Mbiri."[11]

In some cases, Kiano and Matiba proposed alternative methods and approaches for Harambee development efforts, each in the hope that his own approach would be adopted by the constituency and that it would prove effective in assisting the people. The most well known dispute concerned the approach for raising funds for primary schools. Matiba, as vice-chairman of KANU in Murang'a District, wanted a district-wide fundraising campaign which would have the objective of raising Ksh. 20,000 ($2,666) for each primary school in the district.[12] As Chairman of KANU's Primary School Harambee Committee, he had been prepared to put his full strength behind such an effort, mindful, of course, of the prestige and support that a successful fundraising campaign would bring him. Kiano had disdained participation in this venture, claiming that the decision to undertake it was made without his knowledge, despite his membership in Murang'a's KANU Committee. He proceeded with a fundraising for the primary schools within his constituency. Kiano's unwillingness to cooperate in a district-wide effort effectively undermined Matiba's proposal, however, both candidates conducted numerous fundraising events for individual schools.

The campaigning continued in a highly tense, competitive manner, and the election itself was very close. Matiba won 55 percent of the vote. Meantime, the people of Mbiri benefited from the battle being waged for their loyalities, and they became increasingly clever at manipulating the politicans and selecting projects for their support.

Examples of election politics and Harambee involvement are legion. The statistics given in Table 2.6 (p. 30) show that the number of projects completed in the election year, 1974, exceeds those completed in any other year between 1969 and 1978. Records in 1974 and newspaper reports in 1979 suggest that there is an increase in projects undertaken, in rates of project completion, and in the number of fundraising meetings during an election year.[13] Moreover, the efforts of candidates to associate themselves with viable Harambee projects important to their constituencies attest to the importance of Harambee in the electoral process.

The District Development Committee

An important institution operating at the district level is the District Development Committe (DDC). The Committee establishes development goals and priorities for the district, administers the Rural Development Fund (funds of the Central Government allocated to the DDCs for purposes of assisting self-help development projects), makes recommendations to operating ministries, and serves as a forum for discussion and exchange of views. The District Officers (heads of divisions within districts), the Members of Parliament for the district, and the district level officers of operating ministries, and sometimes other prominent members of the community attend the meetings of the DDC. The District Development Committee is regarded as highly political since its members compete, often quite fiercely, for the limited funds allocated to the Committee by the Provincial Development Committee.

A similar process occurs at the divisional and locational levels. In each case a new subset of participants enters the political process. At the divisional level there are District Officers and prominent persons such as the chairman of a cooperative. At the locational level there might be a minister or headmaster in addition to the Chief and Assistant Chiefs and perhaps some other local notables. Assistance for a school here, a dispensary there, a water project a third place are discussed and priorities are established. The Member of Parliament is apt to enter into the negotiating process at the district level, having been well informed beforehand by his supporters within the constituency of the outcome of various lower level committees. Most likely, he has influenced those decisions from "behind the scenes." He may also attend meetings below the district level. For example, records from the mid-1970's show that Kamwithi Munyi, MP for Kyeni and Nthawa, was attending Divisional Development Committee meetings regularly.[14] Thus, those projects which come before the District Development Committee for consideration have been through a process of political negotiation which may have involved both administrative and political figures at all levels of the political arena.

The District Development Committee of each district approves the proposals for self-help grants according to criteria which have been established for this task. These criteria include:

1) Priority for projects nearing completion which already contain a high degree of local contribution;
2) Projects in accord with the national development plan;

3) Reasonable distribution of similar types of projects within the district;
4) Preference for projects which have an economic payoff.[15]

The system of grants from the District Development Committee is a "top down" approach. Projects are recommended from below, but the decisions are taken at the district level, and the levels of participation and autonomy for rural citizens are not necessarily notable. Reynolds and Wallis suggest that the District Development Committees are "becoming the locus of all significant decision-making on development at the local level and therefore need more adequate representation of local interests."[16]

An important contribution made by the District Development grants administered by the DDC is the incentive they provide for communities to organize themselves for purposes of development. These funds are not used as "seed money." They are matching grants or "topping up" funds. As matching grants, they are released when the local community has raised its quota for the project. District Development grants received by the six locations under study during the 1974-1978 Plan were for cattle dips and water projects. There were 14 such projects ranging from one to six per location. Among the six Locations, Nthawa received the most.

The County Councils

County Councils are elected bodies covering the entire district and responsible for the maintenance of some local-level services. County Councils employ the Locational Community Development Assistants and thus have a key role in the process of development through Harambee. The salaries they pay, the kinds of qualifications they establish, the fringe benefits they offer determine the professional caliber of the LCDAs employed.

In 1974, when the Central Government abruptly took from the County Councils some of their sources of financing, many Councils suspended the employment of CDAs for a period. By 1975, these positions were again filled. It was evident from the hiatus in project reporting and communication that the LCDAs at the locational level play a critical role in bringing projects to the attention of appropriate officials, in encouraging local communities to undertake projects, and in facilitating and coordinating self-help. County Councils occasionally make small contributions to the completion of self-help projects within their districts. The Councillors themselves are active initiators of

self-help projects, participate as members of a number
of committees within their area, and, in general,
assist the process of development through self-help.

Harambee and the Bureaucracy

Harambee is closely linked to the bureaucratic
structure of the Government. Harambee projects are
supervised by the Community Development Office of the
Ministry of Housing and Social Services, though not
initiated by that office. Any fundraising endeavor
must be registered with the Community Development
Office through the Locational Community Development
Assistant (LCDA) and funds collected must be recorded
and placed in a bank account under the name of the
project committee. A project may be undertaken with
the assistance of an operating Ministry, such as the
Ministry of Water Development, but management of its
Harambee component comes under Housing and Social Services. While the Ministry formally approves self-help
projects and undertakes some record keeping on contributions to projects, it does not have the capacity for
auditing books or assuring appropriate use of funds.
    The Locational Community Development Assistant
(LCDA). The LCDA is employed by the County Council but
has line responsibilities to the District Office of
Community Development for its operations. The LCDA also works closely with the Chief of the location and
must attend regular locational meetings of Sub-Chiefs
and other public meetings, barazas, when they are
called by the Chief.
    Because he is subordinate to the Chief, political
considerations are part of the LCDA's frame of refer-
ence. The LCDA can easily be swept up in the politics
of the community and not infrequently is used by the
Chief to further political, or personal, rather than
administrative or developmental aims. For example, at
the request of the Chief, the LCDA of Weithaga, Evanson
Mugo, in the spring of 1978, was spending considerable
time talking to women's groups and encouraging them to
purchase shares in a business investment backed by
Matiba, the leading contender for the constituency's
Parliamentary seat then occupied by Dr. Kiano. Mr.
Njuki, Chief of Weithaga was a staunch member of a faction backing Mr. Matiba.[17] In his somewhat ambiguous
role, with commitments both to his department and to
his Chief, and highly dependent upon the Chief for his
effectiveness within the location, the Locational CDA
can find himself in difficult situations with conflict-
ing obligations and concerns. His job is illustrative
of the complex mesh of administrative and political
duties found not only at the local level but at all
levels in the political/administrative system.

73

Civil Servants and Harambee.   In Nairobi many
civil servants find Harambee taxing both personally and
professionally They may give time to Harambee fundraising events, and they often give personal contributions
from their own resources.   The typical civil servant
often feels beseiged by requests for contributions to
this project or that one, and he rarely sees the finished project to which he has contributed.   Except in
regard to projects in his own home area, he is apt to
feel somewhat overburdened by the Harambee "spirit."[18]
     Civil servants in the field are more likely to
perceive self-help as a vital contributor to rural development.   One former District Commissioner for
Kericho District, summarizing the role of Harambee
self-help in building rural infrastructure stated,
"Harambee is a very important part of our development
efforts.   If we did not have Harambee, we would be 20
to 30 years behind where we are now."[19]   The District
Officer for Kiharu Division in Murang'a District
suggested,

     People like Harambee projects.   They can see that
     the rich give more than the poor.   People like to
     participate and are learning to manipulate Haram-
     bee to the advantage of the community.   Harambee
     is not being used simply as a lever to obtain gov-
     ernment resources.   It is a way to release re-
     sources within the community.[20]

Whatever their attitudes toward local-level development through Harambee, it is hard to imagine how little most of the district officials visit the more remote parts of their district, and how cut off from the
lines of communication, Governmental interest, and public support many communities feel.   There are several
causes.   First, many areas are difficult to reach for
several months of the year when it is raining, when
roads are washed out, and when mud makes a route impassable.   Second, the constraints on transport - both
vehicles and gasoline - within the district headquarters are staggering.   The allotment per officer for
trips for conducting any kind of work - implementing
new programs, evaluation, auditing, reporting or merely
exchanging ideas - is very small. Officers must double
up for their trips into the field so that one vehicle
can take several people at a time.   Thus, the work itself does not determine the order and timing of field
contacts, but the availability of transport does.   In
one sublocation in Nthawa, it had been a full year
since any member of the District Education Board or the
District Education Officer had visited the primary
school.   In one remote part of a sublocation in Soin,
the Locational Community Development Officer, responsi-
ible for assisting with Harambee projects, had not

visited the area in the past five months. Such infre-
quency in visits and contact is quite common.   These
communication gaps cause great delays in planning and
implementing projects and complicate the efforts to
integrate development.

HARAMBEE AND NATIONAL-LEVEL ELITES

Leadership in Project Initiation and Funding

Political power and status can accrue to Members
of Parliament, and to other political or administrative
leaders, in a variety of ways.   One way is association
with successful development efforts within their respective constituencies.   For an elected official this
may be significant because it brings willing votes during elections.   To others it may be important for reasons of status, power or influence within the community.   Leaders are assessed by the public, in part, by
the number of development projects which they have
assisted or sponsored, the extent to which they have
helped them, and the performance of these projects.
This is, of course, not the only measure according to
which leaders are judged, but it is an important once.
Throughout Weithaga, for example, one hears repeatedly
how much Dr. Kiano has done for the people of that
area, and what a debt of gratitude they owe him.   If a
location-by-location breakdown of Murang'a constituency
votes were available, it would likely reveal strong
support for Kiano in Weithaga Location, his home area.
That participation in Harambee projects is important to elected officials is evident from the data collected in the six locations.   Among 80 projects for
which data was gathered in the six locations, there
were 98 visits in the course of a five-year period,
from politicians, administrators or other public persons for purposes of fundraising for one of the projects.   Seventy-three percent of these visits were made
by politicians.[21] The sitting Member of Parliament for
the constituency in which the project was located
accounted for 43 percent of the total.
Twenty-seven percent of the guests at fundraising
events in the six locations were not politicians. Some
were prominent members of the civil service at the district or national level; some were religious leaders;
others were people from the area who had become prominent in some field of endeavor.   Group discussions with
Harambee project committees suggest that their members
are becoming increasingly sophisticated and imaginative
in their efforts to get fundraising assistance from a
wide variety of sources.   Much thought is given to obtaining assistance from local people who have prospered
outside the immediate community but are still loyal to

it.   The main effort, however, is directed toward the
MPs.
     Table 3.1   indicates the positions held by the 27
percent of key fundraisers who were not politicians involved locally.[22] Several MPs from other constituencies were invited to fundraising events because of
their particular administrative responsibilities. Some
of the officials shown in Table 3.1 may assist Harambee
projects in a variety of ways in addition to serving as
guest speakers at fundraising events.   District Officers and District Education Officers, for example,
sometimes assist in the collection of funds for projects in their areas.   In some instances, there are
"local notables" who are assuming leadership responsibilities within their communities.   The personal returns are not immediate political benefits, but are
prestige and local influence with, possibly, a later
return in the form of elective office.   Sometimes an
administrator is particularly interested in certain
types of projects and will make a special effort on
their behalf in whatever district to which he may be
assigned.
     Table 3.2 provides some information on nationally
prominent persons who were guests at Harambee fundraisings in mid-1979.   It is based on figures derived from
newspaper reports of major fundraising events and their
guests for the period of May, 1979 through July,
1979.[23] Among the guests listed, 40 percent are not
political figures, although some of them may have
future political aspirations.   Because they have prospered and become prominent, they are called upon by
family, friends and local leaders to assist in the development process of their home area, the area in which
they are working, or the community of a colleague.
     Although such a person may be somewhat selective
in the endeavors he or she chooses to assist by participating in a fundraising event, it is not easy to turn
down such requests.   The person who aids his community
is accorded status and respect.   He also fulfills an
implicit obligation to return to his or her home and
family and to assist them when possible.   Although his
residence may be in Nairobi or in another city, or
town, his loyalties remain with his home community.   He
expects to retire there eventually, and he is willing
to work at the present time to develop it.   His parents, brothers and sisters may rely heavily on funds he
is able to provide to the family and on those services
which his contributions can help build.   Increasingly
local leaders are aware of the opportunity to call upon
this group of people.   With the passage of time there
are more educated and prospering Kenyans on whom to
draw for such assistance.   Consequently, the number of
non-political persons involved in Harambee development
efforts is likely to increase.

Table 3.1
Position or occupation of non-political guests for
Harambee fundraising events in six locations

Guest	Number of appearances at any of 80 projects in six locations
District Commissioner	2
District Officer	1
District Education Officer	2
Minister of Education	2
Permanent Secretary of Education	1
Assistant Minister, Housing & Social Services	1
Chief Archivist	1
Director of Medical Services	1
Church Officials	6
Municipal Officer	3
Police Officer	1
KANU Administrative Official	1
Local Businessmen	3
Foreign Aid Agency representative	1

Table 3.2
Newspaper reports of guests at Harambee fundraising
events

Guests by Position or Occupation	Number of Appearances Nationwide
President	2
Vice President	5
Attorney General	5
Ministers (excluding the Vice President)	5
Assistant Ministers	5
Permanent Secretaries	5
MPs (excluding Ministers and Assistant Ministers)	15
Provincial Commissioners	4
District Commissioners	4
Bank Officers	4
Government Corporations	2
Businessmen	2
Professionals	3
Officials of Political Organizations	3
Other Civil Servants	3
Former First Lady	1

Fundraising Events

Each fundraising event consists of a large public
meeting at which the guest speaks, presents his gift to
the community, and encourages others to make contributions, either outright, or through Harambee fundraising
mechanisms such as auctions. The politician attending
such events receives a lot of publicity and good will
if he does the job well. In all cases, guests at fundraising events are expected to bring sizeable financial
gifts to the project. These may vary from several hun-
dred shillings to thousands of shillings. Following
are some typical examples culled from articles in The
Daily Nation:[24]

> Mr. Pius Kibathi, Nairobi businessman, gave Ksh
> 17,300 ($2,307) to Githinji Primary School in
> Nyandarua District, March, 1978.
>
> Assistant Finance Minister, Arthur Magugu gave Ksh
> 15,000 ($2,000) to Thuita African Independent
> Pentecostal Church in Murang'a, March, 1978.
>
> Deputy Police Commissioner, Michael Arrum, gave
> Ksh 26,000 ($3,467) for a health center in Siaya
> District, March, 1978.
>
> Dr. Kiano gave Ksh 21,000 ($2,800) to Tuthu Sec-
> ondary School, Murang'a District, August, 1979.
>
> Vice President Mwai Kibaki gave Ksh 65,000
> ($8,667) to the Mt. Kenya South Diocese of the
> Church of the Province of Kenya, July 23, 1979.
>
> Mulu Mutisya, Chairman of the New Akamba Union,
> gave Ksh 6,700 ($893) to Kiboko School, Machakos
> District, July 2, 1979.
>
> Dr. Kiano contributed Ksh 300,000 ($40,000) to the
> Kahuti water project from himself and friends, May
> 22, 1978 and at the same fundraising Mr. Matiba
> gave Ksh 121,000 from himself and friends.

As the above list indicates, a guest at a fundraising
will often bring gifts not only from himself but from
friends and acquaintances. In Government offices and
businesses, it is a common occurrence to find a messen-
ger circulating with a receipt book for a project to
which a Minister or other high official is going as an
official guest. Co-workers are asked to contribute to
the projects. Sometimes these requests become "demands" and impose an unfair burden on poorly paid
bureaucrats who can ill-afford numerous contributions.
In fact, it is the urbanite at the lower end of govern-

ment or business employment scales who most often complains of being caught in an unending round of Harambee contributions both to his own home area and to projects in other areas. At times this may amount to a "squeeze" being place on such a person from above as high officials seek to fulfill expectations placed on them to bring generous sums to local fundraising endeavors.

Role of the Member of Parliament

In addition to his role at fundraising events, a skillful MP is often involved in the role of broker, attempting to secure governmental assistance for his constituency. This, of course, takes many forms, including assistance with Harambee projects. Dr. Kiano is widely appreciated in Murang'a District for his successful efforts to secure government assistance for Mumbi Girls' Secondary School which was floundering for lack of funds and which, thanks to him, is now thriving.[25] In other cases, MPs have been known to negotiate with District Planning Officers to obtain small-scale water schemes for their constituencies, to arrange "topping up" funds to complete primary schools, or to secure government funds for maintaining dispensaries. In virtually all cases, the rural populace expects the Member of Parliament to present its needs to the appropriate offices within the civil service. Some MPs are highly skilled in this role; others do not have the connections, requisite skills or interest in a particular group or its problems, and in such cases Harambee projects may languish.

In the locations studied, MPs responded unevenly to the needs of their constituencies. In two cases, Murang'a and Embu, the MPs provided better services to those geographical areas in which their own homes were located (Weithaga and Kyeni) and which were the more densely populated and affluent sectors of the constituency. In both these cases, persons in the neglected section of the constituency (Mbiri and Nthawa) were becoming increasingly eager to do something about the indifference they perceived on the part of the MP.

With access to centrally controlled resources, an effective MP can be a most valuable asset to his community. Local elites know this, and have learned how to manipulate their MP to their advantage in both a collective and personal sense. Advantages may accrue to the community in the form of Government programs or aid to Harambee projects or they may accrue to individuals in the form of licenses secured, jobs obtained and favors done. Clearly then, political clout and political criteria are important in determining allocation of governmental assistance, little though it may be, to

Harambee projects. Development criteria, productivity concerns, and equity issues are also considered, particularly within a constituency or an administrative unit, but the skillful MP who can move his project up to the "head of the line" is a distinct asset to his constituency, and national development priorities are not his major concern.

Impact of Patrons Upon Project Performance

In the locations investigated, politicians most frequently gave support to educational projects. Of 16 secondary schools visited in the three districts, in the course of the study, 12 have been aided by the MP as guest speaker and chief fundraiser at a Harambee event. In four of the 16 schools, the MP's aid has not only been substantial, it has been critical, and without his assistance, financial support, and leadership or administrative skills, the schools might have closed. At best, they would have encountered considerable difficulties. In most instances, the MP has visited the school for fundraising purposes on only one occasion. Five of the schools or 31 percent have, however, held two major fundraising events, both of which the MP attended. Five schools (not the identical five) have also enjoyed the assistance of prominent political figures from outside their area who have come to speak at their fundraising events. Often this is at the request of the MP, and the guest is a friend of the Member from the host area. On at least two separate occasions, President Moi, when he was Vice President, appeared in Murang'a District on behalf of secondary schools in Mbiri constituency.

Mbithi has noted that Harambee projects sometimes get caught in political crossfire and abandoned by politicians who do not want to assist a project started by someone else.[26] Not one of the secondary schools visited in this study has been caught in conflict among politicians. Support by leading politial figures has been steady and productive. For boarding schools the constituency has been sufficiently broad that the entire location or at least several sublocations have been working on the project. With several notable exceptions, day schools have been carefully adjusted to the needs of several feeder primarily schools. They have not received the levels of assistance customary to boarding schools, but the MPs have not neglected them. Among the secondary schools included in this study, there were important controversies and issues including such matters as the appropriate level of pass on the CPE for admission, adequate textbooks, or adequately trained teachers, but the issues were not tied to political loyalties and political questions. One must note, however, that local residents were quick to take advantage of political conflict if they perceived it would serve their interests. Two of the four secondary schools in Mbiri Location had held fundraisings with both the incumbent, Dr. Kiano, and his challenger, Mr. Matiba. Certainly the Mbiri day secondary schools bene-fited from the Kiano-Matiba rivalry.

Nearly three-fourths of the primary schools visited in the six locations had received fundraising assistance from an MP, one time only, most commonly in 1974-1975. Mbiri primary schools, as well as secondary schools, have taken advantage of the Kiano-Matiba con-flict. Two-thirds of the primary schools visited in Mbiri had held two fundraising events, one with Kiano and one with Matiba. Of these, the majority were ex-tremely poor schools and very much in need of the boost that a second fundraising might offer to them.

In addition to obtaining support from political figures, schools receive assistance from religious org-anizations or leaders. Of the primary schools visited, 10 percent had benefited from fundraising efforts on their behalf by the Vicar or Bishop.[27] Thirty-one per-cent of the secondary schools had enjoyed some religi-ous patronage, usually when a church leader served as guest speaker at a fundraising event and brought a large contribution for the project with him. These cases were primarily in Murang'a District.

Only one-third of the health projects visited in the six locations have received assistance from MPs or other national level elites. While politicians are clearly aware of health needs within their communities, they have responded to their constituents' more acute desires for educational opportunities. As Court and Ghai point out,

> Academic education alone produces the formal qual-
> ifications which have been mostly rewarded in the
> period of post-colonial Africanization and eco-
> nomic expansion. That rural communities have a
> strong desire for more and better schools is a
> rational response to a reward structure in which
> salaries are tied to years of formal schooling ...
> and a social structure where there are few altern-
> ative channels of mobility.[28]

To refer back to Table 2.8 (p. 32) on the value of self-help projects, never has the share of educational projects dropped below 50 percent of the total, and re-cently it has been at least 60 percent. It is in this area that the greatest energies of the national-level elites have focused.

LOCAL ELITES AND HARAMBEE PROJECT COMMITTEES

The relationship between Harambee projects and elites works two ways. Support from national-level elites can be important in assuring the success of self-help projects. The reverse is also true; indeed, success of Harambee projects can affect the power and status not only of national-level elites, but also of rural elites. Data from the six locations show that local elites are involved in initiating Harambee projects and in the day-to-day planning, decision-making, implementation and management of projects. They do so primarily as participants of project committees.

In each of the six locations observed, there were between 20 and 40 project committees. These include school management and church management committees. The former are comprised of a membership from the community, some of whom are elected by the parents and some of whom are appointed by the Government and by the school's sponsor, frequently a religious denomination. In general, committees have from ten to twenty members. A member may represent a particular constituency, sub-location or village, or may be chosen by the community or asked by the Sub-Chief to serve.

Typically, a committee member will be an older man with position and status within the community. In Kenyan parlance, he is a "mzee."[29] Usually, in the locations studied, he is a farmer, often with some side business interests such as a small shop or transport, but he may also be a minister, retired teacher or retired civil servant. In many instances these men bring a mature and thoughtful experience to the efforts of the project committee and clearly hold the interests of their community paramount. For example, a retired veterinary officer in Boiwek Sub-location of Soin, Mr. Thomas Tele, is tireless in his efforts to improve services in his community. A founder of the local AIC Church, and a member of the primary school committee, he is organizing the fundraising drive for a water project and is personally helping to build a village polytechnic. In other cases motivation seems more closely related to "filling time" or to personal benefit. Usually, young men or middle-aged men are serving on such committees primarily because of a particular position or function related to the project. For example, the headmaster of a school is always on the committee, and normal procedure is for him or her to serve as secretary to the committee.

Sometimes women are elected to a committee or appointed to a reserved seat providing formal assurance that a woman will have a position and can represent the "women's point of view." This happens most frequently with primary schools. In some cases, a woman is chosen to serve on a committee because she is the mother or wife of an important male in the community. The position may be given to her to honor her, as was the case with Cheborge Dispensary where a woman who was declared "the mother of important sons" served on the committee. Or it may be given to her for more political reasons: she can provide information to or convey the views of her male relative. Finally, in some cases women serve on committees because of their own achievements, and the position they themselves occupy in the community.

The Assistant Chief sits on all committees within his sub-location. He may or may not serve as chairman, depending upon his inclination and the committee's decision. Frequently, the local representative to the County Council, the Councillor, is a member of a committee. A major project such as a secondary school may also enjoy the membership of the Chief of the location and the MP for the area. A KANU representative for the area may also be on a committee, and sometimes there is a member affiliated with an ethnic organization such as GEMA, the Gikuyu, Embu, Meru Association. Boards of Governors of secondary schools often have a distinguished group of members including the directors of various important institutions in the district, as well as persons from the community who have become well known in Nairobi or elsewhere.

Respondents to the questionnaire administered on a random basis throughout the locations were asked about membership on Harambee project committees. Table 3.3 provides information about committee participation by socio-economic groups. Respondents were organized into quintiles according to several measures of affluence and status.[30] Table 3.3 compares the top and bottom quintiles for respondent participation on project committees. Among those who indicated they were or had been members of project committees a disproportionate number were in the top quintile of respondents. Of male members of committees, from 31 to 40 percent were in the top quintile. Add to them the local officials who are automatically members of the committees, and it is likely that a majority of many project committees are from this quintile.

Among women, 28 percent of those who participate on project committees are from the top quintile, while 19 percent are from the bottom quintile. Membership on church committees accounts in large measure for the relatively high representation from the bottom quintile among female committee participants in Kyeni. Male respondents in the bottom quintile were not represented on project committees in four of the six locations. Thus, committee membership is definitely skewed toward the more affluent socio-economic groups, though the most prosperous clearly do not have a monopoly on committee positions.

Table 3.3
Percentage of participants on project committees who
are from the top and bottom quintiles (N = 66)

Location	Top Quintile		Bottom Quintile	
	Men	Women	Men	Women
Soin	38	--	13	--
Nthawa	35	40	--	--
Mbiri	40	36	--	--
Kisiara	38	50	--	--
Kyeni	31	18	6	36
Weithaga	31	23	--	8

Most committees schedule elections every one to
four years. In actuality, however, the composition of
committees changes relatively little over time. The
same people are often re-elected. In one school in
Kyeni, a committee member had served for twenty years.
In many instances, members had served for a number of
years and showed every indication of continuing their
services. There is, of course, a certain prestige and
status involved in serving on various committees. Some
members of committees seem to be oriented more toward
this prestige and accrued status than toward the task
involved. There is no notion of rotation of service,
and of encouraging new ideas and new energy to surface
within a committee structure. Rather, it is a more
common procedure to continue to re-elect a person unless there is specific evidence that he or she is doing
the job badly or there is specific cause for discon-
tent. Hence, preserving the status quo in committee
structures is widespread.

A second aspect of committee membership concerns
the network of committee members. A high percentage of
members of each committee are serving on other committees. For example at Kathenjure School in Kyeni Location, two of the nine members were also serving on the
cattle dip committee; five were on a total of three
church committees, and one was a prominent member of a
local self-help group. At Mufu primary school in
Kyeni, the chairman of the committee was serving on the
Location Development Committee and was also chairman of
the Salvation Army Church Committee. Among his colleagues, two members were on the AIC Church Committee,
two were on CPK Committees, one was on the cattle dip
committee, and one was on the dispensary committee and
the Catholic Church Committee. Clearly, there is a
circulation of local notables among the various committees within a location. Usually, the leadership of the

committees varies, and the chairman of one committee is
not likely to be the chairman of another. He may, however, hold a different position such as secretary or
treasurer. Thus, the committees emphasize continuity
and stability with a minimum of changeover in personnel. Methods for facilitating innovation and change
are not built into the project committee structure.

Given that local elites are well represented on
Harambee project committees, and that decision-making
is highly concentrated within these committees, it is
then important to ask what difference this makes to the
selection and operation of Harambee projects. In the
six locations under consideration, there was a clear
overlapping of interests on the part of all sections of
the community. Most of the residents were small
farmers or involved in semi-pastoral, semi-agricultural
pursuits. In no case was there a clear-cut difference
in economic interests such as one might find if the
more affluent were farmers and the poorer members of
the community were fishermen.

Second, in the communities visited, needs were
very basic and were widely shared. Respondents to the
questionnaires were asked their opinion on the most important needs of their community. In three of the
locations more than 90 percent of the respondents
shared the same view of the area's most important
developmental concern. Some respondents had criticisms
concerning the operation and management of projects.
Few, however, protested the choice of projects, and
those who did focused primarily on the district-wide
projects such as the Murang'a Institute of Technology
which they felt would in no way benefit them personally. Local level primary and secondary schools, water
projects, dispensaries, cattle dips, feeder roads and
similar small-scale projects are widely regarded as
useful and important community improvements. Opinions
on future project priorities did not vary by socio-
economic group within the location.

Some analysts have suggested that self-help in
Kenya constitutes the efforts of the disadvantaged in
the rural areas to rectify the imbalances in benefits
and services within their communities.[31] In the locations studies, this has not been the case. A common
source of initiative for projects is a small group of
people, generally the more educated and/or prosperous,
who are interested in developing the facilities of
their area. These are people who are likely to be
aware of comparative opportunities and advantages of
their home area vis-a-vis other communities. In interviews such people asked about the level of development
in the other areas under investigation and said, "We do
not want our area to be left behind." This possibility
concerns local-level leaders who form an almost interlocking network on various committees. For reasons

both civic and personal, they often appear to be trying
to propel their communities toward higher levels of
development. The poorest groups, the truly rural disadvantaged, do not initiate projects. They cannot
afford to take risks. They respond to the efforts of
those in a leadership or elite position within their
local community.

Thus, self-help serves a variety of functions in
the political process. It links local and national
elites in a complex network of patron-client relationships. It serves as a mechanism for transfer of resources. It provides an avenue by which local communities can gain access to new resources, opportunities
and benefits. Moreover, self-help as an approach to
rural change permeates party politics and bureaucratic
behavior. It is integral to the political process in
Kenya.

NOTES

1. See H.H. Gerth and C. Wright Mills, From Max
Weber: Essays in Sociology (New York: Oxford University Press, 1946), translated, edited and with an introduction by Gerth and Mills. See also James C. Scott,
The Moral Economy of the Peasant (New Haven: Yale University Press, 1976) and Gerald Heeger, The Politics
of Underdevelopment (New York: St. Martins Press,
1974).
2. Heeger, op. cit., p. 10.
3. Ibid., p. 8.
4. See Carl Lande, "Network and Groups in Southeast Asia: Some Observations on the Group Theory of
Politics," American Political Science Review, no. 57,
March, 1973, pp. 103-127; James C. Scott, "Patron-
Client Politics and Political Change in Southeast
Asia," American Political Science Review, vol. 16, no.
1, 1972; or Alex Weingrod, "Patrons, Patronage, and
Political Parties," Comparative Studies in Society and
History, vol. 10, no. 4, July, 1968.
5. John Ducan Powell, "Peasant Society and
Clientelist Politics," in Finkle and Gable, Political
Development and Social Change (New York: John Wiley
and Sons, 1966), p. 536.
6. Gerard Ciparisse, "An Anthropological Approach
to Socioeconomic Factors of Development: The Case of
Zaire," Current Anthropology, vol. 19, no. 1, March-
June, 1978, p. 40.
7. Government of Kenya, Development Plan for
1979-1983, p. 42.
8. Cherry Gertzel, Maure Goldschmidt and Donald
Rothchild (eds.), Government and Politics in Kenya
(Nairobi: East African Publishing House, 1972).
9. Apter, op. cit., p. 732.

86

10. <u>The Daily Nation</u>, April 19, 1979.
11. Peter Kareithi and Hilary Ng'weno, "Guide to Politics in Mbiri," <u>The Weekly Review</u> (Nairobi: Stell-ascope Ltd., 1979).
12. This conflict was widely reported in <u>The Daily Nation</u> and <u>The Weekly Review</u> in mid-1979.
13. See Chapter II, Table 2.4. Newspaper reports on pre-election Harambee fundraising events also indicated that the number was increasing in the election year.
14. Files of the Siakago Office of the Special Rural Development Programme for Mbeere, 1976-1977.
15. The Government of Kenya, <u>Murang'a District Development Plan</u> (Nairobi: Government Printer, May, 1976), p. 28.
16. J. Eric Reynolds and M.A.H. Wallis, "Self-Help and Rural Development in Kenya," Discussion Paper #241, Institute for Development Studies, University of Nairobi, 1976, p. 17.
17. Discussion with Mr. Evanson Mugo, Locational CDA for Weithaga Location, May, 1978.
18. Discussion with Mr. Ruchiami, Office of the President, January, 1978.
19. Interview Mr. J. Onyango, former District Commissioner for Kericho District, February 22, 1979.
20. Conversation with Mr. Mwaisaka, District Officer for Kiharu Division, May, 1978.
21. Data gathered in the course of interviews with project committees and from the district files which have monthly and annual reports submitted by the LCDAs.
22. Data collected in six locations as indicated in Note 21.
23. <u>The Daily Nation</u>, between May and July, 1979.
24. Examples of announcements of Harambee fund-raising events listed in <u>The Daily Nation</u> in 1978 and 1979.
25. Interview with the headmistress of Mumbi School, Mbiri Location, June 12, 1978.
26. See Mbithi, <u>Rural Sociology and Rural Development</u> (Nairobi: East African Literature Bureau, 1974), p. 171.
27. Data obtained in interviews with headmasters of primary and secondary schools in six locations and in the files of the District Office.
28. David Court and Dharam P. Ghai (eds.), <u>Education, Society and Development: New Perspectives from Kenya</u> (Cambridge: Oxford University Press, 1974), p. 12.
29. "Mzee" is a title of deference and respect reserved for older men.
30. Within each location respondents' households were ranked on the basis of land ownership, size of holding, wage employment, level of education of husband

and wife, household amenities, household construction
and possession of basic furnishings. Once rankings
were established, households were clustered into quintiles. Much of the data is evaluated in terms of the
"richest" and the "poorest" quintile of each location.
      31. Mbithi, op. cit.

IV
Patterns of Access and Advantage in Self-Help: The Province, the District, and the Local Community

> Some communities are making great progress through
> Harambee self-help, but others in this district
> have hardly any projects at all.
>   District Development Officer
>   Kericho District

In recent years analysts have observed regional or
geographic inequities, as well as class inequities, in
Kenya's development patterns.[1] The Government of Kenya
has, however, expressed a strong commitment to the objective of increasing equity among all of Kenya's people.[2] What are the geographical, regional and related
ethnic variations in development through Harambee?
What is the relationship between community implementation of local development projects and the objective of
increasing equity among the people of Kenya?
    In 1976, Edgar Winans and Angelique Haugerud, in
their article entitled "Rural Self-Help in Kenya: The
Harambee Movement," observed "sharp disparities between
regions in both volume and value of self-help activity."[3] Analyzing district-level data for 1967, 1968,
and 1972, they state that "prior levels of development
account for a quarter or more of the regional variation
in project rates."[4] Their findings reveal that population density, land potential and ethnic homogeneity are
positively related to self-help development. The
Winans and Haugerud study shows a change over time in
that project frequency was highest in 1967 in areas
with good land potential and high population densities,
but by 1972, the reverse was true. They suggest that
Harambee may be contributing to a regional equalization
of services, particularly educational opportunity.
Their district-level data suggests that self-help
activity is tapering off in many of the more developed
areas and therefore, "if this trend continues self-help
activity would contribute to the equalization of development levels between the regions of Kenya."[5]

Evidence presented in this chapter suggests that Harambee activities are not decreasing in the more developed areas and that the trend noted by Winans and Haugerud is not continuing throughout the 1970s. The more affluent areas are not standing still; many are involved in a continual effort to extend and upgrade the quality of their services. However, it is also true that Harambee is an important means for poor as well as affluent communities to provide some services and opportunities primarily through their own efforts. Hence, the basic facilities and services available in many communities are rising. The variation in Harambee project choice and performance as well as the inclination of more affluent communities to improve facilities and services suggests, however, that the inequities among communities will remain. These observations draw in part on provincial and district-level data collected from 1967 to 1977 and, in part, on the data collected at the locational level through 1979.

PROVINCIAL AND DISTRICT DATA

Over the years, the total national value of self-help contributions per year has increased while the number of projects completed annually has diminished. At the provincial level there has been considerable variation in self-help project completion and value. Figure 4.1 shows the distribution of Harambee project value by province in two years, 1968 and 1977.[6] Central Province leads in value of Harambee projects with high ratings in both years. Rift Valley shows a consistently good performance. Nyanza involvement in self-help has dropped from 24 percent of the total value in 1968 to 11 percent of the total value in 1977, although the province has 19 percent of the population. Eastern jumped from 10 percent to 20 percent of total value. The Coast, Western Province and Northeastern follow with considerably less Harambee activity.

Figure 4.2 shows the distribution of completed projects by province, using the 1968 and 1977 figures. Both Rift Valley and Eastern Provinces sustain major increases in number of projects completed in 1977 over the number completed in 1968. In Central Province the percentage of total projects completed drops slightly while the value has increased, indicative of some of the large projects being undertaken in that area.

Table 4.1, using data from the 1979 census, shows the relative population and value of Harambee projects in the seven provinces, using 1967, 1972 and 1977 as benchmark years.

For five of the seven provinces the value of Harambee activity as a proportion of total Kenyan activity differs by only a few percentage points from

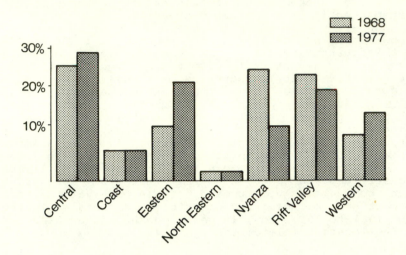

Figure 4.1 Percentage of Total National Value of Harambee
Projects by Province, 1968 and 1977

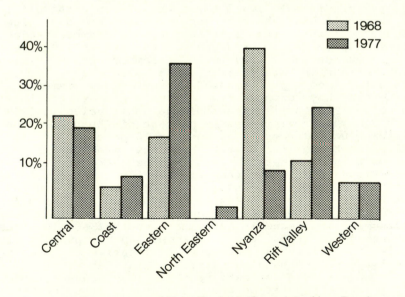

Figure 4.2 Percentage of Total Projects Completed by Province,
1968 and 1977

Table 4.1
Relative population and value of Harambee projects
as a percentage of the total value of projects in
1967, 1972 and 1977

Province	Population as a Percentage of all Kenya	Harambee Value In		
		1967	1972	1977
Central	15	24	32	29
Coast	9	7	8	6
Eastern	18	16	16	20
Northeastern	2	n.d.	2	.5
Nyanza	17	25	15	11
Rift Valley	21	18	20	18
Western	12	10	7	15

Source: Ministry of Housing and Social Services,
op. cit., Self-Help Statistics, Mbithi and Rasmusson,
op. cit., p. 65. The Weekly Review, November 30, 1979,
p. 17.

the proportion of the population living in that province. This generalization holds in most cases for all
three benchmark years. The exceptions are Central
Province where Harambee activity is relatively higher
than the proportion of the total population living in
that province, and Nyanza where it is lower. In 1977,
Harambee projects in Central Province were valued at 29
percent of the total for all of Kenya, whereas the
province contains 15 percent of Kenya's population. In
Nyanza, 17 percent of Kenya's population had 11 percent
of the total value of Harambee projects in that year.
In all the intervening years between 1968 and 1977,
Central Province has ranked first among the provinces
in total value of Harambee activity, according to statistics collected annually by the Ministry of Housing
and Social Services.[7]
    Within the provinces, there is considerable varia-
tion in self-help activity according to district. Using the Self-Help Statistics for 1977, it is possible
to correlate measures of "peoples' contribution" in
each district with comparative levels of wealth within
the districts, as indicated by the Statistical Abstract
for 1976.[8] Table 4.2 ranks the districts according to
wealth and level of peoples' contributions to self-help
projects. Calculations based on these figures for the
districts indicate that the correlation coefficient for
contribution levels and wealth is .73. These figures
suggest that among the districts, self-help development
continues in the mid to late 1970s to be more active in

the affluent districts of Kenya than in the poorer
ones.[9]   Figure 4.3 is a scatter diagram which illustrates the relationship between wealth and Harambee
contributions at the district level.

    Districts are large units with internal variation
in resource distribution, population density and socio-
economic infrastructure, as well as in Harambee activity.   Data gathered in the six locations focuses on
inter-locational variations in Harambee activity and
explores the varying relationships among Harambee self-
help, relative affluence of different communities, and
regional/geographic conditions in greater depth than
the use of district-level data permits.

Table 4.2
Ranking of districts in terms of wealth and in terms
of contributions to Harambee projects in 1977*

District	Wealth	Contribution to Harambee Projects
Mombasa	1	22
Nakuru	2	9
Kiambu	3	2
Kisumu	4	19
Kericho	5	20
Machakos	6	6
Nyeri	7	5
Kakamega	8	1
Uasin Gishu	9	32
Meru	10	4
Murang'a	11	3
Kisii	12	8
Trans-nzoia	13	27
Nandi	14	31
Bungoma	15	11
South Nyanza	16	14
Kilifi	17	23
Embu	18	10
Nyandarua	19	18
Kirinyaga	20	15
Laikipia	21	13
Taita Taveta	22	12
Kitui	23	16
Kajiado	24	11

Kwale	25	25
Siaya	26	21
Baringo	27	17
Busia	28	24
Elgeyo Marakwet	29	29
Wajir	30	35
Garissa	31	40
Narok	32	26
Marsabit	33	36
Isiolo	34	39
Tana River	35	37
West Pokot	36	38
Lamu	37	28
Samburu	38	34
Turkana	39	30
Mandera	40	33

*To establish district rankings of wealth, indicators from the Statistical Abstract for 1976 were used. The figures include earnings from agriculture and forestry, mining and quarrying, manufacturing, electricity and water, construction, wholesale and retail trade, restaurants and hotels, transport and communications, finance, insurance, real estate and business services, community, social and personal services. See Table 252, p. 289.

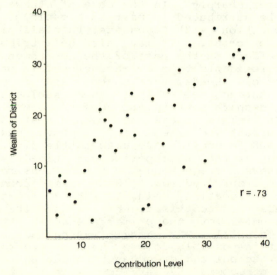

Figure 4.3 District Ranking by Wealth and Value of Contributions to Harambee Projects

LOCATION DATA

Variation in Contribution Levels

Evidence from the six locations suggests that the district-level data obscures wide variation among locations within the same district. Figure 4.4 shows the range of funds raised by the six locations during a five-year period between 1971 and 1978. Kisiara, with the largest sum collected for Harambee over a five-year period, raised nearly four times the amount raised in Soin which collected the least. Both are in Kericho District.

Figure 4.5 shows the flow of contributions within each location for the period of time under consideration.[10] Weithaga has the largest single annual contribution level, surpassing the Ksh. 450,000 mark in 1976 at the height of the coffee boom. Kyeni, an area also prospering from coffee put a large effort into primary schools in the early 1970s but did not sustain the level of interest throughout the period, and contributions there dipped in 1976 and 1977, just as they were peaking in Weithaga. Nthawa and Soin have paralleled each other in terms of total levels of contributions, but with a very different emphasis. Most of Nthawa's efforts have gone into primary schools, whereas the bulk of Soin's fundraising, until recently, has concentrated on cattle dips. Nthawa and Kisiara are the only two locations which show a clear and steady increase in contributions to self-help projects, the former slowly, and the latter sharply. In the case of Nthawa this increase may be attributed in part to a cycle of improved weather conditions with adequate rainfall permitting some return on crops. It may also be attributed to a persistent effort on the part of the Government to encourage the residents to grow cash crops, in particular cotton, sunflower seeds, and tobacco, and to encourage development through self-help.[11] Some sublocations are responding, despite poverty and concerns over land ownership. In Kisiara there has been a systematic and widespread effort to extend and improve educational facilities and to provide adequate cattle dips.

Looking at the same period of time, 1971-1978, Table 4.3 shows average annual contributions for households in the areas studied. These varied from Ksh. 40 in the poorest location, Soin, to Ksh. 87 in the richest, Weithaga. If to this figure is added the building fund requirement for the primary school, typical of each location until 1978 when it was banned by President Moi, it is possible to see what an average family with primary school children has been paying toward the acquisition of community services within each area. Table 4.4 shows the combined Harambee contributions and primary school building fund assessment typical for

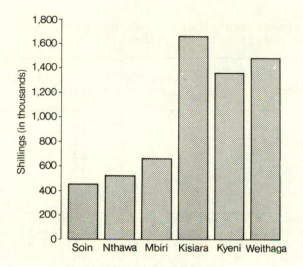

Figure 4.4 Harambee Funds Raised for a Five-Year
Period Between 1971 and 1978*

*All locations had gaps in their statistical
records, but it was possible to gather
information for a five-year period for
each location between the years 1971
and 1978.

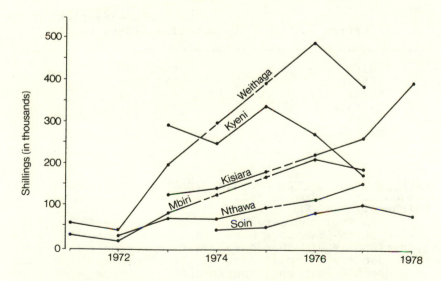

Figure 4.5 Annual Contribution Levels for the Six Locations,
1971-1978

Table 4.3
Average annual contribution per household for a
five-year period between 1971-1878

Location	Average Shilling Contribution Per Household
Soin	Ksh. 40
Nthawa	Ksh. 53
Mbiri	Ksh. 62
Kisiara	Ksh. 46
Kyeni	Ksh. 72
Weithaga	Ksh. 87

*Locations are listed from top to bottom in order of relative affluence, poorer to richer. The figures are based on the population estimates for 1974 and the mean household size of 6.97 persons as used by the Integrated Rural Survey, 1974-1975 of the Central Bureau of Statistics, Government of Kenya.

Table 4.4
Average annual contribution per household plus the
primary school building fund assessment typical for
a five-year period between 1971-1978

Location	Harambee Projects Plus School Building Fund
Soin	Ksh. 100
Nthawa	Ksh. 113
Mbiri	Ksh. 152
Kisiara	Ksh. 146
Kyeni	Ksh. 172
Weithaga	Ksh. 207

each location. The average annual outlay per family varies from a low of Ksh. 100 in Soin to Ksh. 207 in Weithaga.

Data from the survey questionnaire provides information which permits a more accurate assessment of contribution levels than "average annual contributions." Respondents were asked to give their personal estimate of household cash contributions for the five years preceding the administration of the questionnaire. Table 4.5 shows the responses of those interviewed in the six locations. If figures for non-contributors and those

who have contributed no more than Ksh. 20 per year (a
total of Ksh. 100 for the five-year period) are added
together, it is evident that 25 percent of the total
sample has contributed little or not at all to Harambee
projects. This figure varies from a low of 6 percent
in Weithaga to a high of 40 percent in Soin. On the
other hand, some members of the public contribute large
sums to Harambee projects. Twenty-three percent of the
total sample had contributed more than Ksh. 1000 during
the course of the past five years, or approximately
Ksh. 133 ($26.60) per year. Twelve percent of the
total sample indicated that they had contributed over
Ksh. 2000 during the past five years. The three locations which show the largest number of such contributors are those in which a number of churches are being
constructed and in which there is a strong commitment
on the part of many members of the public to building
them. The two locations in Central Province, one prosperous and one resource-poor, and both Kikuyu, have the
highest percentage of large contributors. Kyeni, the
second most prosperous location, follows closely.

Table 4.5
Residents of six locations: non-contributors, low
and high cash contributors for the years 1973-1977
or 1974-1978 (in percent) (N = 500)

Location	Non-Contributors	Contributing Ksh. 1 - 100	Contributing Over Ksh. 1000
Soin	30	10	0
Nthawa	22	17	5
Mbiri	10	7	32
Kisiara	8	2	14
Kyeni	10	2	28
Weithaga	6	0	34

Table 4.6 shows project involvement per family or
household in each location. It indicates the number of
projects to which most households in each location have
contributed or the mode for project contributions.
Household involvement in self-help projects is clearly
greater in richer than in poorer locations. In the
poorer locations many respondents have given to one to
three projects. These almost always include the local
primary school, and they may include the cattle dip, or
a nursery school or dispensary. In Kyeni or Weithaga,
a typical family might have contributed to a primary

school, a secondary school, dispensary, cattle dip,
church, water project or a nursery school.

Table 4.6
Project involvement per household in each location:
the mode

Location	Number of Projects
Soin	2
Nthawa	2
Mbiri	4
Kisiara	4
Kyeni	6
Weithaga	5

   Often the projects in poorer locations are narrow
in scope and are confined to the sublocation in which
the project is found.   In the more affluent locations,
the   scope   of some projects is larger.   A boarding
school for secondary students, such as Kiaganari Girls
School in Kyeni, may require the support of the entire
location.   A dispensary, particularly in the more
densely populated areas, may serve two sublocations and
thereby have the support of residents of both areas.
In part, the participation of residents of poorer communities in fewer projects is a function not only of
wealth, but of geography.   A service must be within
walking distance or it is useless.   In sparsely populated areas a sublocation may not have enough people to
build and support a facility from local effort, and the
area may be too large to combine several sublocations
in the use of one facility. Hence, both space and population density play a role in determining the number
of projects and the level of support found among the
population.
   Self-Help Statistics for 1977 show that in this
year these six locations generated approximately Ksh.
1,213,942 ($161,859) in cash to be used on a variety of
local services and projects.[12] This figure represents
an average investment potential of Ksh. 7.50 ($1.00 at
1977 exchange rates) per capita for the six locations
combined. Table 4.7 shows the self-help investment per
capita in each of the locations for 1977, figures based
on contributions to self-help made by each location's
residents during the course of the year.   This table
reveals that the two locations in Central Province have
the highest per capita figures for investment through
Harambee.   This is based on a low labor input, but

large cash and material contributions. Nthawa ranks
third with relatively low cash and material contributions, but a high labor contribution. Women in Nthawa
are working regularly on building and maintaining primary schools and their labor contributions constitute a
significant portion of Nthawa's 1977 self-help figures.[13] Kisiara ranks sixth in part because of the
large population over which investment figures are
spread.

Table 4.7
Per capita investment in community projects in six
locations in 1977

Location	Contributions (including cash, labor and materials)
Soin	Ksh. 7.70
Nthawa	Ksh. 11.00
Mbiri	Ksh. 12.20
Kisiara	Ksh. 5.50
Kyeni	Ksh. 6.90
Weithaga	Ksh. 14.70

Distribution of Benefits by Location

Just as contribution levels vary substantially
from location to location, so do benefits received.
Ironically, those locations where contribution levels
are high are not necessarily those where a high proportion of contributors receive benefits. Table 4.8
shows, location by location, the percentage of individual project contributions, made by respondents to the
survey questionnaire, which are actually benefiting the
contributor. It also shows the percentage of contributors among respondents who have benefited from all
their contributions and the percentage who have not
benefited from any of them.[14]
The benefits received do not vary according to the
wealth of the particular location. Other variables
must be considered. Weithaga, the most affluent location, Mbiri and Nthawa have the lowest percentage of
contributions providing benefits to the contributor.
In Weithaga it is necessary to consider the broad range
of projects, their scope and complexity, all of which
exceed that typical of other communities. Some projects take considerable time to complete and when finished directly benefit a limited number of people. For
example, the laboratory of Karingu Secondary School in

Table 4.8
Respondents who have contributed to Harambee projects:
appraisal of benefits received from contributions

Location	% of Individual Project Contributions Benefiting Donors	% of Donors Benefiting From:	
		All Contri- butions	No Contri- butions
Soin	90	83	2
Nthawa	59	23	6
Mbiri	49	17	8
Kisiara	85	63	8
Kyeni	83	62	3
Weithaga	65	29	2

Weithaga benefits only those families who have secondary school students in that school who are taking science courses. Further, Weithaga has had a large number
of projects, and its residents have been called upon to
support a variety of Harambee activities both within
and without the location, projects such as the Murang'a
College of Technology or the Kahuti water supply.
Nthawa's poor record in terms of project benefits
stems primarily from the mismanagement of the cattle
dips. Mbiri's poor record relates to mismanagement of
projects and mismanagement of funds as well as to involvement in some long-term projects. In both Weithaga
and Mbiri there has been considerable pressure to contribute to projects. In Mbiri this pressure has combined with mismanagement to produce low returns to contributors. Just under half of all project contributions made by respondents in that location have yielded
any benefits to the contributor.
In all locations the various categories of projects are yielding benefits to contributors at disparate
rates. Table 4.9 shows some of these differences.
Benefits received from contributions to educational
projects vary widely. Whereas only 57 percent of the
contributions to education projects in Mbiri have benefited the contributor, 94 percent of the contributions
in Nthawa have yielded benefits to the contributor.
Nthawa and Soin, characteristic of poorer communities,
show widespread benefits from educational projects
among all groups of the population. Benefits become
narrower as communities begin to concentrate on secondary schools. Thus, locations such as Kisiara, Weithaga
and Mbiri do not show as high a rate of benefits for
contributors to education projects as do the former two
locations. In the locations investigated, most fami-

lies send some children to primary school for several
years or more and consequently get some return on contributions to building primary schools.

Table 4.9
Percentage of contributions to projects which are
yielding benefits to donor respondents

Project Type	Soin	Nthawa	Mbiri	Kisiara	Kyeni	Weithaga
Educational	90	94	57	75	85	68
Economic	95	32	60	90	90	95
Health	63	--	50	82	42	50
Water	--	51	10	--	90	28
Social Welfare	100*	100*	60	80	78	61

*Soin and Nthawa have very few social welfare projects.
Those respondents who had contributed to these projects
were few, but they were unanimous in affirming that
they had received benefits from them.

At present relatively few children go on to secondary school both because of academic qualifications
and because of fees. Mbiri and Kisiara are building
Harambee day secondary schools. Weithaga is building
both day and boarding schools. If the school is a day
school, the funds may be collected through an extension
of Harambee contributions for the primary school. The
parents who have children in the primary school thus
may be involved in contributing to building a day secondary school by virtue of their affiliation with the
primary school. In Kisiara a common procedure is to
designate some classrooms of the primary school for
secondary classes and to call upon the entire community
to contribute to the addition of new classrooms for the
primary school. Hence, in these locations there are
families contributing who do not have children in secondary school. Those communities which are focusing on
secondary schools show lower returns in educational
benefits than do those focusing on primary schools.
Returns on economic projects are high in four
locations. Figures for Mbiri show that only 60 percent
of contributions to economic projects benefit donors.
In parts of Mbiri all households were required to contribute to cattle dips. In some cases households had
lost cattle through tick-borne diseases and did not
have any to dip; in others poor households had never

owned cattle, but were nevertheless required to contribute to the dip. Thus, there is a low percentage of
benefits returned from contributions to economic projects made by Mbiri residents. Figures for Nthawa show
that 32 percent of contributions to economic projects
yielded benefits. This low return relates primarily to
the malfunctioning cattle dips mentioned earlier.

Respondent comments on benefits from health-
oriented projects indicate that approximately half the
contributions bring benefits to donors, with the exception of Kisiara which has a high figure of 82 percent.
Benefits from water projects vary substantially.
Kyeni's water project has been functioning since the
early 1970s; it covers the entire location and shows
the highest percentage of benefits received from contributions. In both Mbiri and Weithaga large water
projects are underway. Contributions have been made by
many residents, and benefits have not yet reached all
areas. The questionnaires of residents of Mbiri and
Weithaga reflected impatience with the length of time
necessary to operationalize the water schemes for their
area. Soin has just started collecting funds for a
location-wide project, but these collections are not
reflected in the data gathered from Soin respondents.
Nthawa has several small-scale water projects in
progress, as well as two dams which have failed and one
water project which is successful.

Finally, social welfare projects have received
attention in all locations. While social halls, can-
teens, youth centers or mosques are included in this
category, the vast majority of social welfare projects
are churches. For many respondents the churches constitute their most important Harambee effort and the
one to which they had given the most generously.

Causes of Variations in Harambee Activity Among Locations

Resource Base. The greater the resource base, the
easier it is for a community to undertake local development efforts through Harambee activity. The more
affluent an area, the easier it is to raise the money
needed for new services. The record of past Harambee
activities in these six locations shows clearly that
the wealthier ones have been more active.

The areas with productive land are more densely
populated than those with poor land. This too facili-
tates Harambee projects because funding requirements
can be spread among a comparatively large group of
households to be served by a particular facility. For
example, the capital costs of constructing a dispensary
or a cattle dip are relatively constant, given some
variation for distances from which building materials

must be transported and for type of material used.   In
Weithaga or Kisiara many more households will be
located within the geographic radius permitting use of
a given dip or dispensary than would be the case in
Nthawa or Soin.
    Although the   District   Development Committees
attempt to take demographic conditions as well as relative affluence into account and to assess the local
population's   contribution   accordingly,   individual
household contributions may be regressive when one compares wealthier locations with poorer ones.   In Kisiara
the public was asked to pay Ksh. 8,000 per dip; in
Nthawa they were asked to contribute Ksh. 3,000 per
dip.   Yet, households paying for construction of cattle
dips in several sublocations of Nthawa were assessed
Ksh. 100 per family with cattle, whereas a typical
assessment in Kisiara was Ksh. 50 per household with
cattle.   Consequently, the overall impact on the location vis-a-vis other locations may have been as the
Government intended - poorer locations   paying less
- but the impact on individual households was harsher
in Nthawa than in Kisiara.
    Figures for other services such as dispensaries or
Harambee secondary schools also show that for a compar-
able effort, the less populated areas pay more for
their construction on a per household basis than is the
case in more highly populated areas.   Add to this the
fact that Harambee contributions are a burden for more
households in the poorer locations than in the wealthier locations and the problem is further magnified.
This, of course, relates to the greater levels of coercion experienced by those in the poorer locations than
by those respondents in the wealthier locations.   It
also accounts for the greater willingness in the
wealthier locations to overlook non-payment on the part
of its poorer inhabitants.
    Complexity of Project.   Both performance and the
nature of benefits received vary according to the complexity of the project.   In this there are substantial
differences among the locations.   Primary schools are
quite simple to construct.   It is possible to obtain
the technical skills from the local area, and no special expertise is needed.   This is not the case, for
example, at Karingu Secondary School in Weithaga which,
as indicated earlier, has just completed a new laboratory facility.   To build this laboratory, a contractor
from a neighboring district was employed.   It was an
expensive and complicated undertaking.   Examples come
not only from education but also from other sectors.
Building a maternity ward is a more expensive and complicated undertaking than building a dispensary.   A
communal water supply requires more complex technology
and organizational skill than does a cattle dip. Without belaboring the point, it is obvious from the re-

spondents in all six locations, that the less complex the project, the more rapidly benefits were received and the greater the number of people who enjoyed them. In general, Soin and Kisiara have been involved in fewer complex, long-term and open-ended projects than the other locations and they show the highest percentage of contributors receiving benefits from all their contributions.

Local Leadership. The nature of local level leadership affects the level of Harambee activity and the performance of projects. The key roles of both the Chief and the Sub-Chief in terms of local development efforts should not be underestimated. Chiefs and Sub-Chiefs are appointed by the District Officer (DO) of the Division in part because of their potential leadership skills in the development process. The Chief is the top Government administrator in the location and the Sub-Chief (or Assistant Chief as he may be called) is the top administrator in the sublocation.

To fill these positions the normal procedure is for the DO to request applications from local residents. A Sub-Chief is always a long-time resident of his sublocation, as is the Chief for the location. Since both officials must have widespread support within their respective areas, these positions are filled with great care.[15] Nevertheless, at present the quality of Kenya's Chiefs and Sub-Chiefs varies. Some have been in office since well before Independence, and have obtained their positions for reasons which may or may not be related to development concerns. Others have been selected more recently when there has been a clear emphasis on leadership in development. Two adjacent sublocations in Kisiara Location are illustrative. In one a venerable elder is Sub-Chief, and he does not concern himself very much with development efforts. There is a Sublocational Development Committee, but it did not meet during the first four months of 1979, and given that "there was nothing to discuss," he indicated it would meet only "if some member feels it is a good idea."[16] In the other sublocation, a young and progressive Sub-Chief is actively encouraging several development projects including a maternity wing for the health clinic, an expanding secondary school, and some innovative women's groups.

It is most often the Sub-Chief (also called Assistant Chief) who has the key role in initiating local development efforts, in fostering interest and enthusiasm, and in responding to the concerns of the community. A Sub-Chief who takes his responsibilities seriously can guide his community in developing needed services through self-help, even in remote areas which are cut off from the rest of the country for several months of the year. Assistant Chief Obed Kibicho Iego of Gangara Sublocation, Nthawa, is an example. He comments,

> The Assistant Chief's role in regard to self-help
> projects in the area is very great. As Assistant
> Chief, I am the promoter of all existing projects.
> My responsibility as the Chairman of Gangara
> Development Committee is extensive. It is my concern to organize the committee in such a way as to
> produce the best fruits. After this my committee
> carries out the duties related to organizing various self-help groups and injecting a good spirit
> in them.[17]

Interest in projects is often stimulated by the Assistant Chief. For example, in Mbiri, the Chief and some Sub-Chiefs struggled in barazas (public meetings) to persuade the population that cattle dips would be beneficial to them. Five years after the dips have been in operation, many people in several of Mbiri's sublocations are enthusiastically enjoying the benefits of the dips and are increasing their purchases of cross-breed and grade cattle. However, without the persistence of the Chief and Assistant Chiefs, such benefits would not have been forthcoming.

A similar example comes from Soin where the Chief and various field officers struggled in the late sixties and early 1970s to persuade the residents to plant sugar cane. In baraza after baraza the Chief lectured and cajoled on the benefits of sugar cane as a cash crop. It was not until the late 1970s that he began to see the results of his efforts, and now there is widespread enthusiasm for growing sugar cane. In fact, the nearby factory cannot handle the supply of cane coming from the area.

Under the present administrative arrangements, little development occurs within a community without a competent Assistant Chief who is motivated by a genuine concern for the people of his sublocation. Should the Assistant Chief be unconcerned, unmotivated or inclined to place personal interests before public ones, as was the case in some sublocations visited, a situation not only stagnant but exceedingly detrimental to the community can develop. Those locations and sublocations in which projects have been rapidly and successfully completed and which are well managed have not lacked astute, honest, reliable leadership. In interviews and in private conversations, Kenyans commented that the quality of local level leadership varied widely. Most leaders were considered sufficiently honest and competent, but a number, it was felt, put personal, especially business, interests before their administrative responsibilities – to the detriment of local development projects.[18]

Internal Politics. While resource base may affect the choice, number and complexity of projects, it is not necessarily the determining factor in the performance of projects. Internal politics have a major effect upon Harambee projects and activities. Among the six locations, local politics varied. Two locations were characterized by severe factionalism which was determining local development through Harambee efforts. These locations were Kyeni and Mbiri. In Kyeni, for example, there had been a recent drop both in number of ongoing projects and in size of household contribution. Many respondents related this trend to dissension within the location resulting from the coffee boom. In this case, the problem stemmed from a plethora of unexpected riches. In Kyeni, coffee politics had so affected the atmosphere that self-help projects had, for the time being, dwindled well below their record in the earlier 1970s. Unprecedented prosperity had brought with it intense competition and rivalry.

The Kyeni Coffee Cooperative Society had been in existence since 1951. It was chaired by Noah Ndwiga who was also Chairman of the Embu District Cooperative Union with which the Kyeni Coffee Cooperative Society was affiliated. This society had 2,861 members. In the mid-1970s a group of farmers in Mufu Sublocation became unhappy over the management of the Kyeni Coffee Cooperative Society and the six factories operated by this society.[19] They broke away, forming the Kiangwa Farmers Cooperative Society with 755 members. The problem was to find a way to divide the assets. The factories, as well as the land on which they were situated, were valuable, and it had not been possible to make a decision on a division of assets to which all parties could agree. The Kiangwa Cooperative had constructed a factory of its own, but the question of the other property remained unresolved.

Meanwhile, as coffee prices dropped, the decision, made during a more prosperous period, to form an independent society appeared dangerously irrational. Issues remained unresolved; acrimony was considerable, and the various sections of the community did not care to work together. This mood pervaded coffee issues and other concerns as well. The Harambee efforts to build the community suffered as a consequence of coffee politics. Mr. Rua, Headmaster of Kegonge Boys Secondary School in Kyeni, contrasted the problems of his all-location Harambee boys school in raising funds within the location, with the ease an adjacent location, Kagaari, had enjoyed in funding three Harambee secondary schools with the boon of coffee profits. "Coffee politics and new wealth," he lamented, "have torn these people apart."[20]

In Mbiri factional politics at the locational

level had become intricately involved with the competition between J.G. Kiano and K. Matiba. Some sublocations felt "left out" from Harambee efforts because
they had been aligned with "the wrong side" in the 1974
elections.[21] In some instances, projects had been
allowed to stagnate because the Chief and Assistant
Chief did not agree politically. The Chief of the
location was pro-Matiba; if an Assistant Chief was from
a rival faction, then his programs and development
projects did not get any support at the locational
level. As the election drew closer, all communities
were able to turn the rivalry to some advantage, but
not without earlier cost to morale and to self-help
projects.

Harambee development efforts are affected by other
conditions operating in a community which may not be
political in origin but which have political implications. In the Mbeere section of Embu (where Nthawa is
located), land adjudication is underway. Title deeds
are just now being obtained. There is a lot of confu-
sion and dissension about decisions related to these
deeds, and many decisions are being contested.[22] People have become distrustful of one another and unsure
that they will be in a position to benefit from a particular project in a few years' time. Animosities over
land have developed and these rivalries have led to an
unwillingness to work with other persons in some instances. A KANU official in Mbeere Division summed up
his perspective, stating, "Jealousy is everywhere.
Clan rivalry is fierce. It is impossible to get people
to work together."[23]

Brokensha and Njeru emphasize the relevance of
Chinua Achebe's theme in Things Fall Apart to the rapid
disintegration of Mbeere society because of land adjudication.[24] "There are many more quarrels; there is
deception and dishonesty as people try to win land dis-
putes; there is inter-clan and inter-family confrontation; and the various customary rights to free use of
land for grazing livestock, collecting timber, burning
charcoal, collecting firewood, collecting wild fruit or
placing beehives have drastically altered."[25]

Projects which require cooperation, trust, contributions in the form of both labor and cash, and confidence in the future of the project and its utility to
each family do not flourish in such an environment. In
the case of Nthawa, one can add low levels of economic
productivity and well-being of the local population to
an explanation of the relatively poor record for self-
help.

Conversely, those locations characterized by relative political unanimity seem to have an easier time
fostering support for Harambee projects. Disagreements
over project choice, methods of fundraising, location
of project, management and performance are less likely

to surface and are more readily managed if they do.
Such is the case for Weithaga, for example, where in
several situations, two or three sublocations have successfully joined together for implementing projects.
Kisiara also has a good record in this regard.

Patrons. The relationship with important leaders
or patrons both within and outside the community
affects the success of self-help projects within a
location. Among the locations included in this study,
there was considerable difference in the community's
relationships with the Member of Parliament or with
other patrons whose status and position might bring
benefits. In the case of the three more affluent locations, close ties existed between the community and a
local person from the area who was prominent in the
national Government. Such relationships clearly serve
mutual needs: the patron brings funds, organizational
skill and motivation to the local community. For example, Kamwithi Munyi, Assistant Minister for Power and
Communications, has been instrumental in developing the
Karurumo Village Polytechnic into a strong institution.
Kiano, as Minister for Water Development, has assured
that his constituency is among the first to receive a
major water project. In return, such patrons as these
acquire political support and are accorded power, position and affection within the community.[26] These relationships can lead to significant levels of outside
assistance for a community, to strong motivation and
contribution levels from within the community and to
high rates of project completion.

In the three poorer locations, the links between
patron and local community have not been strong. The
momentum for projects and project assistance generated
by patrons has not been as great as in the wealthier
areas. Neither Munyi nor Kiano has done as much for
the poorer locations within their constituencies as for
the more affluent ones. Evidence from both Mbiri and
Nthawa support this observation. Mbiri's disenchant-
ment with Kiano and readiness for a change in the last
election suggest an awareness on the part of those residents that perhaps they were being shortchanged.[27]

In part, the weaker links with patrons relate to
lower levels of organizational effort, a lower density
of population, greater communication problems, and a
general inability of poorer locations to make the same
level of demand upon the Members of Parliament and
other patrons. At the same time, they do not return
the number of votes that the more densely populated
areas are able to mobilize. Residents also have
achieved lower levels of education, and even now do not
have a large group of people politically aware of the
potential relationships between patrons and local development.

The more affluent locations have learned to capit-

alize on the power and position of their "successful
sons" and to make demands on those who have done well
on a broader national scene. Their loyalty is an important asset to the community. In Central Province,
this loyalty has been organized on a large scale.
Murang'a District has the benefit of the Murang'a
Harambee Development Fund organized by leading Murang'a
citizens from Nairobi, Mombasa, Thika and Nakuru in
order to provide a systematic approach to raising funds
for development within Murang'a District. This Fund is
set up as a public corporation. Anyone willing to pay
Ksh. 1,000 may become a Life Member and may participate
in electing the Trustees who include "all Members of
Parliament who come from Murang'a and prominent leaders
in all walks of life from Murang'a."[28]

The Trustees have established development priorities for Murang'a. They have determined that all people of Murang'a should contribute to meeting the development goals, such as the Murang'a College of Technology. The Trustees have specified that all employed
persons "are expected to make contributions in respect
of Murang'a College of Technology" on the basis of an
annual contribution equivalent to 20 percent of one
month's salary. A levy on tea growers, coffee growers
and milk producers was established. The rate was one
cent per pound on tea or coffee until the Ksh.
10,000,000 target for the College was reached. Owners
and employers of businesses such as bars, restaurants,
transportation or barbershops were all assessed a specific sum, payable to the Chief of the location in
which the person was resident or employed. Would these
assessments for Murang'a development, made by the
Murang'a Harambee Development Fund, be considered legal
if someone chose to contest them? Probably not. Was
this procedure successful? Very.

Naturally both Weithaga and Mbiri benefit from the
efforts of the Murang'a Harambee Development Fund. For
the Mbiri resident, however, these assessments are far
more likely to be a burden than they are for the
Weithaga residents. A number of Mbiri respondents
noted their displeasure over the required contribution
to the College of Technology, indicating that it was
excessive and that they did not expect to benefit.

Even in Murang'a, project by project, the wealthier locations are receiving more attention and benefiting more from the activities of patrons than are the
poorer ones. The comparative Harambee development
efforts in Weithaga and Mbiri provide evidence to this
effect. Only in 1978-1979 with Matiba's strategy for
winning the Parliamentary seat has this situation
started to change.

Attitudes of the Public. The centralization of
power at the local level and the personalization of
much that is official business leads to an unwilling-

ness on the part of the general public to criticize
publically and openly when there is dissatisfaction
with the conduct of projects. Evidence from this study
shows that only in the more affluent areas with higher
levels of education and somewhat greater experience in
projects, were people becoming willing to assert themselves and to question the actions of a committee or
its leadership. This willingness is both limited and
tenuous.

Weithaga provides several examples. At Kianderi
Girls School in Kahuti Sublocation there were widespread concerns on the part of parents about misuse of
funds by the Headmaster and the Chairman of the School
Committee. These concerns led to a series of meetings
and eventually resulted in interim supervision of
school affairs through the Bishop of the Anglican
Church. The parents have been satisfied with this
arrangement.

In another case in Weithaga, residents of Wanjengi
Sublocation were distressed that their dispensary/
maternity ward had never been completed and that aid
they were promised had not been forthcoming. Although
they had not been willing to organize themselves to
present their grievances in a careful and systematic
manner to the District Commissioner, they were quick to
press the story of their problems upon anyone who, they
felt, might be in a position to assist them. Their
irritation was widely known. They had not been successful in redressing their grievance, in part because
the Chief opposed their preferred solutions. By contrast, residents of the poorer locations have taken no
action when projects have failed. In Mbiri, collection
of funds for a social hall and a village polytechnic,
neither of which materialized, has not galvanized people into any form of protest. Likewise in Nthawa,
broken cattle dips aroused individual complaint, but no
community action.

Even within project committees, members may hesi-
tate to protest a decision or activity with which they
disagree. This is in part because of authoritarian
leadership patterns. The chairman is accorded great
respect, and along with two or three key members, he
often determines committee policies. The other committee members may concur willingly, but they often do so
in silence. A widespread exchange of views is not a
common occurrence. One respondent to the questionnaire, commenting on the lack of opportunity to participate in discussions about projects, stated, as explanation, "Even if I am on the committee, I am not the
Chairman."[29]

Relations with Nairobi. Of the six locations
studied, Mbiri is the one most closely involved with
Nairobi in relationships with varied and sometimes
harmful social and economic consequences. The survey

in Mbiri revealed that a high percentage of males are
working outside the location, primarily in Nairobi. Of
households interviewed, 60 percent had a member earning
a wage or a salary at least some of the time. For some
this has meant substantial increases in income. Many,
however, are employed at unskilled labor or low levels
of skill with low wages and unreliable access to jobs.
The second largest group of Mbiri residents were those
relying completely on subsistence agriculture with no
other income-generating opportunities. This group comprised 23 percent of the respondents interviewed.
Thus, it would appear that in Mbiri there is an increasing differentiation between rich and poor.

Low productivity of the land and a withdrawal of
labor to the cities has meant that there is a high percentage of female headed households accompanied by relatively high poverty levels. The competition between
Dr. Kiano and Mr. Matiba helped counter the demoral-
ized atmosphere which respondents say has characterized
Mbiri Location for some years. It has helped bring resources into the area, along with releasing some local
resources for public purposes. Matiba's campaign was
built on Mbiri residents' feelings of impoverishment
and neglect, and, clearly, he hit a responsive chord.

All the locations are affected by their relations
with the center and by their ability to obtain and
utilize funds, personnel and other resources from
Nairobi. The more affluent locations have been more
successful in this regard, despite genuine efforts of
the District Development Committees to direct funds
toward the resource-poor locations. The small sums
which these committees have at their disposal simply
provide no counterweight to the informal techniques developed by more affluent areas for obtaining needed
assistance from outside the locality. The Murang'a
Harambee Development Fund is one of the more sophisticated and effective among them.

Project Clustering and Structural Supports. Projects tend to cluster, a phenomenon explored more fully
in Chapter V. A sublocation may have a nursery school
attached to the primary school, a day secondary school,
a clinic and a church. Another sublocation may have
only a primary school. This pattern suggests that
lateral linkages develop among projects. These linkages may be based on the principle that "success begets
success" or on some of the conditions mentioned earlier: strong leadership, a highly motivated Assistant
Chief or patron, or a particularly strong resource
base.

Gangara Sublocation is illustrative. A primary
school in this remote sublocation had been on its present site since 1956. Built of mud and wattle, the
buildings required constant maintenance because of
termite damage. The community was constructing a new

stone building, and four of the seven classrooms were complete. Parents came once a week to work on the schools, both old and new, and a turnout of 80 parents, mostly women, out of approximately 100 families, was customary.

The school was set on spacious grounds, and the parents had started an acre of cotton which was to be used to supplement school funds. They perceived that their biggest need was water. Gangara is one of the sites of a dam which had been damaged, and they were eager to repair it. If they could solve the water problem, they wanted to build a secondary school. Thus, a locally initiated project, the primary school, had the potential for involving this community in two more projects: water supply and secondary school. The projects were locally planned, initiated, and implemented. They had received a small amount of assistance for the school from the Office of Community Development, and it was welcome, but not critical. Such would not be the case for a water project. Outside help would be essential for the local community lacked the technical expertise to undertake it.

How has the central Government contributed to or facilitated this potential "clustering" of projects in Gangara, which also has one of Nthawa's few functioning cattle dips and a church constructed by self-help? First, it would not have been possible without the road development component of the Special Rural Development Program (SRDP), an intensive development effort undertaken in Mbeere Division with the assistance of NORAD, the Norwegian Development Agency, between 1970 and 1975. The road to Gangara was a mere track before SRDP, and even now is impassable at certain seasons of the year. Stones from Siakago had to be hauled by truck to Gangara, a task not feasible six years ago. The road also facilitated bringing iron sheets for roofing the building, and, in general, made transport of materials possible.

Second, the Government activated its agricultural service on behalf of cotton production during the SRDP. While the cotton blocks failed because of drought and inappropriate organization for the area, individual farmers now grow cotton in good years using more modern methods. With the favorable rains of 1976-1979, approximately 50 percent of the farmers in Gangara Sub-location were growing cotton. The average acreage varied between one-fourth and three acres per household. Yields per acre, in 1978 prices, were Ksh. 2,080 for high quality cotton, with costs of less than Ksh. 200.[30] For "B" quality the yields were about Ksh. 1,000 per acre. The returns from this cash crop brought increased prosperity to the area and encouraged more families to send their children to school. This resulted in an increased interest in the quality of education being offered by the primary school and in the opportunities for further education for the children of that community.

It is possible to draw similar illustrations from many projects in other locations. They have started in the sublocation as a result of widely shared interests. The project has drawn on the resources of the immediate community and has slowly led to other projects. The procedure has worked upward and outward using supports the Government provides, and integrating them into the project.

In addition, some locations have an emerging social infrastructure which is central to the success of their Harambee activities. That is, the local women's group may have built the nursery school or contributed to the dispensary. A church may have actively contributed to and supported the building of a day secondary school. A women's group in Weithaga planned to open a library in its social hall. The Coffee Cooperative in Kyeni helped finance two secondary schools, and coffee cooperatives in Weithaga gave generously to the Kahuti water project. Slowly a new social infrastructure is emerging in some communities. Groups and activities begin to reinforce one another in useful ways and to provide a network for fostering community activities and services.

IMPLICATIONS OF THIS VARIATION IN HARAMBEE ACTIVITY

Some communities have mobilized far higher levels of Harambee activities than have others. These same communities have strong networks and linkages enabling them to take advantage of resources from outside the area and enabling them to draw on loyalties of patrons successful in other parts of Kenya. Nowhere is this more evident than in the record of newspaper accounts of major fundraising events and their guests for the period from May, 1979 through July, 1979, referred to in Chapter III.[31] Dividing Kenya's 40 districts into quartiles according to wealth and comparing the number of outside visitors for fundraising purposes received by the districts in each quartile for those three months, a startling picture of the skewed nature of outside support for local Harambee activities emerges. Of the 67 fundraising events and guests noted during that period, 57 percent visited the ten most affluent districts for fundraising purposes. In the second quartile, districts ranking 11 through 20 in terms of wealth, there were 25 visitors or 37 percent of the fundraising visits. The third quartile of districts received 5 percent of the visitors, and the poorest quartile received one percent. Clearly the access routes for both formal and informal assistance for development efforts are better established in the wealthier areas.

Moreover, exactly half of the fundraising visitors to the ten most affluent districts were visiting the two Kikuyu districts of Central Province, which rank among those in the most affluent quartile. Add to those the fundraising visitors to Kikuyu districts among the second most affluent quartile of the districts, and 51 percent of the fundraising guests noted in The Daily Nation during the specified period of time, were visiting Kikuyu areas. Since the Kikuyus occupy as a majority of residents only 5 of 40 districts and constitute only 15 percent of the total Kenyan population, these figures represent a clear thrust toward Harambee activity within the Kikuyu community. In December, 1979, the Acting Provincial Commissioner for Central Province, David Musila, reported that people in that province had raised Ksh. 113,312,000 ($15,108,026) for Harambee projects between September, 1978 and October, 1979.[32] Central Province has ranked first in self-help among the provinces since the statistics have been collected beginning in 1967. This data suggests that Kikuyu "access" far exceeds that of other groups and communities.

NOTES

1. See Colin Leys, Underdevelopment in Kenya (London: Heinemann Educational Books, Ltd., 1976); or ILO, Employment, Incomes and Equality (Geneva, 1972).
2. Government of Kenya, Development Plan, 1979-1983, Part I (Nairobi: Government Printer, 1979), pp. 5-6.
3. Edgar V. Winans and Angelique Haugerud, "Rural Self-Help in Kenya: The Harambee Movement," Human Organization, vol. 35, November, 1976, p. 10.
4. Ibid, p. 16.
5. Op. cit.
6. Provincial data is drawn from Ministry of Housing and Social Services, Department of Social Services, Community Development Division, Research and Evaluation Unit, Self-Help Statistics, 1977, mimeographed report, 1979, pp. 5-19. Also, from the files of the Ministry of Housing and Social Services, Reports on the Status and Value of Self-Help Projects, 1967-1977.
7. Records in the Ministry of Housing and Social Services indicate that Central Province is first in self-help value, 1968-1977, among the provinces. Also, Ministry of Housing and Social Services, Self-Help Statistics, 1977, op. cit., p. 30.
8. Government of Kenya, Central Bureau of Statistics, Statistical Abstract, 1976 (Nairobi: Government Printer, 1976), p. 289; and Ministry of Housing

and Social Services, <u>Self-Help Statistics, 1977</u>,
<u>op. cit.</u>, pp. 20-23.
        9.   This method of measuring correlation from
rank uses Spearman's formula. See Herbert Arkin and
Raymond Colton, <u>Statistical Methods</u> (New York: Barnes
and Noble, 1964), p. 85.
        10.   Figure 5 is based on data collected from the
District Files of the Community Development Office.
These figures are found in the Annual Reports presented
to the CDO by the Locational Community Development
Assistants.
        11.   Interview with Miss Nguyo, Divisional Agri-
cultural Officer for Mbeere, Siakago, April, 1978.
        12.   All locations had complete records for 1977.
These figures are based on the contributions listed in
their annual reports by the LCDAs.
        13.   Most of the schools in Nthawa Location are
constructed of mud and wattle. They require constant
maintenance. This is done on a regular basis by women
in the community who have children in the school.
Their labor contribution is given a monetary value, as
is all labor contributed to self-help projects. In the
case of Nthawa, this labor accounts for a high percentage of the total value of self-help.
        14.   This section on benefits excludes incidental
contributions such as one might make to a church in a
neighboring community.
        15.   Conversations with District Officers in
Mbeere, Embu and Kiharu Divisions, April and May, 1978.
        16.   Interview with Assistant Chief, Roret Sub-
location, Kisiara, May, 1979.
        17.   Interview with Assistant Chief, Gangara Sub-
location, May 4, 1978.
        18.   Observations on Chiefs and Assistant Chiefs
are based on a number of conversations with District
Officers, Locational Community Development Assistants,
Community Development Officers, and residents of the
communities.
        19.   Interview with Mr. Buhl-Nielsen, Nordic Ad-
viser in Management and Planning, Cooperative Department, Embu, April, 1978; and with Mr. Ndwati, Coopera-
tives Officer in Embu District, April 27, 1978.
        20.   Interview with Mr. Rua, Headmaster, Kegonge
Secondary School, Kyeni Location, March, 1978.
        21.   Conversations with several shopkeepers in
Makuyu Sublocation, arranged through the LCDA, Rose
Njeri, June, 1978.
        22.   See David Brokensha and E.H.N. Njeru, "Some
Consequences of Land Adjudication in Mbeere Division,
Embu," Working Paper #320, Institute for Development
Studies, University of Nairobi, 1977.
        23.   Interview with KANU Official, Mbeere Divi-
sion, Embu District, April, 1978.
        24.   Brokensha and Njeru, <u>op. cit.</u>, p. 5.

26. In spite of the fact that he has lost the Mbiri seat in Parliament, Kiano is still a very power- ful Kenyan politician, and is one of the most influen- tial Kikuyus on the national scene.

27. While many people of both Weithaga and Mbiri respect and admire Dr. Kiano and feel he has done a great deal for the people of Murang'a, there was also a feeling that he had been in power a long time, that he had not paid full attention to some portions of the constituency, and that it was time for a change. Kiano has not retired from politics, and it would be surpris- ing if he did not compete for the Mbiri seat in the next Parliamentary election.

28. Murang'a Harambee Development Fund informa- tion sheet, P.O. Box 8793, Nairobi.

29. Respondent, Mbiri Location, May, 1978.

30. Interview with Miss Nguyo, Divisional Agri- cultural Officer for Mbeere Division, Siakago, April, 1978.

31. The Daily Nation, May through July, 1979.

32. The Daily Nation, December 5, 1979.

V
Self-Help Community Projects:
From Rhetoric to Reality

> In most cases contributing to a project is as routine as buying sugar or tea leaves.
>   Respondent
>   Mbiri Location

Analysis of the important characteristics of Harambee community projects in the six designated locations draws on data collected in the course of interviews with project committees of more than 80 projects. It also uses data derived from records and reports found in the files of the Community Development Offices in Embu, Murang'a and Kericho Districts. We investigate how projects are chosen, funded, implemented, and managed. In addition, we explore the characteristics of different types of projects as well as the attitudes of the general public toward self-help community projects.

METHODS FOR SELECTING AND INITIATING PROJECTS

When questioned about the kinds of development projects needed by his community, one Assistant Chief answered, "Anyone can tell you - roads, water and health care."[1] To date, however, these three areas have not been the major focus of self-help efforts. Table 5.1 shows the types of projects which residents have undertaken within the six locations. In 1979 there were 304 separate institutions, services or facilities which had been undertaken or were under construction by self-help community efforts in these locations. Of these projects, 181 or 60 percent are related to education. Economic-related projects rank second with 82 or 27 percent of the total number of projects. Health facilities account for 5 percent of the total projects and social welfare facilities for 8 percent.

Table 5.1
Community projects completed and current in six
locations,* 1965-1979

Project	Soin	Nthawa	Mbiri	Kisiara	Kyeni	Weithaga
Primary school	18	14	12	24	15	13
Secondary school	3	1	5	11	2	9
Nursery school	8	7	5	5	7	18
Health services	3	1	--	5	4	3
Cattle dips	18	6**	7	21	7	5
Water supply	1	4	1	--	1	1
Road/bridge	4	--	--	4	--	--
Village Poly-technic	1	--	1	--	1	1
Social	1	--	6	2	6	10
Dams	--	2***	--	--	--	--
Total	57	35	37	72	43	60
Ratio of projects: people	1:184	1:316	1:343	1:532	1:498	1:335

*Locations: these are listed left to right, poorer
... richer
**Of these six cattle dips, all were completed; four
are inoperable
***Both dams were completed; neither is functioning

In the official Government statistics, primary and
Secondary schools are usually listed on the basis of
individual units.[2] That is, a primary school project
may be a classroom, teacher's house, latrine, fence,
office or storeroom. A secondary school project may
include classrooms, office and storeroom, laboratory or
library facilities, teacher's house, dining hall, lava-
tories or dormitories. All schools visited had ongoing
projects. A school may have completed six classrooms
and be starting construction of teacher's houses, or it
may be adding new dormitory space or expanding other
facilities. Building schools, whether primary or secondary, is a long-term process, and no school claimed
to be "finished."
    The figures conceal some important differences in
quality and scope of the undertaking. For example, in
Weithaga, seven of the primary schools had fully com-

pleted classrooms constructed of permanent materials, stone or cement blocks. In Soin, five schools were building classrooms of permanent materials; the remaining 13 were constructing classrooms of mud, wattle and stone. Only two of the nursery school buildings in Soin were permanent; the remainder were semi-permanent. By contrast, almost all of the nursery schools in Weithaga were of stone or cement block construction.

The Assistant Chief's comment suggests that there is much unanimity within communities concerning need for common facilities. The data collected in the survey in each of the six locations would support such an observation. Table 5.2 indicates the percentage of respondents in each location who named identical first and second choices for projects needed by the community. The notable exception to the high levels of unanimity in first and second choices for local development projects is Kisiara where satisfaction on health and education issues is paramount, but a wide variety of economically-oriented projects are suggested by local residents. Thus, in most locations and sublocations, there is widespread agreement on development needs. There are, however, differences on order and sequence of projects, on siting of projects, and on magnitude or quality of projects to be undertaken. Some, for example, may prefer to start with a health clinic; others with a secondary school; some may advocate a day secondary school; others a boarding school. In some cases in the locations surveyed, relations among sublocations have become tense as they fought over projects. For example, the health clinic in Wanjengi Sublocation of Weithaga has been a source of bitter contention between Wanjengi and Kirogo Sublocations.

Table 5.2
Percentage of respondents sharing opinions on first and second choices for needed community projects

Location	First Choice	Second Choice
Soin	94	58
Nthawa	90	75
Mbiri	86	75
Kisiara	56	42
Kyeni	91	81
Weithaga	83	70

It is in seeking funds from the District Development Committee (DDC) that competition is likely to become acute. The District Development Committee, as indicated in Chapter III, considers recommendations for use of funds from the Divisional Development Committees. Divisions are comprised of several locations, and the Divisional Development Committee must decide on its priorities before requesting funds from the DDC. These funds are allocated in small sums according to well understood criteria and allocation procedures. Nevertheless, they can cause serious competition, for the scraps are small and the need is endless.

The decision to proceed with a self-help project is usually made at a <u>baraza</u> (public meeting) held at the locational or sublocational level. Normally there is not much controversy or discussion in such public meetings, though its open forum style might lend itself to such. Differences of opinion are worked out beforehand, and the public meeting is more likely to be used as an opportunity for the Chief or the Sub-Chief to inform the public of priorities and to suggest steps to be taken. Residents will be well aware of the purpose of a particular baraza and may have had an informal opportunity to discuss the issues with local leaders.

For example, in Kathanjure Sublocation of Kyeni Location, residents are very concerned about providing secondary school facilities for their children. In 1977 that sublocation alone had enough children passing the CPE at the end of primary school to make up four Form I classes. These children did not find places in the Government secondary schools outside the location. Some residents want to convert one of the primary schools into a girls boarding school and then convert a second primary school into a day secondary school while building new primary school facilities. Jackson Ireri, the Assistant Chief, has informally polled all the households in his sublocation to obtain their views on the need for these schools and their ability and willingness to contribute to them, particularly through their coffee earnings.[3] In the process, he learned that there were only three of 1,000 households which were not growing coffee and which did not have some source of cash income. He also learned that the concerns over educational facilities for primary school completers were widely shared. Further, he learned that residents were interested in the possibility of having some sort of trade school, such as a village polytechnic which would teach skills in carpentry, agriculture or masonry. Before coming to a baraza with a proposal, Ireri will have a clear idea of the community's attitudes, the approach toward educational changes which most favor, the possible location for a school, and a timetable for the sublocation to follow.

There are, of course, Assistant Chiefs and Chiefs

who do not bother developing this kind of support for projects. They may gather the local residents for a baraza, using a "chief's order" to insure complete attendance by all adults, and then harangue the community about what should or should not be done. Such an authoritarian approach is not uncommon. Exhortation, at times flamboyant, is considered by some an important means for motivating the public. It does not always motivate, but it clearly does inform.

In a number of cases, there is a recognizeable pattern to the selection and initiation of projects. The first project in a sublocation is usually the primary school and this may become a catalyst for other projects. If the school is relatively good, and a substantial number are passing the examination for the Certificate of Primary Education (CPE) at the end of Standard 7, then the pressure builds to open a secondary school. This pressure exists because only a small number of students from any one primary school will be admitted to a Government secondary school. As in the case of Kathanjure, many students who actually qualify for a place in a secondary school still cannot find an opening. At the other end of the primary educational system, there may be pressure on places in Standard 1. This is particularly true of some of the densely populated areas such as Weithaga and Kyeni. There, teachers of Standard 1 are reluctant to admit children into their classes if they have not attended nursery school. In these two locations, families are eager to use nursery schools in order to insure that their children will not only have a place in Standard I, but will do well.

Projects other than primary schools may also serve as catalysts. Cattle dips have led to the formation of women's groups involved in raising funds for the purchase of imported, or grade, cattle. Likewise, churches have started schools - primary, secondary, nursery and polytechnic. Projects may call on the services of a local village polytechnic, thereby generating business opportunities which strengthen the latter institution. Kiaganari Girls Secondary School Committee in Kyeni employed carpenters and masons from Karurumo Village Polytechnic to construct classrooms and teachers' houses. Thus, for a variety of reasons related to need and to other conditions, as suggested in Chapter IV, projects tend to cluster and to build upon one another.

COSTS AND FUNDING

Once a community has determined to undertake a project, there are several ways to proceed to raise money. People from the community will be expected to give cash, labor and occasionally material. The Project Committee will determine the specific amount to be contributed by each family. It will decide whether the cash contribution will be based on a flat sum per family or a sliding scale according to wealth. (Household contributions in relation to different socio-economic groups within a community are discussed in Chapter VI.) Labor contributions will be a requisite number of days of work; material may be a required two poles for a fence, or a similar form of assistance for the project. Sometimes a resident who has sand or stone on his land, or a truck which can be used for hauling, will donate such an item with a cash value attached to the contribution.

The Committee obtains permission from the District Community Development Office to collect funds for the project; it opens a bank account in the name of the project. The Project Committee is responsible for collecting the required funds from community residents. Typical payments per household, using a flat rate would be in the Ksh. 20 to 50 range. Using a sliding scale, payments might vary from Ksh. 30 to 300 as in the case of a cattle dip in Koitaburot Sublocation in Soin, from Ksh. 30 to 500, as with the Cheborge Primary School in Cheborge Sublocation in Kisiara, or from Ksh. 10 to 1,000 for the Murang'a College of Technology in Weithaga and Mbiri.[4] (See Chapter VI for a discussion of coercion in collecting Harambee "contributions".)

In some cases the Project Committee issues receipt books to residents of the community and their friends who then solicit contributions for the projects. Receipt books are used widely in cities or towns by Kenyans who collect small donations - five or ten shillings - from friends and colleagues and carry these funds back to their home communities to contribute to the local school, dispensary, church or other project.

Once a project is fully initiated, the community may try to obtain Government or private agency assistance. This is primarily in the form of "topping up" aid. The Government, CARE, Charity Sweepstakes, or another private agency may provide iron sheets for a roof, cement for the floor, or windows and doors. Such assistance offers an incentive for a community to get the building "up to the lintels." The cash value of such assistance for a school varies from just over $100 in a typical Government contribution to $1,500 in one of the more generous CARE grants to a primary school. Cattle dips have received $1,000 to $1,500, and the cash value of outside contributions to water projects is much greater. For example, the people of Gitiburi Sublocation of Nthawa have collected the nearly Ksh. 10,000 which is their cash contribution to a water project in their area. The Government is contributing Ksh. 91,000 ($12,133). The people themselves are dig-

ging the trenches for the water pipe and through a combined labor and cash contribution will bring their
total contribution to the water project to approximately 30 percent of the cost.[5]   Nevertheless, as noted in
Chapter II, such outside assistance accounts annually
for 6 to 15 percent of the total value of Harambee
projects in the years 1967 to 1977.   Table 5.3 indicates the percentage of projects, among those investigated, which have received outside donor aid.[6]

Table 5.3
Percentage of projects in six locations which
have received outside aid from various sources

Type of Project	Kenyan Gov't	Foreign Gov't Aid	Int'l PVOs	Kenyan PVOs	Other
Secondary schools	31	0	13	43	6
Primary schools (building program)	48	0	14	10	0
Cattle dips	22	67	11	--	--
Health facilities	68	--	--	--	--
Social welfare	--	--	--	42	--
Village polytechnics	25	50	--	50	--
Nursery schools	--	--	--	--	33
Water	80	--	20	--	--

Finally, it is customary for a Project Committee
to organize one or two fundraising events for the benefit of a particular project.   These will vary according
to the size of the undertaking.   For a secondary school
fundraising, a committee will make elaborate plans.
Guests of honor will include the local Member of Parliament and any other dignitaries to whom the community
has access.   The advance publicity will be extensive,
and the occasion itself will be part fair, with a public auction of contributions ranging from cups to cows,
and part politicking and speech-making.   At these fundraising events the Committee gives the contribution-
in-kind, perhaps a goat or chicken, baskets, mug or
torch, a cash value and enters it in the books as a
material contribution.   The cash received for each of
these items is entered into the computation of cash received.   When cash, material and labor contributions
are totalled, there is a form of double bookkeeping

which leads to inflated values in the self-help statistics collected by the Locational Community Development
Assistants and submitted to the Community Development
Office. Because the material listings include both
actual contributions to building, such as stone and
timber, as well as auction items, without distinguish-
ing between the two, it is impossible to determine the
size of the double counting procedure.

Nevertheless, material contributions make up a
relatively small share of total contributions. In
1977, for example, they accounted for 17 percent of the
total.[7] This problem suggests that district-level statistics must be used with caution, but it is possible
to make comparisons and to suggest the relative magni-
tudes of local-level contributions. Donations from the
Government of Kenya or from outside agencies such as
CARE, Danida or Charity Sweepstakes are listed separately in the Community Development Office records.
Contributions brought by guest speakers at fundraising
events are included under "people's contribution."

One misleading aspect of fundraising concerns the
overly zealous promises of some contributors at the
Harambee fundraising events. It is not unusual for
persons, carried away by enthusiasm, and perhaps also
by the public limelight, to promise a larger contribution than they can realistically make. Several days
after such events, checks may bounce or truckloads of
promised supplies may fail to materialize. The headmaster of Kegonge Secondary School in Kyeni, Mr. Rua,
indicated that the Ksh. 90,000 which guests publicly
announced they were giving at a major fundraising event
in 1977 turned out to be only Ksh. 50,000 ($6,667).[8]
Weithaga High School had a similar shortfall at a fundraising in 1978.[9]

The problems with the funding methods for self-
help projects are numerous. One of the most difficult
is the combined effect of the time it takes for a community to raise a large sum of money and the current
inflationary economic cycle. The escalating cost of
building materials means that by the time a community
has collected enough money to begin work, it is likely
that the costs have gone up and their original assessment of costs of construction and transport of materials was inadequate. This is particularly a problem
for communities which may need to transport building
materials from some distance and which face sharply increasing gasoline prices. Primary School Committees
estimated that in the six years between 1972 and 1978,
their costs had risen by approximately 67 percent.[10]
For a school such as Kamasega Primary School in Soin
which has had to transport stone from a source 40 miles
away and sand from 30 miles, transport costs have been
substantial. Rising world gasoline prices have ad-
versely affected the ease with which a remote rural

community, such as Soliat Sublocation in Soin, can undertake a self-help project.[11]

Second, in some cases there is not an adequate system of recordkeeping. Accounts are not properly maintained, and records of funds collected and expenditures sustained by the committee are either inadequate or non-existent. In one case, the headmistress of a secondary school which had received major Governmental funding, as well as high levels of community support, acknowledged that there were simply no proper records of funds.[12] In another case, the school committee chairman kept the receipt books at his home, and even the headmaster did not have an exact idea of receipts versus expenditures.[13] The national Government has become concerned about management of Harambee secondary schools, and these schools are now being required to submit monthly audit statements to the Provincial Education Board.

There is no doubt that misuse of funds is a problem in the case of many Harambee projects. The misuse is occasionally flagrant, as in the case of a village polytechnic in Mbiri Location where Ksh. 4,000 ($533) simply disappeared and where sand and stone worth Ksh. 12,000 ($1,600) "drifted away."[14] More often it consists of "skimming" or pilfering funds or supplies. Examples would be a few iron sheets for the headmaster's house while the classrooms are being roofed or a kickback for a committee chairman when purchases of stone or sand are being made.[15] A related problem is shortchange of supplies, such as cement, on the part of unscrupulous contractors or workmen. Mr. Wahome, Provincial Director of Social Services in Eastern Province, a man with long experience in the Community Development Offices of several districts, suggests that such problems are widespread at low levels of misuse.[16]

This form of misuse clearly slows the rate of project completion. If excessive, it also discourages the public from becoming involved in such projects. Evidence from the six locations suggests that the narrower the scope of the project, the easier it is to assure that the funds collected, or most of them, reach their objective. Concrete evidence of a classroom going up or the cattle dip being built means that the committee has not "eaten the funds" as one respondent indicated sometimes happens.[17] The most difficult kind of project to control is one which is long-term and open-ended. Some committees start with the idea of a project such as a dispensary or a water supply, and begin collecting funds in a rather vague manner, with the objective of beginning work when they have collected enough. They indulge more in wishful thinking than in concrete planning. This may go on for years with little or no progress being made. In such situations, financial arrangements are apt to be haphazard and money is likely to slip through fingers.

In the course of interviews with project committees it was impossible to determine in any precise way
whether or not project funds were being misused, and,
if so, to what extent. That is, it is clear that funds
have been misused if a project has not moved past digging the foundation and Ksh. 7,000 which were collected
are no longer in the bank account.[18] What is not as
easy to ascertain is whether the classroom which is
nearly completed should have been finished two years
ago and was not because funds set aside for it found
their way to personal uses. Project committees did not
readily share perspectives on misuse of funds with an
outside researcher. Insights and frank comments on the
problem came primarily from officials who did not have
responsibility for particular projects and from the
occasional school headmaster, committee member, or community resident interviewed privately who thereby felt
more free to offer his opinions than he would have in
the presence of others.[19]

A SELECTIVE EXPLORATION OF PROJECT TYPES

Educational Projects

The purpose of investing in schools is a long-term
increase in earning power and productivity of the children of a family, not easily measured unless one is ob-
serving both generational and community change.   There
is no doubt that schools are considered very desirable
and important by the majority of Kenyans in the locations studied.   Only in Nthawa did any respondents indicate that they preferred keeping their children out
of school and did not like the influence of new ways.
Even here, these respondents were a small minority.

Table 5.4 shows the percentage of respondents in
each location who had contributed cash to schools. The
two poorest locations have the lowest levels of involvement in school projects.   In Soin 20 percent of
the households of respondents were living at a subsistence level, and in Nthawa 29 percent were at a similar
economic level with no regular cash income from employment or sale of crops or other commodities.   This partially explains the low levels of cash contributions to
educational projects.

In Mbiri, however, where 23 percent are living at
a subsistence level, 80 percent of these poorest households had managed to contribute to school projects.[20]
In some cases this was simply the Ksh. 10 required of
all women (unless they were employed) for the Murang'a
College of Technology.   Nevertheless, the long Kikuyu
involvement with education and the pressure felt by
this community to improve economic opportunities

through education, account in some measure, for the educational emphasis among even the poorest residents of Mbiri. Important too is the emphasis within the Kikuyu community on communal solidarity and joint effort to develop their area, as indicated by the existence of the Murang'a Harambee Development Fund. In Mbiri, 91 percent of those respondents living at subsistence levels had contributed something at some time to Harambee projects.[21]

Table 5.4
Percentage of survey respondents who have contributed cash to Harambee school projects

Location	% of Respondents Contributing to School Projects
Soin	64
Nthawa	56
Mbiri	82
Kisiara	92
Kyeni	90
Weithaga	88

Primary Schools. The quality of educational institutions varies widely. Local residents are very much aware of the quality of their primary school, and for purposes of judging its effectiveness they have a useful measure: the Certificate of Primary Education (CPE). This is a nationwide, standardized examination given at the end of Standard 7 and used for admission to secondary school. Primary school headmasters keep careful records of results of the CPE among students at their school. Should the numbers who receive passes and gain admission to Government-sponsored schools be increasing, there is considerable pride and pleasure on the part of headmaster and staff. The school will be sought by parents of adjacent communities who would like their children to have the opportunity for good training in Standards 6 and 7.

Most of the primary schools visited were characterized by a slow but steady improvement in CPE scores. Should a school have a setback in numbers of CPE passes, there is likely to be considerable effort to address the problem and to make improvements. In one instance, a school in Mbiri found the CPE results declining over a several year period, and the school committee requested a new headmaster to take on the job of reversing the process.

While schools may be valued for purposes of long-term improvement in individual income earning powers and productivity, they often play an immediate role in increasing productivity, incomes and employment of adults in the community in three ways. First, many schools have income-earning activities. Second, schools involved in building programs provide jobs for local skilled and sometimes unskilled labor. Third, schools make local purchases and increase levels of local business.

Primary school income earning activities are usually agricultural. Fifty percent of the schools visited had school gardens ranging in size from one-half acre to two acres and earning from Ksh. 800 to 4,000 annually. The variety of crops included coffee, bananas, potatoes, maize, beans, napier grass and cotton. Money earned was used for a variety of school related expenses, usually furniture and teaching materials. Sometimes it was used to augment funds being collected for building purposes. Several schools had sufficient land that they were able to rent out several acres for a small fee.

In four of the six locations of the study, all primary schools were involved in a process of upgrading or adding to their buildings. This endeavor is directed primarily toward creating a school built of permanent materials, as opposed to a mud and wattle structure which is vulnerable to termites as well as to wind and rain. In two of the more prosperous locations more than half of the primary schools had completed their classroom building program. The component spent on skilled labor for the construction of a classroom was approximately one-fifth of the total cost. Records kept by the schools on building fund expenditures and the costs of construction were inadequate or non-existent, so only estimations are possible. If, however, we make a conservative estimate of the average cost of building a classroom between the late 1960s and 1979 at Ksh. 12,000 for a permanent structure, then Ksh. 2,400 of that sum has been paid to skilled laborers. If an average school has constructed six classrooms, then it has generated employment and increased income to the value of Ksh. 14,400 ($1,920).[22]

In the sample of schools, 26 percent of the skilled laborers were hired from outside the immediate area, and, therefore, the income generated did not benefit the particular sublocation. The remaining 74 percent of skilled laborers, usually masons or carpenters, were local people. The benefits to the community in the form of income generation through school building programs are, at present, skewed toward the more affluent communities which have completed more school buildings as permanent structures than have the poorer communities.

Finally, primary schools generate business in the
local community. This may relate to materials, such as
sand, stone and timber, needed for building purposes.
It may be the need for school furniture or for material
and tailoring for school uniforms. It may be for
lunch, an egg or some ugali (porridge) to be purchased
by teachers or school children. The latter may not be
significant activities, but they do generate a bit of
business for local residents.
Secondary Schools. It is impossible to overesti-
mate either the level of interest in building secondary
schools on the part of the Kenyan public or the impact
which this interest has had on local communities. In
the last decade Harambee secondary schools have virtually burst onto the Kenyan rural scene. The Government
has become concerned about the rapid expansion of secondary education and gives little support to Harambee
secondary school programs. Nevertheless, many communities are committed to developing secondary school
opportunities. Table 5.5 shows the change in relative
numbers and percentages of Government-aided schools and
private, primarily Harambee, schools for Kenyans. Enrollments in 1977 were 128,324 (40 percent of the
total) in Government-aided schools and 191,986 (60 percent) in unaided schools.
There is a form of assistance to Harambee secondary schools from the Government called the Harambee
Package Programme. It was started during the 1974-1978
Plan, and included primarily the assignment of
Government-paid Teacher Service Commission teachers to
Harambee secondary schools. Only eight percent of the
Government's funds for recurrent expenses for secondary

Table 5.5
Secondary schools in Kenya

Year	Government Aided #	%	Unaided (primarily Harambee) #	%
1945	4	100	0	0
1957	21	84	4	16
1967	226	40	336	60
1977	444	30	1042	70

Sources: J.E. Anderson, "The Harambee Schools: The
Impact of Self-Help," in Education in Africa, Richard
Jolly (ed.) (Nairobi: East African Publishing House,
1969); and Government of Kenya, Development Plan, 1979-
1983, Part I (Nairobi: GovD ernment Printer, 1979), p.
157.

schools, anticipated in the 1979-1983 period, is allocated to Harambee secondary schools, even though
they constitute nearly two-thirds of all secondary
schools.[23]

The facilities constructed by communities for secondary schools vary substantially. Day schools range
from two classrooms, borrowed from the local primary
school for the use of Forms I and II, to one with nine
classrooms, a laboratory and a staff house. Boarding
schools range from several in which the students are
being taught in two classrooms (Forms I and II) and are
using a third classroom for the dormitory, to the well-
established Kianderi Girls Secondary School in Weithaga
with its 385 students accommodated in four dormitories,
its eight classrooms, laboratory, dining hall, kitchen
and four staff houses. This school opened in 1970.

Costs vary substantially as well. A day school in
Soin has just built two classrooms for approximately
Ksh. 20,000 ($2,667).[24] Construction materials were in
abundance nearby and this school was able to minimize
costs for materials and transport. In several other
cases, costs for recently constructed classrooms have
been nearly Ksh. 35,000 each.[25] One small school has
cost to date, Ksh. 40,000; one large secondary co-
educational day school, Karingu in Weithaga, complete
with nine classrooms, laboratory, staff house, office
and staff room has cost Ksh. 334,000 ($44,533).[26]
Kianderi Girls Boarding School cost in excess of Ksh.
500,000 ($66,666).[27]

Committees and staff constantly work on upgrading
these schools. One boys' school had only three classrooms and an office when it opened in 1964, and it now
has eight classrooms, four teachers' houses, laboratory, book store and staff room, and two permanent
stone hostels under construction. Another, a day
school with good facilities, opened in 1972 with only
one classroom and 26 students in Form I. A third, a
boarding school, started as a day school and operated
in that form for several years before it was able to
build accommodation for resident students.

Although slow improvement is the normal pattern,
there are some schools which are just barely functioning given few facilities, and insufficient and ill-
trained teachers. In two of the locations, two secondary schools had closed down because there had not been
enough students to fill Forms I and II and to support,
out of current fees, the costs of hiring teachers. In
one case the school reopened several years later. The
Assistant Chief indicated that the sublocation's interest in secondary education had been premature; there
had not been enough primary school completers to war-
rant a secondary school, in spite of high level of interest. Now, with increased primary enrollments, they
anticipate no problem with the reopened school.

In the early period of Harambee secondary school

expansion, admission procedures were somewhat chaotic, and Harambee schools earned the reputation of having low standards of admission and correspondingly low results on the Junior Secondary School Examination (EACE) given after Form II and the "O" level examination after Form IV. Now, however, it is customary to have formally selective admission procedures to Harambee secondary schools. A minimum number of points on the CPE is established as an entry requirement. After the examination results are announced, the headmasters of the constituent primary schools in the area meet with the headmaster of the secondary school to go over the records of their respective students on the CPE. Admissions are made on the basis of marks on this examination.

Some Harambee secondary schools have two streams or groups of students: a Government stream and a Harambee stream. There is a nationwide competitive admission based on CPE scores for the Government stream, for which the Government pays the tuition and boarding fees. For the Harambee stream, individual students from the immediate locality are accepted on a competitive basis, but they pay their own fees. Students from any part of the country may be assigned to the Government stream of a school. In some instances Government and Harambee streams are actually taught separately; in most cases they are mixed in the classroom.

One headmaster noted a considerable difference in the EACE results for his Government stream and Harambee stream students.[28] Whereas 69 percent of the Government stream passed the examination, only 22 percent of the Harambee stream passed. He proceeded to implement selective admissions procedures for the Harambee stream, selecting two boys from each primary school in the location, if there were two who met the minimum pass on the Certificate of Primary Education given at the end of Standard 7. Two years later, the passes for both streams had increased, and the Harambee stream was narrowing the gap with 51 percent as opposed to 84 percent passes.

The presence of a Harambee stream or a fully Harambee secondary school is important to a community. Observers have been under the impression that Harambee schools are eager to become Government schools and want nothing more than to become fully aided. Such is not the case. The Harambee secondary schools are eager for assistance, particularly in the form of qualified teachers who are paid by the Government's Teacher Service Commission. However, in most cases they are not eager to be taken over by the Government. In such situations they become open to students from the entire country and no longer serve the local community.

For example, the Weithaga High School, a boys

school for both day and resident students, opened in
1965 as a Harambee secondary school. In 1972 it
started its first Government stream, that is, a fully-
aided, Government-maintained Form I. In 1974 the last
Harambee class graduated, and the school was a fully-
aided secondary school including Forms I through IV.
In 1977 the school, because of community interest and
pressure, opened another Harambee stream, and it continues at present to have both Government-supported and
Harambee students. The latter are primarily from the
local community.

Overall, communities have been pragmatic in their
approach to building secondary schools. Usually the
community has started "small" and expanded its school
facility over time. Where there have been resources
based on cash crop earnings and substantial fundraising
from outside the community, the schools have improved
satisfactorily. Where funds are extremely limited and
outside support negligible, even the construction of an
additional classroom or two can be quite a burden for a
community, and the payment of teacher salaries out of
current school fees can be an overwhelming problem.
Building an institution is difficult under the best of
circumstances. Building them when there are few guidelines, when resources are limited, and when expertise
is minimal is quite an achievement. The view of these
schools, at any point in time, suggests that there are
numerous problems in acquiring adequately trained staff
and appropriate teaching facilities and materials; the
view over time attests on the part of many of these
schools to a determination to persist and even to suc-
ceed in the face of some very difficult problems.

Cattle Dips

Cattle dips are illustrative of a simple type of
project which is economically productive for village
people. Because of the clear-cut immediate returns on
a dip, its impact on productivity and incomes is relatively easy to evaluate. There are a number of tick-
borne diseases in Kenya which afflict and ultimately
kill cattle which are not indigenous to the area.
Local cattle are relatively immune to these diseases,
but they produce very little milk and are not a potential source of income to a family. In fact, a local
cow scarcely produces enough milk for the use of a single family. However, imported breeds, such as Hol-
steins, called grade cattle in Kenya, and cross-breeds
produce sufficient milk that some can be sold enabling
the family to have an additional source of income.
These cattle, however, cannot survive without being
dipped in a chemical once a week to kill the ticks.
Therefore, the process of upgrading the quality of the

cattle and achieving an increase in milk production necessitates the use of cattle dips.

A cattle dip is actually a simple structure. It consists of a narrow trough about 12 feet long, cement-lined, with a narrow opening at one end so that cattle can be moved through one at a time. It involves stone or cement blocks and cement for construction, iron sheets for the roof, and fencing for the corral into which cattle are put while awaiting the dipping process. Costs vary somewhat depending upon the proximity of building materials, but most of the dips in the locations visited were constructed for a sum of roughly Ksh. 15,000 ($2,000).[29]

In the early 1970s, the Government of Kenya determined that a policy of upgrading the quality of cattle in Kenya would be beneficial to rural Kenyans and to building the dairy industry. It sought the assistance of outside aid agencies, particularly the Government of Denmark, in the construction of cattle dips and in an expanded program of veterinary services. The Government offered to assist local communities with the construction of dips on a cooperative basis. Some funds were to be raised by a community, and the remainder was to be supplied by the Government or an aid agency. The precise ratios varied by community, but the Government or aid agency in most cases provided from half to three-fourths of the funds. The community was to provide the unskilled labor free of cost.

Initially the Government, working through the veterinary officers and through the Chiefs and Sub-Chiefs, tried to interest farmers in the cattle dips. In some areas they met much resistance. The idea of dipping cattle was new, and people did not understand the value in dipping them. The cost of constructing the dip, plus the weekly charge of dipping at Ksh. .30 (the charge from 1971-1978, a rate set by the Government) per cow caused some villagers to react negatively to the suggestion. In only one of the locations visited was there sufficient experience with cattle and with the benefits from increased milk production that people did not have to be persuaded to assist with dip construction. In the remaining five locations, there were a few community leaders and a few of the more prosperous farmers who perceived the advantages of constructing a dip. In these locations those people, clearly in a position to benefit from dip construction, tried to persuade their neighbors to proceed with building dips. Their arguments, however, were not always persuasive. Since the Government was fully behind dip construction and was urging local communities to undertake these projects, it was not difficult for the Chief and Sub-Chief to take an additional step and obtain permission to assess individual households in the community for dip construction.

134

Procedures for raising funds were handled in a variety of ways, varying by sublocation rather than by location.[30] In two sublocations only those who had cattle were asked to contribute. In one of the poorest sublocations, people who had cattle were asked to contribute Ksh. 100 per household. In one of the wealthiest sublocations people with cattle were asked to contribute Ksh. 20 per household. In a third sublocation residents were asked to contribute on the basis of Ksh. 10 per adult male and Ksh. 5 per adult female. Those with employment were asked to pay Ksh. 20. In yet another sublocation every household, whether or not they owned cattle, was asked to contribute Ksh. 26. One sublocation, where there was considerable animosity toward the idea of constructing a cattle dip determined to raise most of the funds by brewing pombe (beer) and selling it at barazas and other public meetings. This they did many times during the course of the year in order to raise funds. In addition, every household was asked to contribute something to the dip, but there was no fixed contribution. Finally, in one sublocation the contribution requested was based upon wealth, and residents were assessed between Ksh. 30 and 300. People in that sublocation felt it was not fair to ask everyone to pay the same amount, and the majority were happy with this arrangement.

For several reasons work on the cattle dips proceeded quickly, and most were completed within a year. First, the sum of money to be raised by the local community was manageable, carefully defined and limited. Second, the counterpart funds were immediately available, and there were technicians, in many cases, who were ready and able to supervise construction. Finally, the work to be done was not complicated, and much of the tedious labor could be accomplished expeditiously by a large number of workers from the community.

Two kinds of problems developed, however, one in the construction process and one in the management process. Construction demanded some technical expertise. It also required, as does all construction, contractors or workmen who are honest in their use of materials, and close supervision to assure that technically competent and fair work is being carried out. In most locations these requirements were met. In one, Nthawa, there was clearly misuse of materials and four of six dips cracked before or upon initial use. These were not repaired, and were not usable.[31] The remaining two dips of Nthawa which were functioning were located in quite remote sublocations. There everyone contributed a small amount to the dip; the Assistant Chiefs supervised the building activities very closely, and the commitment on the part of each community was high. In each case, the Assistant Chief put a lot of time and effort into persuading his community that the dip would be valuable.[32]

The second problem to surface related to manage-ment costs. The chemical used in the dips costs approx-imately Ksh. 700 ($93) every six months. According to the plan, the charge for dipping animals was to cover the cost of this chemical. However, since dipping was not mandatory, many did not bother to dip their cattle. Since few had grade cattle, and since there was no real need to dip the indigenous breed, the dips were used relatively little in the early stages. This meant that it was difficult to earn the money for the purchase of the chemicals. Given a Ksh. 700 expenditure every six months, and a need to earn a minimum of Ksh. 117 per month, it is necessary to run nearly 100 cattle (at Ksh. .30 a head) through the dip on a weekly basis. Only with that number could the dip function properly.

The evidence from the six locations is quite clear. In Kisiara and Soin where there are a lot of cattle and where residents had some basis for judging that dips would benefit them, the cattle dips have functioned well; repairs had been made expeditiously at low cost to the community; and supervision of the dips has proceeded efficiently and fairly. In several other locations the dips operated but the chemicals were not used appropriately and were not purchased according to schedule. As a result they did not benefit the few grade cattle that were being dipped. In Wanjengi Sub-location of Weithaga, some of the wealthier farmers contributed funds to the Cattle Dip Committee for the purchase of chemicals.[33] Slowly in this location the ownership of grade or cross-breed cattle spread, so that the dip became self-supporting. The number of cows in this sublocation increased in five years from 200 to nearly 400, and the shift to ownership of better quality animals was dramatic. The number of grade cat-tle had increased by 333 percent, from 30 to nearly 100 and comprised one-fourth of the cows of the area in 1979.

In not all communities was the financial problem this easy to solve. Until people could see the bene-fits of owning grade cattle and bringing them to the dip, thereby insuring a cow's health and longevity as well as its production of milk which could be sold, they were unlikely to purchase such cattle and to re-quire the use of the dip. However, until there were enough people with grade cattle using the dip, the dip could not be self-supporting and function effectively. It was a vicious circle. Ultimately the Government stepped in, and began taking over the management of the dips.

In both locations in Murang'a the transition had just taken place, and the dips by 1979 were under Gov-ernment management. In the process, the dipping of all cattle had become compulsory; the Government supplied the chemical and paid an attendant a minimal salary to operate the dip. In the remaining four locations of the study, the Government had not yet taken over the dips. In the two locations in Kericho District, the dips were operating effectively without Government intervention. Though the residents were looking forward to Government management which would relieve them of responsibility for the dips, it clearly was not a necessary Governmental function for these communities were managing very well on their own.

In Embu District, the Government had not yet taken over the dips. In the location where dips had not functioned from the beginning, Nthawa, there was absolutely no incentive for people to try to repair the dips and get them into operation. They did not have grade cattle; they did not have good veterinary services; they did not have a way to sell milk on a large scale. They were not in any way integrated into a growing dairy industry. Furthermore, the area is dry and grade cattle which require good grazing conditions might not survive difficult years. In addition inflated estimates for repairs were given and what cost Ksh. 300 to repair in another location was estimated at Ksh. 6,000 in Nthawa. Thus the dips continued to stand unused and malfunctioning. It would take a lot more than Governmental management of cattle dips to establish an effective dairy industry in that community.

Water Projects

In five of the six locations studied, water supply was ranked by respondents among the first two priorities for future self-help projects. Residents were eager to improve access to potable water. Water projects in the locations visited were designed for household use, not for irrigation purposes. In one of the locations, Kyeni, a water supply was installed in the early 1970s with communal water taps to cover the entire location. By the late 1970s all homes had access to a communal water tap; 1,400 homes had water piped to the premises. There were 150 communal water taps which were spaced throughout the location on the basis of population density. With the high returns from coffee in the mid-1970s, demand for individual installation of water pipes to Kyeni homes had risen dramatically.[34] In four locations water projects are currently underway. These vary from the initial stages of fund collection in Soin to Phase III of the Kahuti water project which is bringing water down through Weithaga and parts of Mbiri to the edge of Murang'a town.

The water projects in Weithaga and Kyeni are massive projects undertaken by the Ministry of Water Development. They have a self-help component, and

local residents contribute both cash and labor. By
contrast, the projects in Nthawa, where the need for
water is acute, have lacked strong Government backing
and have been initiated by local leaders, particularly
county councillors. Such is the case in Gitiburi Sublocation where Seraphino Nagari, a teacher, County
Councillor and Secretary for the Water Project Committee, has been instrumental in organizing the water
project along with B.G. Mwangario, the Committee Chairman.[35] Soin is slated for a major Government water
development program, but the initiative for bringing
the water into the various market centers of the sublocations resides with local leaders. This is in
marked contrast to the two most wealthy locations which
have received backing from prominent national leaders
for their water projects and therefore have not had to
orchestrate the slow mobilization of effort to obtain
improved water supply.

Water projects are handled in one of two ways.
They may follow the normal self-help procedures whereby
a community decides to begin a project, seeks approval
from the District Community Development Office, and
ultimately may seek funding through the District Development Committee. Alternatively, there is a Self-Help
Division of the Ministry of Water Development, and this
Ministry along with the District Development Officer
can assist a community in the organization of a water
project. In either case, there is a major self-help
component, and the people of the area are asked to
raise a certain portion of the cash for the project as
well as to contribute in the form of unskilled labor,
usually by digging trenches and laying pipes.

Illustrative of a community rural self-help water
project is the Mathai-Kabaci project in Siakago Sublocation of Nthawa.[36] There an enterprising group of
local residents has been working on improvements in the
local primary school and on establishing a nursery
school. They have also banded together in what might
be called an informal neighborhood improvement association which involves two villages, Mathai and Kabaci.
This group decided that a water supply would be of
great benefit to the school. They sought community
support with the notion of later expanding such a water
project throughout the sublocation. With the assistance of the Chief, they got advice and support from the
District Water Development Officer of the Ministry of
Water Development. Working through the Location and
Division Development Committees, they procured assistance of Ksh. 60,000 from the District Development Committee for a project which, in present terms, they
estimate will cost Ksh. 200,000 when complete. It
will be phased over time. The immediate objective is
to collect Ksh. 20,000 in order to begin construction,
and to that end they have already collected Ksh. 11,000

138

from the local community. The Committee was asking
Ksh. 20 from every adult, planning a fundraising occasion, and keeping careful records of funds collected.

Recognizing that the total cost was well beyond
the means of the community, these villagers hoped to
obtain material assistance from an organization such as
CARE which is known to provide water pipes for such
projects. Their strategy is to implement the project
in stages, collecting what funds they can, and accom-
plishing as much as they can at each step along the
way. It is a strategy frought with problems for a
variety of reasons. It leads easily to frustration
when insufficient funds are collected to undertake the
next segment of work; it leads to delays and problems
in coordination since the work is done in a piecemeal
way; it can lead easily to mismanagement and misuse of
funds since there is no carefully delineated work plan
and procedure; it can also lead to cost overruns related to delays in carrying out work. It is, however,
an approach that most rural people seem to find comfortable, and perhaps it is the only approach open to
them without massive Government aid and commitment. It
is nevertheless clear that undertaking such projects on
a protracted, piecemeal basis can be a frustrating and
discouraging venture.

Another case is illustrative of these problems.
In Soin Location which is large, stony and dry, the
Ministry of Water Development is planning a Ksh.
10,000,000 ($1.3 million) water project to bring water
to each of seven sublocations. The residents of the
location have established a Harambee project to collect
money permitting the installation of pipes to bring
water to each market center within the sublocation.
They are hoping to collect Ksh. 520 ($69.33) from each
family which will give them the currently estimated
cost of installation.[37]

Data from the survey questionnaire indicates that
only 15 percent of the men in Soin have any kind of
employment, casual or regular, and 20 percent of households have no cash crop or regular source of cash income. It seems unlikely, therefore, that all families
will be able to make such a payment. Location and sublocation leaders are nevertheless optimistic. They believe families in the location are enthusiastic about
the opportunity to install a water supply and are willing to sacrifice to acquire it, as long as they are
confident that their actions will lead to the implementation of the project.

An outside observer is less likely to be sanguine.
Because of the scarcity of resources, the project operates in a financial and time vacuum. The residents do
not have a clear idea of what the cost will be, and
they do not have any idea when sufficient money will be
collected, or when the project will be started or fin-

ished. Nevertheless, they have started collecting
funds for their share of the total costs.
What does the provision of a water supply mean to
village people?   Obtaining water for family use is a
time-consuming task for many rural women.   Table 5.6,
based on information from respondents to the survey,
gives some indication of the distance women must travel
in the locations studied in order to obtain water for
home use.   In Weithaga and Kisiara the water supply is
relatively plentiful and constant, and even those who
travel more than one kilometer to a water source, rarely have to travel more than three or four kilometers.
In Nthawa and Soin distances of five to ten kilometers
to obtain water are quite common during the dry season.
Thus, obtaining water can be the better part of a day's
project several times a week.   The installation of a
water supply which would eliminate long walks for rural
women would free their time for other activities and,
in particular, would give them more time for agricultural or other income-earning pursuits. In addition to
the time saved, access to water for a small vegetable
garden or for poultry or animal care would augment family welfare.

Table 5.6
Distance travelled to obtain water for home use (in
percent)

Location	Water at Home	Less Than 1 Kilometer	More Than 1 Kilometer
Soin	0	48	52
Nthawa	9	48	43
Mbiri	9	35	56
Kisiara	6	38	56
Kyeni	71	29	0
Weithaga	30	52	18

Besides the value to the individual family, rural
water supplies are central to the development of rural
institutions and rural industry. The establishment of
a village polytechnic, a rural clinic or small-scale
rural industry becomes possible when there is a constant and uninterrupted supply of water. This is a
fundamental step in the process of rural development.
There is no doubt that the people in the six locations
studied are well aware of the importance of water to
the development of their areas and are eager to do

everything within their power to foster self-help projects related to water supply.

Health Projects

Health projects have the poorest record of completion and performance among the self-help projects observed. In general, the more complex the health project, the more likely that it will be incomplete, languishing for lack of funds, organization, management, and purposeful interest on the part of the local leadership. Most particularly, maternity wards have encountered these problems. In three of the four efforts to construct maternity wards, the wards are not yet functioning although two have been under construction since 1966. In one of those cases, a highly political situation revolved around the siting of a dispensary and maternity ward in Weithaga Location. The Chief preferred Kirogo sublocation to Wanjengi sublocation and was able to mobilize funds to complete a health project in that area. Meanwhile, Wanjengi residents completed a dispensary without outside aid. A prominent Nairobi businessman from Wanjengi arranged a Government grant of Ksh. 20,000 for a maternity ward to accompany the Wanjengi dispensary, but local residents felt they had done well to raise the Ksh. 30,500 to build the dispensary, and they were not interested in the additional fundraising necessary for a maternity ward.[38] Desultory contributions have permitted the building to come near to completion. However, it remains unfinished and without equipment. It is unlikely that the Government will provide staff for this ward when the other one is not far, and it is clear that the local residents could not and would not care to sustain the recurring costs of staffing it. Embroiled in local politics, the buildings – both dispensary and maternity ward – remain unused except as meeting places for committees and groups.

The Wanjengi project stands out as one in which local enthusiasms, local wealth and local politics combined to create an untenable situation for local residents. Now it is impossible for them to turn back. While local residents use the building for other purposes, they keep hoping that eventually it will be used as a maternity ward. However, it is an objective toward which they are not willing to put much effort and attention, and most believe that even if they do so, locational politics are such that their effort will not be to much avail.

Further complicating such situations is an absence of planning and advice on the part of the District Health Officer. The Ministry of Health has involved itself very little in planning and advising local communities on health facilities. In the locations studied, initiatives have come exclusively from the local communities without the benefit of official consultation and guidance. Since most communities sorely need improved medical care, it is not surprising that whenever possible, residents have tried to mobilize efforts to build health facilities.

Among the health services visited, one was particularly well managed. This was the Mufu Dispensary which had been constructed by two sublocations, Mufu and Kathari in Kyeni. The project was characterized by careful planning and thorough committee work guided by an energetic and enterprising Assistant Chief, Alexander Miviyango.[39] It was executed in manageable stages, and at every point, all residents of the two sublocations were involved. The community first constructed the dispensary in 1968 out of temporary materials, on land which had been set aside for public purposes and which was provided by Mufu Sublocation. The Project Committee was organized on a geographical basis so that all residents of the two sublocations had a role in selecting someone from his or her immediate locale to represent him or her on the Committee. The Committee organized work on the dispensary on a geographical basis with areas rotating work days under the supervision of their particular committee member until the project was completed.

The dispensary was widely used by residents of both Mufu and Kathari, and by the mid-1970s, the community determined that the facility was too small. Further, the residents decided they would like to enlarge the dispensary, construct it out of permanent materials, and construct a staff house for the nurse. The Committee estimated that the dispensary would cost Ksh. 45,000 ($6,000) and assessed each household Ksh. 30 toward its construction. In the meantime, the Government agreed to take over the provision of staff and medicines for the new dispensary which in 1979 was almost complete.

There are several keys to the successful performance of this project: 1) Careful management on the part of the Assistant Chief and the Committee insured widespread community knowledge about the project and willing support for it. 2) The project was undertaken in manageable stages so that visible benefits and successful operation were attained within a relatively short period of time. There was tangible, positive feedback to the community. At a later point the community was ready for a larger and more demanding project. People had been able to see and experience the benefits of their first effort. 3) Finally, Mufu and Kathari are densely populated areas on high potential land with a strong resource base. Moreover, by the mid-1970s, these sublocations were enjoying the coffee mid-1970s, these sublocations were enjoying the coffee boom, and for most families a Ksh. 30 contribution was not a hardship.

The Mufu-Kathari dispensary contrasts with the Kaitui maternity ward in Soin. Here the sublocation started in 1966 with the idea of building a maternity ward, not a dispensary. By mid-1979, they had spent Ksh. 28,000 and the building was nearly finished.[40] Furnishings, equipment and painting remained. There had been three fundraisings which yielded a total of Ksh. 20,000 and the Community Development Office made a small donation of doors and ceiling board. The Committee asked each family to contribute Ksh. 50. Although the community leaders agreed that cooperation had been quite good, progress had been slow, and other projects had had priority, particularly two cattle dips in the sublocation, and nearby schools. With approximately 300 households, in an area that is not prosperous, it is clear that these projects represent a major burden and responsibility. It is not surprising that, despite initial enthusiasm, a maternity ward has received low priority in that sublocation.

Observations based on the self-help projects related to health suggest that some broad policy issues are relevant. There is tremendous concern about health care in the locations visited, and there is a great need for improved care and facilities. Rural residents, in their efforts to establish facilities, are encountering a system which is not geared to the provision of widespread, low-cost medical care, particularly preventative care directed to the greatest possible number. For example, Nthawa is a large location with health facilities only at the clinic in Siakago. There is no public transport going to the various sublocations, and people walk wherever they must go. A woman with a sick child living 10 to 15 miles from Siakago would leave her home late morning, carrying the child, a few belongings, and, if lucky, an umbrella for protection against the sun, and would walk to Siakago where she would find a place to spend the night in order to be at the clinic when it opened at 8:00 a.m. the next morning. She would try to be among the first in line so that she would be able to walk the return distance home before nightfall.

The health care system focuses on district hospitals and related facilities of a relatively high quality which can service complicated medical needs at the district level. It does not attempt to maximize its reach to the sublocation or to villages on matters of routine respiratory and intestinal illnesses, the causes of most medical problems in rural Kenya. It is this, along with post-natal and early childhood care which most families are seeking. Consequently, locally perceived needs and Government health programs do

not coincide.   Self-help health projects constitute an
effort to   address these needs, but without   the requisite resources and planning they often flounder or per-
ish.

NOTES

     1.   Interview with the Assistant Chief, Koitaburot
Sublocation, Soin, May, 1979.
     2.   District Community Development Offices keep
large work sheets set up to serve as a running tally on
the state of self-help within the district.   Projects
are divided into two broad categories: social and economic.   Within social are listed educational, health,
social welfare and some assorted "domestic" projects.
Within economic are listed water supply, transportation
and communications, agriculture and "other projects."
This information is based upon reports submitted to the
District Office by the Locational Community Development
Assistants, and it is forwarded annually to the Ministry of Housing and Social Services for its use in com-
piling statistics on self-help.
     3.   Interview with Jackson Ireri, Assistant Chief,
Kathanjure Sublocation, Kyeni, April, 1978.
     4.   These figures were all obtained in interviews
with committees or, in the case of Cheborge School,
with the headmaster of the school.   Figures for the
Murang'a College of Technology are taken from a publication of the Murang'a Harambee Development Fund.
     5.   Interviews with S. Ngari and B.G. Mwangario,
Gitiburi Water Project Committee, March, 1978 and with
the Water Development Officer, Embu District, April,
1978.
     6.   Information on outside aid to Harambee proj-
ects is contained in the district files.   The LCDAs include it in their reports.
     7.   Government of Kenya, Ministry of Housing and
Social Services, Department of Social Services, Community Development Division, Self-Help Statistics, 1977,
p. 2.
     8.   Mr. Rua, Headmaster, Kegonge School, Kyeni
Location, March, 1978.
     9.   Interview with the Principal, Weithaga High
School, May, 1978.
     10.   Figures on increased costs for primary school
construction came from several school committees including Mufu Primary School Committee, Kyeni; Gikuyari
Primary School Committee, Nthawa; and Cheborge Primary
School, Kisiara.
     11.   Interview with the Kamasega Primary School
Committee and the Assistant Chief of Soliat Subloca-
tion, Soin, April, 1979.
     12.   Interview with the Headmistress of Siakago

Girls Secondary School, Nthawa, March, 1978.

13. Interview with the Principal, Karingu Secondary School, Weithaga, June, 1978.

14. Information obtained in conversations with the LCDA, from Mbiri Location, June, 1978.

15. Examples are from situations known to Mr. Benson Kibutu, teacher at Kangaru Secondary School, Embu and research assistant for this study.

16. Interview with the Provincial Director of Social Services, Mr. Wahome, Eastern Province, May 25, 1978.

17. Respondent to the survey questionnaire, Mbiri Location, June, 1978.

18. This would seem to be the case with the Cheborge dispensary in Kisiara Location.

19. A number of people were willing to generalize broadly about the misuse of funds without giving particular names and institutions. The LCDAs had a clear idea of what was happening within their locations; some were willing to talk more openly than others. Two Assistant Community Development Officers at the district level, Rose Muguchu in Murang'a and Enid Miriti in Embu, also provided insights on this issue.

20. These figures are based on the Mbiri respondents to the questionnaire and the evidence they provided on contributions to educational projects.

21. The group of respondents who were part of the 23 percent living at subsistence levels, were examined for contributions to Harambee projects.

22. These figures are rough estimates based on an examination of statistics provided by the School Committees interviewed.

23. Government of Kenya, Development Plan, 1979-1983, Part I (Nairobi: Government Printer, 1979), p. 158.

24. Interview with Boiwek School Committee, June, 1979.

25. Interview with the Principal, Weithaga High School, May, 1978 and with Gikandu Secondary School, June, 1978.

26. Interview with the Principal, Karingu Secondary School, Weithaga, June, 1978.

27. Interview with the Headmaster, Kianderi Girls Secondary School, June, 1978.

28. Interview with Mr. Rua, Kegonge Boys Secondary School, March, 1978.

29. Figures on the costs of cattle dips are found in the district files, and in the SRDP files of Mbeere Division. The LCDAs are also completely familiar with the costs of the dips.

30. Information on methods of raising funds for the dips came from the interviews with Cattle Dip Committees, from the LCDAs, and occasionally from Assistant Chiefs of several sublocations.

31. Of the dips in Nthawa, Siakago, Gitiburi, Kaungu and Kirii were not functioning in 1978; Rukira and Gangara were operating. Data is drawn from interviews with Cattle Dip Committees and from the SRDP records in the office of the Mbeere SRDP, especially the Final Report of Mbeere, May, 1977.

32. Conversations with Assistant Chief Iego, Gangara Sublocation.

33. Interview with the Wanjengi Cattle Dip Committee, July, 1978.

34. Discussion with the location water engineer posted at Kathanjure, Kyeni Location, March, 1978.

35. Interviews with S. Ngari and B.G. Mwangario, Gitiburi Water Project Committee, March, 1978.

36. Interviews with the Gitiburi Water Project Committee and the Mathai-Kabaci Water Project Committee, March, 1978. Figures are confirmed by the Water Development Officer for Embu District, April, 1978.

37. Interview with Thomas Tele, Chairman, Water Project Committee and with the Assistant Chief for Boiwek Sublocation, Soin, April, 1979.

38. Interview with the Wanjengi Health Center Committee, June, 1978 and conversations with Mrs. Pelis Manyeki, Divisional CDA for Kiharu Division in which both Weithaga and Mbiri are located, June, 1978.

39. Interview with the Mufu Dispensary Committee, Kyeni, March, 1978.

40. Interview with the Kaitui Maternity Dispensary/Maternity Ward Committee, Soin Location, May, 1979.

VI
Self-Help and Rural Stratification:
Who Wins and Who Loses?

> In 20 years, I think the population here will be
> very great. Some people will be rich but many
> will be jobless and landless. There will be a lot
> of unrest and chaos unless we begin now to take
> measures.
>
>   Respondent
>   Weithaga Location

Some analysts of self-help have suggested that
community projects are a method for taking cash and
labor resources from the poor and using them to serve
the purposes of the wealthier segments of the community. Several studies from Eastern Province support
this perspective. Hill, drawing on his work in Kitui,
suggests that it is the rural progressives who tend to
benefit from self-help projects.[1] Musyoki, utilizing
evidence from Mbooni Location in Machakos District,
states that "the poor are most active in self-help
efforts and contribute the most in cash, labour and
materials, while the elites are the ones who benefit,
with the consequence that the Harambee movement en-
hances and perpetuates inequalities within the rural
areas."[2]

Evidence from the six locations in Embu, Murang'a
and Kericho Districts supports a different perspective
on the role of self-help in rural communities. It suggests that Harambee projects are a means for drawing
higher levels of resources from the more affluent
socio-economic groups and using them for the benefit of
the entire community. To permit such an assessment, a
method of rating a household's economic position within
the community was established. This drew on information concerning sources of income, existence of a cash
crop, and the presence of various household amenities
and furnishings. Information concerning contributions
to Harambee projects and benefits received from them
was then evaluated for the most affluent 20 percent and
the poorest 20 percent within each location.

146

CONTRIBUTIONS

Cash Contributions

Levels of Cash Contributions in the Sample Investigated. Figure 6.1 summarizes in the form of a histogram the data collected from the six locations on the contribution levels of the most affluent 20 percent of the sample and the poorest 20 percent for the five-year period preceding the administration of the questionnaire. This figure shows that the modal contribution for both the most affluent quintile and the poorest quintile is Ksh. 101-500 over the five-year period. The median contribution for the poorest quintile was Ksh. 101-500, whereas the median contribution for the wealthiest quintile was Ksh. 501-1,000. Among the poorest, the second largest category of respondents did not contribute at all. Three percent in that quintile contributed in the Ksh. 2,000-3,000 range. They were from Weithaga Location, and, while relatively poor within their own community, on a national scale would not be among the least affluent. Among the most affluent, the second largest category was in the Ksh. 500-1,000 range; the third largest in the Ksh. 1,001-2,000 range; and the fourth largest in the Ksh. 2,001-3,000 range.

Figure 6.2 is a scattergram which indicates the size of contributions and number of projects assisted over the five-year period by both top and bottom quintiles. It shows clearly that respondents in the top quintile have contributed larger donations to more projects than have those in the bottom quintile.

Table 6.1 shows the distribution of contributions of the top and bottom quintiles by location. In all locations there were households in the poorest quintile which did not contribute at all to Harambee projects. The median contribution for the poorest quintile ranged from zero in Soin Location to Ksh. 501-1,000 in Weithaga. In two of the three most affluent locations, there were no households in the top quintile which had contributed less than Ksh. 100 to Harambee projects during the past five years. In three of the locations — Kyeni, Weithaga and Mbiri - 10 percent of the most affluent had made contributions exceeding Ksh. 3000. In Kisiara and Nthawa the largest contributions were in the Ksh. 1,001-2,000 range. As Table 6.1 indicates, data from each individual location support the conclusion that within the locations, the wealthier strata are paying more for projects than the poorer strata.

A more precise understanding of the relationship between wealth and contribution levels can be developed by comparing measures of wealth and relative contribu-

148

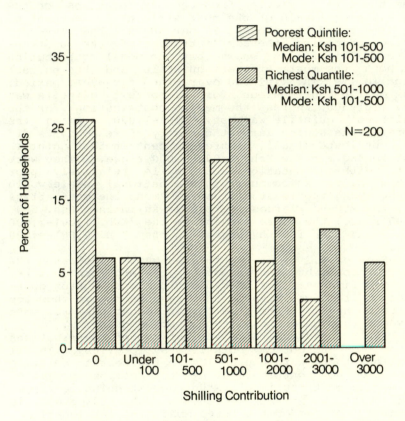

Figure 6.1 Six Locations: Composite of Contribution Levels of Poorest
Quintile and Richest Quintile of Total Sample for a Five-Year
Period

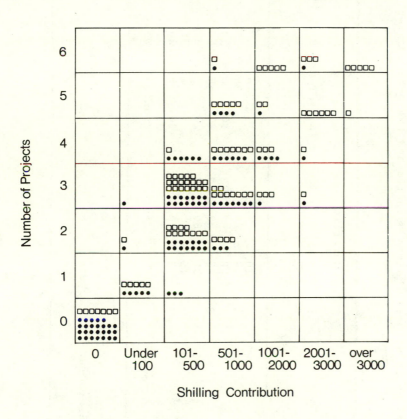

Shilling Contribution

• Poorest 20 percent
□ Richest 20 percent

Figure 6.2 Six Locations: Composite Summary of Poorest Quintile
and Richest Quintile Harambee Contributions,
1973-1977, 1974-1978

Table 6.1
Distribution of contributions by location: the top quintile and the bottom quintile (in percentages)

	Quintile											
	Soin		Nthawa		Mbiri		Kisiara		Kyeni		Weithaga	
Shilling Contributions	B	T	B	T	B	T	B	T	B	T	B	T
Over 3000						10				10		10
2001-3000						15				25	15	15
1001-2000						10		30	10	30	20	5
501-1000	40	70	5	15	30	25	20	40	40	30	20	40
101- 500	10	10	45	45	50	30	60	30	20		20	30
Under 100			15	20	10	5					5	
0	50	20	35	15	10	5	20		30	5	20	
Location	Soin		Nthawa		Mbiri		Kisiara		Kyeni		Weithaga	

B = Bottom Quintile
T = Top Quintile
Locations are left to right: poorer ... richer
N = 200

151

tion sizes for the top and bottom quintiles. Since
accurate assessments of income are extremely difficult
to obtain through single interviews of rural residents,
a proxy measure has been used. This is a measure of
the size of land holdings. For each location, average
size of land holdings and average size of cash contributions for a five-year period have been computed for
the top and bottom quintiles. The resulting ratios,
shown in Table 6.2, indicate that in all but the
wealthiest location, Weithaga, the ratios of contribution levels between poor and rich exceed the ratios of
differentiation in size of land holding. This, of
course, is a rough measure, but it does suggest that at
least in terms of cash contributions, Harambee is mild-
ly redistributive in five of the six locations studied.

Table 6.2
Comparison of average size of land holding and average
size of Harambee contribution for the richest 20% and
poorest 20%

Location	Ratio of average size of land-holding richest: poorest	Ratio of average size of contribution for 5-year period richest: poorest
Soin	3.8:1	5:1
Nthawa	2.3:1	2.5:1
Mbiri	1.4:1	3:1
Kisiara	1.5:1	3:1
Kyeni	2:1	3:1
Weithaga	2.5:1	1:1

The foregoing evidence indicates that the wealthier segments of the population within the location are
paying more for self-help projects than the poorer segments, both absolutely and relatively. It is necessary, however, to look more closely at the 26 percent
of the poorest quintile (as shown in Figure 6.2) who
did not participate in any project. In particular, it
is important to know whether this group has been in any
way barred from participating in and benefiting from
Harambee projects.
This concern leads to a consideration of the
school building funds. The building funds have, until
recently, been in an anomalous position vis-a-vis
Harambee self-help. The Ministry of Education informed
the public shortly after Independence that the Government would provide faculty at the primary level but

that each community was responsible for building, up-grading and maintaining primary schools. In order to implement programs for improving facilities, most schools established building funds to which each family with children in the school has had to contribute, even though there have been no tuition charges for primary education through Standard 5. These building funds have ranged from a low of Ksh. 60 per year to a high of Ksh. 210 asked per year per family. Some families have not sent their children to school simply because of the building fund requirement. This fact was noted by President Moi when he banned the imposition of building funds in primary schools in late 1978 and made primary education free through Standard 6.[3]

In examining questionnaires from the 26 percent in the bottom quintile who did not participate in any project, it is useful to see if any of them were pro-hibited from sending their children to school by the mandatory building fund fees. Among those respondents, 15 were not in a position to contribute to or benefit from several types of projects. This group included very young households with children under school age. It included old people without school-age children, without cattle and without social affiliations which might have led them to participate in Harambee proj-ects. Also in this group were several widows and wid-owers or bachelors obviously living a marginal exist-ence. Of the remainder, seven households did not send their children to school because of the costs, primar-ily in the form of the building fund. Hence it seems fair to state that approximately one-fourth of the non-contributors in the lowest quintile were being effec-tively barred from sending their children to school be-cause of what was in reality a mandatory Harambee fee in the form of the school building fund. This situation was observed only in the three poorest locations.

Assessment/Contribution Patterns. The pattern whereby the wealthier members of the community are con-tributing more to Harambee projects than are the poorer members of the community can be attributed to three factors: 1) an increasingly sophisticated form of assessment closely related to a type of graduated tax; 2) an informal skill which both officials and the gen-eral public have developed for "squeezing" a bit more out of their wealthier neighbors for the benefit of the community; and 3) the clear benefits they can receive from some types of projects.

As noted in Chapter V, assessments vary according to two patterns. The Project Committee may charge a flat rate per household or impose a graduated assess-ment according to the wealth of the household. In gen-eral, the poorer communities almost always use a flat rate, whereas the more prosperous communities sometimes impose a scaled or graduated rate of payment. Two

schools in Kericho District are illustrative.[4]   One, a
school in Soin, was being constructed by two remote
villages in order to reduce the distance their children
must walk to school from five miles to about three
miles.   Parents in these two villages were eager to
have the school, and each family was committed to a
contribution of Ksh. 300, not all of which was to be
paid at once.

In Kisiara an established primary school was expanding the number of classrooms.   The Assistant Chief
and the residents of the sublocation drew up a committee of 44 members with an equal number from each village involved.[5]   This committee was then responsible
for a careful assessment of funds required from each
household for the construction of the classrooms.   Each
man and each woman were assessed.   In the case of the
men, assessments ranged from Ksh. 100 to Ksh. 500, and
for the women from Ksh. 30 to Ksh. 200, the Ksh. 200
being required from one woman in the sublocation who
had a salary.   In addition, each adult was required to
bring a specified item to the fundraising event sched-
uled in August, 1978.   These items ranged from a hammer
to a cow for men, and from a cup to a goat for women.
These items were specified according to a careful consideration of ability to pay or contribute.   Typed
records were available for all to see, and public support for the procedure was widespread.   Almost all persons had paid the amount requested; a few women had
paid less than the amount asked.   The Committee indicated that these were the poorer families in the community and that it was not considering steps to ask
them to pay the remainder of their assessment.   This
was no doubt in part because the August fundraising had
been very successful.   In general, however, the more
prosperous communities tend to ignore or overlook those
instances of non-payment, particularly if people are
poor, whereas the poorer communities are more likely to
take action against recalcitrant contributors.

In the case of the Kisiara school, the community
in effect established an advisory council with broad-
based community support for the purpose of developing
an equitable procedure for obtaining funds.   The procedure is not dissimilar from those used by local communities in other parts of the world where revenues
collected are based on size of landholding, valuation
of buildings on the property, and, perhaps, a percentage of earned income.

Some have suggested that the self-help approach is
a more effective way to gain local as well as outside
contributions and to release local resources than is
taxation.   The argument is that local elites often find
ways to circumvent tax collection and to coopt the system for their own purposes, which they are less likely
to do with Harambee, based as it is on customary value

154

and sanctions.[6]   The County Councils of the three districts in the study have indicated that they have difficulty with tax collections, and a member of one specified that the Council was lucky in any given year to collect taxes from 50 percent of the population.[7] Table 6.3 shows the percentage of households contributing to projects in the six locations.

Table 6.3
Percentage of households contributing to Harambee projects

Location	Percentage of Households Contributing to Projects
Soin	70
Nthawa	79
Mbiri	90
Kisiara	92
Kyeni	90
Weithaga	94

The figures in Table 6.3 suggest that contribution levels exceed the present local-level capacity to collect taxes.   In the district where officials felt they were unlikely to collect from 50 percent of the population, the tax was Ksh. 22 per adult.   Most households contributed between Ksh. 100 to 500 over a five-year period, and as Figure 6.1 shows, many households exceed that level of contribution.   The evidence from the survey was supplemented by interviews with several officials who indicated that local communities were becoming increasingly skillful at assuring that their more prosperous citizens carried their full share of the development effort.[8]   Community pressures supported by notions of loyalty, duty, ethnic solidarity or responsibility to one's home, may be a more effective and compelling approach to obtaining resources for local development than local taxation in situations where local administrative capabilities to enforce payment of taxes are negligible.
    Levels of Coercion.   Problems of forced cash payments to Harambee projects have received some publicity in recent months.[9]   Project committees generally believe that they have community support for obtaining payment for those projects agreed upon by the community and for which an assessment has been specified.   One committee in Nthawa, for example, indicated that it would soon have to make an effort to collect the Ksh.

40 outstanding from several households in payment for a water project. In this case, the community is endeavoring to raise Ksh. 10,000 as its contribution in cash in order to obtain a District Development Committee grant to bring water to the sublocation. The community is eager to get the water; the Government does not begin work until the community's portion is in hand, and there is a general feeling that insufficient payment on the part of a few should not deny the community its water supply. Obviously this attitude creates hardships for some households.

Action toward those who are not making their payments may include outright forcible extraction of payment through confiscation of personal goods, denial of services such as the use of a cattle dip or fairly gentle verbal reminders. Personal pressure by leaders, public embarassment of non-contributors, and subtle reminders of favors or services to be withheld are also "coercive" measures sometimes used. Table 6.4 indicates the percentage of project contributions made by the total 500 respondents in the six locations, about which the respondents indicated they experienced a measure of coercion.

Table 6.4
Percentage of project contributions for which respondents experienced some measure of coercion

Location	Coerced Contributions
Soin	12
Nthawa	15
Mbiri	13
Kisiara	3
Kyeni	4
Weithaga	2

Those locations with a higher percentage of people on subsistence or living a marginal existence show a comparatively high level of coercion in regard to Harambee project payments. Again, these figures exclude the building fund which has been, in effect, a mandatory fee for a Harambee project. This obviously has prevented some children from attending school. It has also had both coercive and punitive aspects, particularly for primary school children. In most cases, partial payment or indication of intent to pay was sufficient to keep a child in school, but there were instances in which children were sent home until the parent appeared with the fees.

In the six locations studied, forcible extraction seems to have been an uncommon procedure (building fund aside) and people did not expect to see committees appearing at their doors ready to take any object in sight. Persuasion, with reminders of coercive sanctions which could be imposed, was a more commonly used approach.

In general, the more immediate the project and the greater the sense of urgency, the more likely it is that some coercion will be applied. Those projects for which the community is trying to raise a specified amount in order to meet the requirements of a grant more easily lead to measures for assuring the money will be forthcoming than do open-ended projects, such as dispensaries or social welfare projects in which there is no outside aid component. On the other hand, communities are usually eager for any outside assistance they can get and welcome the incentive which that assistance provides for collecting larger amounts. While the more affluent may contribute more funds and may give more rapidly than the poorest groups, such an approach does create difficulties for poorer households.

Is there a legal basis for the application of coercion in order to obtain Harambee "contributions?" Clearly there is not. One would not find among Kenya's legal statutes the basis for forced contributions. In fact, in July, 1979 Attorney General Njonjo publicly reprimanded District Commissioners and Chiefs who have, by administrative fiat, forced people to make Harambee "donations."[10] However, in many rural communities Harambee development exists in the interface between customs or mores and statutory law. If the community has approved a project, the Chief, Sub-Chief and/or Project Committee will act as if the force of the community, if not of the national law, is behind them.

Labor Contribution

Nature of the Labor Contribution to Self-Help Projects. Contributions to Harambee projects are also given in the form of labor, both skilled and unskilled, though primarily the latter. In all six locations, the community is involved in providing unskilled labor for projects which are being undertaken. This includes such tasks as assisting masons in building cattle dips, constructing nursery schools, clearing bush and digging the foundation for village polytechnics or dispensaries, making bricks or constructing and maintaining semi-permanent buildings. Typically, heavier work of digging and clearing is done by men, whereas women do hauling and carrying as well as mud and wattle construction and maintenance. For the most part, the community assists until the project is completed. This, however, is often an intermittent and occasional process.

On a more regular basis, the community of parents with primary school children is responsible for providing labor for the school. This may be used for building purposes; it may be used for maintenance; or it may go into income-earning activities generating funds for the school. Fifty percent of the schools visited in the six locations have agricultural income-earning activities. In two of the most affluent locations, Weithaga and Kisiara, the common procedure is for the school to employ laborers to cultivate the land. In the other four locations, parents, usually the women, are organized to do the agricultural tasks required according to season. Depending upon the nature and size of the task, all families may be asked to participate on a given day, or parents may be divided into groups which rotate their services to the school. In general, if there is a good cash crop in the area, parents are more reluctant to work at the school and are eager to provide cash for the employment of laborers.

Levels of Labor Contributions in the Six Locations. Mbithi and Barnes have suggested that Harambee projects demand labor from the poor whereas the more prosperous do not have to contribute in this way.[11] Evidence from the six locations shows that labor and cash contributions are not interchangeable. Both cash contribution and labor contribution may be required from a household. A labor contribution cannot be substituted for a cash contribution. The School Committee normally establishes a fine of Ksh. 2 per work session which it imposes if the family fails to provide its assigned labor contribution. A community may decide that it is permissible to make a cash payment instead of contributing labor; the option is not normally available on an individual basis for making a labor rather than a cash contribution.

Table 6.5 reveals some comparisons between the top quintile in affluence in each location, and the poorest quintile in terms of labor and cash contributions to Harambee projects. The cash category includes materials. These figures suggest that those who contribute labor to self-help projects come from a broad spectrum of the community. Among those who give cash only, twice as many are found in the affluent group as in the poorest group. Both top and bottom quintiles contain approximately the same number of respondents making contributions of labor to projects.

The use of community labor for purposes of providing unskilled labor for building programs has both benefits and costs for the individual while providing quite significant benefits for the community. Normally

Table 6.5
Contributions to Harambee projects by most affluent
quintile and least affluent quintile in six locations
(in percent)

	Poorest 20%	Richest 20%
Cash and labor	56	58
Cash only	17	35
Labor only	1	0
No contribution	26	7

N = 200

five or six days of effort per household over a period
of time is sufficient input to a widely shared community responsibility. Typically, a woman with primary
school children may contribute about 40 to 60 hours a
year to the school, spending 15 to 20 mornings assisting with a variety of tasks such as plastering walls
with mud, or carrying sand and water for construction.
        Costs to parents of such an arrangement are pri-
marily in the alternative uses of time. In those areas
where parents are becoming involved in cash crops with
a labor-intensive component, they are beginning to sub-
stitute financial support for labor support of the
school. This is usually accomplished by a collective
decision that all labor for the school will be hired
rather than an individual decision based on family
preferences. Respondents were asked in the questionnaire what they felt they would prefer to be doing during the time they were contributing labor to schools
and other projects. Some indicated that they would
prefer to be cultivating their fields, but most expressed willingness to give this kind of assistance to
developing community services.
        Thus, evidence from this study of Harambee proj-
ects in six locations suggests that, within a community, contributors come from across the spectrum of
socio-economic groups with the larger cash contributions coming from the more affluent rather than the
poorer segments of rural society. This is a different
perspective from the widely held view that Harambee
takes labor and cash from the poorer groups to support
the interests of the wealthier segments of society. It
is important, of course, to look at the other side of
the question. That is, who benefits from Harambee
projects? Having determined that contributors do not
come primarily from the poorest groups in the six location studies, it is necessary to see who benefits and
how they benefit from Harambee projects.

BENEFITS

Distribution of Benefits According to the Respondents in the Interview Sample

Respondents were asked to give specific information concerning contributions to projects and benefits
received from them. Contributions included cash, labor
or material. Not included in this assessment were
minor contributions of a shilling or two such as one
might give to a friend's organization or a church in a
neighboring community.

One useful way of addressing the question of benefits from Harambee projects is to look at the total
number of contributions which have been made by the respondents interviewed and then to assess the percentage
of contributions for which they have actually received
benefits.[12] Table 6.6 is based on information about
contributions made by all respondents and specifically
those from the wealthiest and poorest quintiles of each
location. It shows the percentage of contributions
which have brought benefits to the contributing household.

Table 6.6
Percentage of individual project contributions which
are benefiting contributors among respondents

Location	Total Sample	Richest 20%	Poorest 20%
Soin	90	94	86
Nthawa	59	67	52
Mbiri	49	54	56
Kisiara	89	95	89
Kyeni	79	77	79
Weithaga	68	68	70
Average	72	76	72

N = 500

The averages given at the bottom of Table 6.6 show
that appropriately three-fourths of the contributions
made by the total sample, by the richest 20 percent and
by the poorest 20 percent are yielding benefits. While
there is considerable variation among the locations,
within each of them (except Nthawa) the percentage
points vary little between the top and bottom quint-

iles. This suggests relative uniformity in numbers of project contributions bringing benefits across socio-economic groups. It does not suggest that the benefits received are identical. Obviously the family with six children in the primary school benefits more than the family with one child in the school. The household with ten cattle benefits from the cattle dip more than the household with one cow. The family which is sick often benefits more from the nearby clinic than the family which is rarely sick. There are important distinctions in nature and scope of benefits received.

It is useful to consider briefly the nature of assets being created by benefits introduced through Harambee projects. These assets might be healthy cows which are producing milk in sufficient quantity for the household to sell some. They might be improved employment opportunities for children or time saved which can be used for agricultural labor. Naturally, those who have more productive capital will benefit more from the project. In this sense, some kinds of projects have a bias toward the more affluent members of a community. However, it seems that most communities attempt to strike a balance between providing services through a widespread community effort and requiring additional payment from those who are benefiting the most.

In effect, there is a user tax on some of these services. A cattle dip may be built by contributions from all members of the community, but there is a small fee per animal for those who use the dip. Those who benefit the most from the use of the dip are paying somewhat more for the service than those who benefit minimally. In another example, students at village polytechnics pay a fee for their training while the community puts up the buildings and the Government provides funds for teacher salaries.

Thus, there is an effort to find a middle ground whereby some basic services are provided to a community, quite equitably across the population and not just to a limited income group. Yet, acknowledging that some may benefit more than others, charges are made accordingly. Moreover, it is evident that many of the respondents, whether currently benefiting from a project or not, welcome the opportunity to keep their options open in preparation for the day when they might have children in secondary school, cattle to be dipped, or sick family members needing medical care.

Distribution of Benefits by Project Type

Evidence from all locations indicates that project choice is similar for both the top and bottom quintiles. The only significant difference is in contributions for social welfare projects, especially churches,

for which the most affluent have contributed nearly
twice as often as the poorest group. For both quintiles approximately half the contributions have gone
into educational projects. Table 6.7 shows the allocation of contributions for the wealthiest and poorest
quintile. Table 6.8 relates benefits to contributions
by project category. According to this table, contributors in the poorest quintile are benefiting a bit more
from educational projects than those in the top quintile, while the wealthiest quintile is benefiting somewhat more from economic projects. The wealthy clearly
have a better return on their contribution to water
projects than do the poor for reasons made evident in
Chapter V.

Table 6.7
Project choice for contributions from the top and
bottom quintiles (in percent)

Project Type	Richest 20%	Poorest 20%
Education	50	49
Economic	16	19
Water	13	13
Health	10	13
Social Welfare	11	6

Table 6.8
Percentage of contributions yielding benefits to
respondents in top and bottom quintiles

Project Type	Richest 20%	Poorest 20%
Education	79	83
Economic	85	77
Water	54	31
Health	56	56
Social Welfare	75	80

Like water projects, health projects offer a low
return on contributions made by rich and poor alike.
Contributions for social welfare projects yield somewhat greater benefits for the poorest quintile, in part

because those households are not as involved in building complex and expensive stone churches as are the
more affluent households.

   In assessing the distribution of benefits from
self-help projects, it is useful to look at one additional group: the non-contributors. Table 6.9 shows
the percentage of non-contributors in the total sample,
as well as in the top and bottom quintiles. It also
gives the percentage of non-contributors who indicated
that they had benefited personally from one or more
Harambee projects in their area.

Table 6.9
Non-contributors and Harambee project benefits
(in percent)

Respondents	Percentage Represented by Non-Contributors	Percentage of Non-Contributors Enjoying Benefits From One or More Harambee Projects
Total sample	14	68
Top quintile	7	57
Bottom quintile	26	65

N = 500

   Non-contributors in the poorest quintile are nearly twice the percentage of the total sample and approximately three and a half times that of the richest
quintile. As a group those households are receiving
benefits from Harambee projects at a rate slightly below that of the total sample average, and eight percentage points higher than that of the top quintile.

Spin-Off Benefits From Projects

   The above assessment of benefits made by respondents does not give much indication of the nature of
these benefits or their spin-off effects. We may know
that a respondent has children in the local primary
school, receives health advice and medicines from a
local dispensary, or takes a cow to the dip regularly.
However, the real return on educational investments and
improved health care may be quite long-term and diffuse
for the families involved. Benefits from churches or
other social welfare projects may be of great personal
importance.
   Several types of economic projects constitute

great labor-saving services, particularly for rural women. Water projects which bring a water supply to a communal tap represent an important saving in time for women who, in this sample, walked anywhere from a few meters to 10 kilometers for water, depending upon the area and the season. Mills for grinding maize into corn meal represent another saving in time for many women who must carry headloads of maize to a mill several times a week. A nearby mill can greatly reduce the time involved for this task. Feeder roads for villages, another type of Harambee project, can greatly ease problems such as bringing supplies into the village or taking quantities of milk or produce out. Such benefits, if difficult to quantify, are very important to the villagers involved, and were mentioned by many respondents to the questionnaire.

Perhaps the economic projects most readily assessed are the cattle dips. They can bring significant benefits to the individual households. Two sublocations, one in Mbiri, Muchungucha, and one in Kisiara, Cheborge, give some indication of the full measure of these benefits. In 1973 there were no grade cows in Muchungucha Sublocation. By 1974 the cattle dip was in operation and households began to acquire grade cattle and cross-breeds By 1978 approximately two-thirds of the cattle in the sublocation were grade or cross-breeds with the remaining third being local cattle. They were owned by just about every family in the sublocation. If the cross-breed was a second cow for the family with most of the milk going for sale, the minimum cash return per month in this location was approximately Ksh. 430 and the average was Ksh. 500, an important supplement to a family's income.

The benefits of acquiring cross-breed or grade cattle, which produce much more milk than local cattle but which must be dipped weekly to prevent tickborne diseases, have been so evident in such a short time that one off-shoot of the construction of the cattle dip has been the formation of the Kabanga Women's Group in Muchungucha. This group of 240 women was raising Ksh. 4,800 each month to be divided among eight members, most of whom were using the money for the purchase of grade or cross-breed cows.

Cattle dips are illustrative of a type of Harambee project which can be linked effectively with Government support services to develop a productive economic infrastructure with high benefits to the local population. For example, Kisiara had smoothly functioning, community-operated cattle dips. There was an active Artificial Insemination Program in the location and easy access to a Kenya Cooperative Creameries factory. From the area surrounding Cheborge's Mekunyet cattle dip approximately 850 cattle were brought, per week, for dipping. In 1973 when the cattle dip was built,

approximately 20 percent of the cattle were cross-
breeds, and there were no grade cattle. By 1979
approximately 70 percent were cross-breed, 20 percent
local, and 10 percent grade. Farmers had made liberal
use of the Smallholders Credit Scheme for purchases of
improved livestock. According to the respondents interviewed in Kisiara Location, earnings from milk range
from Ksh. 100 per month to Ksh. 800 per month. Clearly, in Kisiara Harambee efforts and Government services
were complementing one another in ways advantageous to
the local population.

Respondent View of Benefits Versus Opportunity Costs

What are the opportunity costs engendered by the
contributions to Harambee projects? For the family
contributing under Ksh. 100 a year, in small amounts,
it is difficult to specify the nature of a tradeoff in
utilizing household funds. For a household making
larger contributions, it is likely that Harambee contributions bite into funds that might otherwise be
spent with greater economic utility on fertilizer, improved seeds or other agricultural inputs. Respondents, however, were not inclined to weigh immediate
economic benefits against long-term social or economic
returns on their cash or labor contributions to Harambee projects. In fact, the vast majority of respondents in the communities visited were eager to develop
social services as well as economic opportunities within their area.
Eighty-eight percent of the entire sample favored
further development of their communities through the
implementation of self-help projects. First choice for
projects included health services for two locations,
water supply for two, schools for one, and cooperative
agricultural projects for one. Many respondents suggested very specific types of economic projects they
would like to implement through self-help processes,
projects such as construction of coffee factories, corn
mills, or jointly owned and managed sugar cane farms.
The interest in new directions for self-help endeavors
is clearly evident among many of the respondents interviewed, as is a willingness to support them. However,
very real questions remain concerning the mechanisms
for implementing these projects. As we have observed
in Kyeni and Mbiri, the implementation process can be
both difficult and divisive.
Are self-help projects effective as a means of resource distribution within communities? Do they provide benefits across social and economic strata? Are
there increasing levels of community welare and productivity? Evidence from this study suggests that in com-

munities where most are smallholders sharing similar problems and needs, local residents select projects with broadly based benefits. Many communities have demonstrated a capacity to determine contributions equitably and to insure fair management of projects so that there is minimal discrimination in favor of some residents. In fact, discriminatory practices were mentioned by respondents in only one location and that was in regard to ill-managed cattle dips. This is not to suggest, however, that competition and disagreement over project implementation and management do not exist. Issues of timing, location, sequence, and maintenance can become acute as the altercations over Wanjengi and Kirogo dispensaries and maternity wards indicated. It does suggest that these conflicts do not necessarily follow class lines.

In the six locations observed, there were no structural biases in the Harambee projects which consistently favored the wealthier members of a community over the poorer members in terms of contribution levels or benefits received. If anything, there was a bias in favor of the poorest quintile in self-help projects, for in the sample surveyed, 26 percent of the poorest never contributed to self-help projects while the majority of them benefited from one or more Harambee projects. In fact, non-contributors represent only 14 percent of the total sample and 68 percent of them received benefits from Harambee projects.

These figures suggest that the "free riders" benefiting from community service without paying for them constitute a relatively small percentage of the population and are comprised primarily of the less affluent rather than the wealthier members of the community. This data, as well as other evidence regarding contribution levels presented in this chapter, suggest that Harambee projects do play a positive role in resource distribution at the local level. Funds as well as labor are directed from individual sources to community benefits in which the poorer strata partake as well as the higher income groups.

NOTES

1. Martin Hill, "Self Help in Education and Development: A Social Anthropological Study in Kitui, Kenya," 1974 (cyclostyled report). Nairobi: University of Nairobi, Bureau of Educational Research.
2. Rachel Musyoki, Socio-Economic Status of Families and Social Participation: A Multi-Dimensional Analysis of Commitment and Alienation in Rural Kenya. Nairobi: University of Nairobi, Department of Sociology, thesis, 1976.
3. President Daniel Arap Moi in his Independence

Day Speech, December 12, 1978.

4. Interview with the Project Committee for
Kamasega School, Soliat Sublocation, Soin, April, 1979.

5. Interview with the headmaster, Cheborge Primary School, Kisiara, May, 1979.

6. Discussion at the Institute for Development
Studies seminar, July, 1979, on Working Paper #354,
"Rural Development Through Local Initiatives: An
Assessment of Kenya's Experience with Harambee Projects
in Selected Rural Communities" by Barbara Thomas.

7. Interview with the Clerk of the County Council, Embu District, April, 1978.

8. Conversations with District Officer Mwaisaka
for Kiharu Division; with Benson Kibutu, Teacher at
Kangaru Secondary School; with Bishop Gitari, Bishop of
the Mt. Kenya East Diocese of the Church of the Province of Kenya; and with the Principal of the Murang'a
College of Technology.

9. See, for example, The Daily Nation, November
6, 1978 or The Daily Nation, May 1, 1979. Both newspapers have articles about coercive practices regarding
Harambee fundraising in Western Province.

10 A statement by Attorney General Njonjo, quoted
in The Daily Nation, July 26, 1979.

11. P. Mbithi and C. Barnes, "A Conceptual Analysis of Approaches to Rural Development," Discussion
Paper #204, Institute for Development Studies, University of Nairobi, 1974.

12. This assessment excludes minor contributions
of a few shillings given to help an institution or an
organization in a neighboring community.

VII
Women's Self-Help Associations: Agents for Change or Techniques for Survival?

> If our group continues to have its spirit of coop-
> eration and hard work we shall soon be managing a
> small shop in addition to our maize mill and
> nursery school.
>
> Chairman
> Kaptebengwo Women's Group

Self-help in Kenya has led not only to community
projects but also to the emergence of a variety of
groups oriented toward development. These groups may
be involved in their own income-generating activities,
or they may assist in building community facilities.
Hence, there are links between community self-help
projects and the self-help groups. In recent years,
the Government has perceived these links and has been
encouraging the formation of these groups as a way of
generating resources for development in the rural
areas.

Self-help groups include women's groups, clan
groups, loan associations, neighborhood associations,
and church groups. These groups have evolved from both
traditional and non-traditional sources. Membership is
based on a common interest and is attained by joining.
In some cases there are specific requirements such as
clan or church membership, sex, or residence in a particular locality. Most common are women's groups,
which were present in five of the six locations under
investigation. They have been selected as the focus
for this examination of self-help groups.

Exploration of the origins and activities of
women's organizations in rural Kenya offers insights
concerning:

- women's responses to socio-economic change;
- group activities in the context of household
  survival strategies, national policies, and
  development planning; and

167

        - the public policies which have affected the functioning of women's associations.

In Kenya women's associations have constituted a significant response to important socio-economic changes in the environment - both needs and opportunities - and to a specific national and international political climate. In particular, they have emerged throughout much of rural Kenya as a response to economic, social, political, and technological changes arising from the colonial experience, from participation in a cash economy, from the systemic linkage of rural communities to a world beyond Kenya through export cash crops, and from the policies and politics of independent Kenya. These organizations provide a range of benefits, supports and opportunities to their members which differ from those found in traditional modes of social organization and which relate closely to broad structural changes taking place in rural Kenya.

    The Ministry of Housing and Social Services estimates that there are approximately 5,000 such associations functioning primarily in the settled, agricultural areas of Kenya.[1] This analysis of the role of women's organizations in Kenya is based on interviews with 44 women's associations in five Locations. There were in the late 1970's approximately 26 women's groups in Weithaga Location with a total membership of over 1,000; there were 25 in Mbiri with a membership of 1,600; seven in Kyeni with a membership of 240; 15 groups in Nthawa with 450 members; and eight in Kisiara with 300 members.[2] Only Soin did not have women's self-help groups. Evidence is also drawn from the questionnaires administered to 250 female respondents.

THREE WOMEN: A PORTRAIT

    Wanjeri Kofia lives in Murang'a District, not far from Mount Kenya. Nancy Ngari lives in Gitiburi, several miles down a dirt track off the murram road running between Embu town and Siakago, the headquarters for Nthawa Location, a flat, semi-arid section of Embu District. Far away on the other side of the Rift Valley lives Rodah Koech midst the tea and maize of Kisiara Location in Kericho District. Like other rural women throughout much of Kenya, these three are engaged in a variety of activities as members of women's organizations.

    Twice a week Wanjeri Kofia meets with her group for a morning of work on a nearby coffee farm. Setting out in the early morning, she knits a sweater for her son as she walks the mile and a half to the farm where 20 women of Kahuti Women's Group are gathering to weed and mulch two acres of coffee. Like most of the women in her group in this prosperous region of Kenya, Mrs. Kofia has been to primary school and can read and write. Her husband and their five children live on their own small plot of one and 1/2 acres growing coffee, maize and bananas.

Once a week Nancy Ngari hoists her baby on her back and leaves behind her own half acre of cotton to spend a morning working in the fields of other members of her Gikuyari Women's Group. Sometimes they work an additional morning at the primary school where the women cultivate a half acre of cotton, the proceeds of which will be used to purchase supplies for the school and perhaps bags of cement for constructing a desperately needed classroom. Mrs. Ngari is glad to help with the school project and eager for her young children to have the advantages of an education. She can neither read nor write, and while she does not consider this lack much of a disadvantage, she hopes her children will be "modern." These sentiments are widely shared by other members of her group. Mr. Ngari is not at home on a regular basis. Much of the time he works as a casual laborer in Embu town, the District headquarters, and sometimes he finds employment in nearby Siakago. On several occasions he has tried seeking employment in Nairobi, but without success.

Rodah Koech meets frequently with the Kaptebengwo Women's association to administer their maize mill and nursery school and to make plans for the small store they intend to open in a portion of the building which houses the mill. A sturdy woman of about 50, Mrs. Koech is a commanding presence with a sure manner and a quick smile. Despite an inability to read and write, she is clearly a leader in the group, though she relies on a younger woman, the group's secretary, for record keeping. Mrs. Koech and her husband are prospering smallholders in Kisiara, growing both tea and maize on a portion of their 15 acres. Her children are grown, although several are still at home. Despite their educational attainments - one son has completed Form IV at a Government secondary school - the sons have had difficulty finding employment in Kericho, the District headquarters, or even in Kisumu, the nearest large town.

These three women are typical of rural women, particularly in the settled, agricultural areas of Kenya. Participation in women's associations is an important part of their lives.

RURAL WOMEN'S ASSOCIATIONS: AN INTERPRETATION

A Definition

    Research in Murang'a, Embu and Kericho Districts
suggests that there are three types of women's groups.
First, there are associations which focus on income-
generating activities.   These tend to be small and cohesive, with 25 to 30 members.   Their income-generating
activities vary widely and may include working as a
labor force at agricultural tasks, cutting and selling
firewood, operating a maize mill, raising chickens or
pigs, making and selling pots, or working at various
handicrafts.   Money earned may be divided among them
according to some established procedure or it may be
used for a particular purpose on which group members
have agreed, such as building a nursery school or contributing to a dispensary.
    A second type of women's association is a revol-
ving loan association.   These groups vary in size with
the smallest of those in the Locations investigated
numbering about 24 and the largest 240 members.   These
associations collect funds on a monthly basis and designate one or more of their members as recipients of
the money.   The organization follows a carefully specified system of rotation. The first person to receive a
share is obtaining an interest free loan from the rest
of the membership; the last is participating in
"forced" savings as she extends credit to the other
members of the association.   The others alternate between debtor and creditor positions.   In essence, a
member of the group is saving until she receives her
share of the fund, after which she begins to repay the
loan in installments.   In some instances the association purchases items for the individual member; in
others, the member is given the money to spend as she
wishes.   Sometimes the group determines what the membership is to do with a given "round" of loans; in
others the decision is left to the recipient.   Loans
are most frequently used to finance iron sheets for
roofing, water storage tanks, school fees, cows, goats
and household utensils or furnishings.   However, women
have also used these loans to purchase agricultural inputs such as fertilizer and coffee seedlings.
    The third category consists of groups which serve
primarily as a form of social security for their members.   They may, in addition, undertaken income-earning
projects or have a system of loans, but often these are
conducted on a somewhat desultory basis, and the underlying function is the provision of some measure of
social and economic security.   Some of these women are
old; some are widowed; some have husbands living elsewhere and receive very little support, financial or
otherwise, from them.   These women may assist one an-

other with agricultural tasks and child care. Generally, these groups provide a support structure which is
lacking to the particular family.

For many groups, functions overlap all three categories. A group which is primarily organized around an
income-generating activity will be quick to come to the
assistance of a sick member. Some groups combine a revolving loan system with earning money for a group
project. The categories are flexible.

Profile of Group Members

There are several misperceptions about participants in women's groups.[3] One stereotype is that of
the affluent ladies' sewing circle. Another is that of
the struggling elderly widow. While a few groups with
members characteristic of both of these stereotypes
were interviewed, they in no way represent the majority
of cases. The group members were of all ages, although
relatively few were in their teens or 20s. The average
rate of literacy for group participants was below the
average among adult females for the location according
to the survey questionnaires.

Very few women participating in such groups had
wage employment. The number of unattached women in any
given group ranged from none to 71 percent with the
average being about 25 to 30 percent. This figure included divorced or abandoned women as well as widows.
It also included women managing on their own with husbands employed elsewhere and infrequently at home.
This phenomenon was particularly common in Mbiri where
one group indicated that 75 percent of the husbands
worked in Nairobi or elsewhere. It was virtually non-
existent in Weithaga where all groups claimed that the
vast majority of husbands were employed on their own
farms or nearby.

Patterns of membership vary by location. In Mbiri
many who originally founded a women's group are still
members. Moreover, the groups are growing. In
Weithaga only 20 percent reported that the original
membership is still largely in the group. In Kyeni,
participation is constant or increasing with original
members still very much involved in group activities.
New groups were organizing themselves in Kisiara.

Modes of Participation

Decision-making processes within a group vary in
part according to the size of the group. In the majority of cases there is a committee composed of officers
who make recommendations for group activities. These
recommendations are then taken to the entire group for

approval or ratification. Although deference is shown to the chairman or group leader, group members indicate that opinions are widely shared and consensus on any issue is generally obtained.

Among members, group activities and responsibilities are fairly shared. Women are expected to do their portion of cultivation if the group is working as an agricultural labor force and to make their financial contributions on time. Usually the group imposes a fine for failure to contribute labor in cases where the group is working as a collective agricultural labor force.

Benefits and rewards of participation are systematically and fairly shared. A roster of members is kept and loans are given out according to turn. Departure from the group as soon as one has received the loan is quite rare, although it has happened. One group in Weithaga indicated that a woman had absconded from the group immediately after receiving her share of funds early in the rotation cycle, but the Assistant Chief had helped retrieve the money. The largest group interviewed, 240 women in Mbiri who give Ksh. 600 to each of eight women every month, keeps careful records and claims never to have had any defaulters or "sudden departures."[4] Nthawa, the poorest location with women's groups, is the one which has had the most difficulty with careless supervision of funds. There were several instances among respondents to the questionnaire in which women had left groups because responsibility for funds had been abused by group leaders. For the most part, however, group sanctions, group solidarity, and carefully watched bank accounts prevent such occurrences.

Origins

The traditional mutual aid system provides firm underpinnings for the activities of women's groups.[5] Traditionally women have worked together in small groups of two, three or four, sharing tasks according to agricultural season. There is a qualitative and quantitative jump to the kinds of endeavors in which women's groups are involved today, but the basis for mutual cooperation and mutual enterprise can be found in a social tradition.

The existence of women's groups is also supported by the firm dichotomy between male and female roles and the tradition of both male and female solidarity. Women's roles have traditionally involved agricultural labor and related tasks, as well as home and child care. Women's groups are building upon the customary responsibilities and duties of women. The groups do not lure women off to new hitherto unrelated interests and concerns. They offer many women an opportunity to expand their successes within a traditional domain: providing more satisfactorily for the care and nurture of children and the welfare of their homes. Where the groups are edging into business, it is through the link with women's major roles as cultivators and providers of food. Only as women's associations move into cultivation of fields for cash crops or ownership of shops or equipment and technology are they diverging from traditional roles. So far, community support for these new roles exists. An indication of this support lies in the actions of the County Councils. In all three Districts, these local governing authorities have given women's associations permits to open shops or maize mills, and the Councils have leased or occasionally allocated land for the use of women's groups.

Nevertheless, the women's associations operating in the five Locations under investigation are quite different phenomena from local agricultural support groups or age-group collectivities. Many originated in the 1970's with the encouragement and support of the national government and political leaders. National government policy continues to support the formation of women's groups. This policy derives in part from a growing international interest in women's issues, from the United Nations impetus behind the International Year of Women in 1975, and a worldwide strengthening of women's organizations. Interest has focused on the differential impact of various modernization processes on women, the ways women can be more fully involved in the development process, and their roles in economic and social change.

In addition, opportunities for funding women's programs became available through the increased interest of international aid organizations. The Ministry of Housing and Social Services (now the Ministry of Culture and Social Services) responded to these opportunities and pressures by reassessing and restructuring its efforts to organize and assist rural women. It established a Women's Bureau for the purpose of implementing various programs and services directed toward Kenyan women. Thus, until the mid-1970's, there was not much official interest in women's groups.

Despite the existence of the Women's Bureau, support of the Kenyan Government has been primarily verbal, focusing on staffing at the District level, rather than specific resources which actually reach local women's groups. The Ministry of Housing and Social Services has placed a female officer in most Districts to foster programs and to assist women in their organizational efforts. These officers are often energetic and dedicated, but they are hampered in their work by extremely limited budgets and resources. This Ministry sponsors seminars to train female leaders and provides

guidelines for group registration and for financial
accountability.

The Department of Community Development has also
encouraged Chiefs and Assistant Chiefs to support
women's groups. Such support has most frequently consisted of exhortation to form women's associations for
development purposes. Occasionally, Chiefs or Assistant Chiefs have allocated specific resources, such as
land, for the use of a group. Also, upon occasion,
local leaders have used these groups for political and
personal purposes. In sum, the Government has been a
key actor in encouraging the formation of women's
groups although it has not often provided them with resources.

Economic Activities

Loan Sharing. Most of the groups interviewed were
involved in income-generating and/or loan-sharing
activities. The most common source of funds for
women's groups was the monthly contribution which members made individually to the group and which provided
revolving credit. For the most part, contributions
ranged from Ksh. 2 to Ksh. 20 per month and came from
the woman's earnings from her garden produce, from
earnings as an agricultural laborer or from milk sold.
While Ksh. 20 saved by an individual once a month may
seem an insignificant amount, the collective effort can
be an important stimulus to community and household
welfare.

A good illustration of the links between women's
groups and development projects leading to improved
household welfare can be found in Muchungucha Sublocation of Mbiri where a women's group was formed in response to the installation of a cattle dip. As discussed in Chapter V, the cattle dip permitted local
residents to own grade and cross-breed cattle which are
far better milk producers than are the local breed of
cattle.

The women were not slow to perceive these benefits. Consequently one off-shoot of the construction
of the cattle dip was the formation of the Kabanga
Women's Group. This group of 240 women, formed in
1976, was raising Ksh. 4,800 each month to be divided
among eight members, most of whom were using the money
for the purchase of improved breeds of cattle. For
this group, the loan-sharing mechanism was so successful that when they had finished a complete round for
purposes of enabling each family to purchase a cow,
they intend to undertake a new round of investments,
probably for water storage tanks. The effectiveness of
this women's association in Muchungucha illustrates the
potential for multiplying the benefits of development

efforts by linking local organizations and project infrastructure.

Procedures for allocation of funds earned or contributed vary from group to group and from area to
area. Some groups allocate funds exclusively to individual members for their use. Others allocate only to
social or community projects selected by the group.
Some allocate for long-term investment purposes, and
some combine all three uses of funds, allocating some
funds to individuals on a rotating basis and reserving
some for donations to community projects or for investment purposes. Women's groups in the wealthiest community, Weithaga, and the poorest one, Nthawa, are
oriented toward community projects. In the other three
locations groups are focused almost exclusively on individual gain to the women whether through a group investment or loan-sharing arrangements. Three-fourths
of all groups provide rotating loans to individual members.

Collective Agricultural Labor. After monthly contributions, the second most widely used means of generating funds for a group was employment as an agricultural labor force, an activity pursued by more than
half the women's groups interviewed. For the most
part, the women had limited education and skills to
offer on the job market. By combining their efforts as
an agricultural labor force, they could compete collectively during peak agricultural seasons, assuring each
individual a regular opportunity for weekly earnings.
For example, groups located in coffee-growing areas
found seasonal employment on smallholder coffee farms,
weeding, mulching, picking coffee or doing a variety of
tasks. A typical group might earn as much as Ksh 400
($53) or Ksh 500 ($66) per month for half the year,
working two mornings a week for 26 weeks annually.
Some groups alternated activities, working one day a
week for a group member, at no charge, and the other
for an outsider at their standard fee. Such opportunities depend, of course, on land potential and weather
conditions. They exist more or less continuously in
Weithaga or Kyeni and only periodically in Nthawa or
Mbiri.

In three of the five Locations, two-thirds of the
women's groups were involved in cultivation of a cooperative shamba. Usually the shamba was a small plot of
one-fourth to one acre. Land was on loan from the
Assistant Chief or from a friend of the group and could
be reclaimed at any time. In Murang'a where land is at
a premium and population pressures are great, neither
location had women's groups with cooperative shambas.
In those locations where there were shambas, earnings
were not large. Crops included sunflowers, cotton,
potatoes, maize, tomatoes, and beans. Vegetables were
generally consumed at home. Crops such as sunflowers

or cotton generated funds for group activities or donations to community projects such as nursery schools or
clinics.

Hopes for Handicrafts. Most of the women were
involved in handicrafts on an individual basis -
knitting, crocheting, embroidery, pottery, basketry.
In fact, all groups expressed keen interest in expanding income-earning capabilities through handicraft production. However, only two of the 44 groups interviewed had been able to organize their efforts in handicraft production to include bulk purchasing of supplies and marketing through the national women's organization. Even this was not entirely satisfactory as
delays in payments were inexplicably long. Low returns
on all handicrafts were commonplace. Marketing problems and the lack of requisite entrepreneurial skills
to make handicrafts a commercial enterprise were apparent.

The Lure of Investment. Finally, groups were becoming interested in investment opportunities. The
list of interests and potential activities was quite
long and included such pursuits as owning and operating
a maize mill, a canteen or small shop, owning and operating a handicraft store, cultivation of land for cash
crops, or purchase of a tractor or other vehicle. The
concept of a group investment was new, and it was a use
of funds in which a number of women's associations were
increasingly interested.

What is the potential of the women's groups for
fundraising and investment purposes? Only one of the
districts, Murang'a, had records providing data from
the early 1970's. Its records showed that the women's
groups in Mbiri and Weithaga had, over a seven or eight
year period, raised and distributed a total of Ksh.
653,757 ($87,168) to both individual members and to
community projects.[6] In 1977 alone, the funds generated in Weithaga came to Ksh. 101,824 ($13,577) for 26
groups with 1,013 members.[7] In Kisiara (Kericho District) one group in one year alone raised Ksh. 57,000
($7,600) for the purchase of a maize grinding machine.[8]
These figures suggest that the women's groups in the
area of high agricultural potential do have fundraising
and investment possibilities.

To date, most groups have not made long-term investments in group-owned activities but have used a
portion of their earnings for community projects. Many
groups have build nursery schools. Some have built
meeting halls. Others have made contributions to primary schools, dispensaries or other community facilities.

WOMEN'S ASSOCIATIONS AND SOCIO-ECONOMIC CHANGE

Increasing Responsibilities of Rural Women

The roles of rural women changed dramatically
under the impact of colonization, the emergence of a
settler economy, the introduction of export cash crops,
the growth of urban areas, and involvement with the
cash economy. For the most part, women's responsibilities have increased. The Central Bureau of Statistics
has recently determined that in just under one-fourth
of all rural households, the husband is either absent
for long periods, usually for employment purposes, or
is deceased.[9] Thus the traditional division of labor
between men and women has been modified by the departure of large numbers of men from rural areas to seek
employment in the cities or labor opportunities on
large farms.

Among the Locations studied, the men remained at
home if they had adequate land in an area in which production of a cash crop was well established. In the
resource-poor areas, in particular, women have had to
assume more responsibility for agriculture, including,
in some cases, the introduction of cash crops, as well
as the management and care of traditional food crops
for home consumption and marginal sale.

These responsibilities have been compounded by
the fact that most rural children are now attending
primary school, leaving the mother short of traditionally valuable assistance for cultivation and for household tasks. It is not uncommon for a woman to have
major agricultural and domestic responsibilities, to be
caring for six or seven children, to be, if she is
lucky, managing a side-operation in brewing "pombe"
(local beer) or selling milk, or perhaps working as a
casual laborer, and, to have her husband at home only
for very short visits throughout the year. This pattern of family life with the husband employed in a dis-
tant place, and the wife and children remaining in the
rural community is common in Kenya today. In some
measure, it may account for the rising success and pop-
ularity of women's groups which provide a useful support structure, as well as new opportunities for rural
households.

Evidence from the locations investigated in this
study suggests that increased responsibilities for
rural women may lead to increased levels of activity in
women's groups. Mbiri Location is illustrative of the
situation in which men are commonly drawn away from the
community to seek employment, sometimes on a seasonal
basis, sometimes permanently. Among the Locations investigated, Mbiri was characterized by two phenomena:
it had the highest rates of male out-migration, and it
had the greatest involvement in women's associations.

In two-thirds of the women's groups interviewed in that
Location, the husbands of the majority of women were
employed elsewhere or were no longer part of the family. While other conditions may contribute to the formation of women's groups, this correlation between out-
migration of males and the establishment of women's
associations is striking.

Dealing with the Cash Economy

One of the main benefits of a women's group is
that it permits women to save small amounts of cash until there is enough to meet a major need - something
which is very difficult for the average household to
accomplish when cash is in short supply. Even for a
relatively self-sufficient household where there is
enough land to produce most of the food required by the
family during years of cooperative weather, there still
are some minimal demands for cash. These include cash
for school fees and uniforms, cash for occasional use
of public transport, cash for clothing and for the in-
cidentals of sugar, tea, salt, soap and a few other
commodities. These would be considered quite basic expenses. Beyond this minimum, of course, there is a
wide range of goods and services which people may desire or require.

A women's association is able to generate and provide cash in sizeable amounts. Moreover, the association controls the cash and can to some extent determine
its allocation and use. This is a significant departure from the customary division of responsibility in a
rural household. Traditionally a woman is entitled to
control her earnings from vegetable produce, eggs or
other farm products which she can sell. However, these
are small amounts quickly used on household maintenance. Large sums of money, such as those from cash
crop earnings or a salary are normally controlled by
the husband and allocated as he sees fit. In many instances, of course, there is no such source of income,
and the opportunities for saving are few.

With the traditional subordinate status of the
married woman, particularly in rural society, most
women seldom have opportunity for saving and spending a
sum of money on a major purchase. The women's groups
which have the rotating savings and loan scheme permit
women this opportunity. The money belongs to the
group, and the group can designate the way in which it
is to be spent, or can leave the decision to each individual. In any case, it is not the privilege or the
right of any other family member to determine the use
of these funds. Thus, the women's groups in their increasing emphasis on cash income and on sharing mechanisms help to circumvent some of the traditional con-

straints on women's abilities to save and to make decisions about cash expenditures.

Moreover, as indicated above, the women's groups
are stronger in those locations which are more tightly
linked into the cash economy than in those which are
relatively peripheral to the market/cash nexus. This
is the case not only because there are income-earning
opportunities in those locations with strong ties to a
cash economy, but also because the groups can play a
role in assisting women in this new mode of economic
behavior. The location in which the groups have been
the most popular - among the locations observed - is
the one in which women are most commonly heads of
household in a marginalized situation with some opportunity for cash income.

Meeting Needs, Capturing Opportunities

In more prosperous Locations, the women's associations are born less out of economic hardship than out
of economic opportunity. Consequently these groups
have been able to address both individual and community
objectives. In Weithaga, for example, the community
interests to which the groups have contributed over
time are dispensaries, churches, social halls, nursery
schools, and primary schools. These contributions or
investments are in addition to their loan-sharing procedures for individual members.

Since the members of these groups have few skills
other than those pertaining to agriculture, their
income-generating opportunities are most often directly
related to the productivity of the land and the cooperation of the climate. A favorable climate as well as
strong agricultural potential, such as that found in
the three more prosperous Locations, translate into
economic opportunity leading to successful income-
generating activities which enable groups to function
effectively over time. If, in addition, there is favorable pricing, such as there was for coffee in the
mid-1970's with escalating international prices, then
income-generating opportunities can proliferate, as
they did in Weithaga at that time.

In the other locations, climate and soil conditions are not as favorable, and opportunities for
women's groups to generate income have been negligible.
In the poorer locations where cash is not readily
available, it is commonplace for a group to contribute
labor to a particular community project. Cash is hard
to obtain in Nthawa, for example, and a Ksh. 2 per
month contribution may strain a woman's financial capability as compared with Ksh. 20 per month in Weithaga.
Neither income-generation nor loan-sharing were significant for most Nthawa groups. Instead, group activity

took the form of a labor contribution to a common endeavor, such as making bricks for the construction of a nursery school. Any loan-sharing which did take place was usually directed toward immediate household needs rather than a major purchase since the sums to be shared were small. Regardless of the enthusiasm which may exist among some women's groups in such a Location, the opportunities for income-generation simply are not there.

In fact, some economic activities, such as poultry raising, have been introduced to groups in resource-poor areas by the Government and have, on the whole, not been successful. These new projects often require a level of infrastructure, such as support services and marketing arrangements, which are not present. They also frequently require a level of organization and continuing financial resources which groups may find very difficult to build and to sustain over a period of time.

For example, one women's group in Nthawa found itself Ksh. 400 in debt trying to feed 200 chickens given to the group by UNICEF under the Special Rural Development Programme.[10] Because of the drought women had trouble buying the feed. They also found it very expensive at Ksh 20 per day. As a result they were not buying much, and the hens were underfed and were not laying. The project was costing rather than benefiting the group and the members eventually gave up.

Political Pressures and Political Savvy

In all the locations there is a new vulnerability, as well as opportunity, for the women's groups as they focus on cash earnings and sharing as opposed to labor sharing activities. Public awareness of the potential of women's groups for generating cash is increasing, and there is growing pressure on these groups to use the cash in a variety of ways, some of which may not be beneficial to the majority of group members. This pressure occurs in the context of Kenya's patron-client, electoral politics with competition for power and resources under conditions of scarcity. The situation with WANGU investment firm is illustrative. WANGU is a firm organized for investment purposes by people of Kiharu Division of Murang'a District. A prominent politician/ businessman has been behind the venture.

In 1977 WANGU purchased a farm in Meru District and some buildings in Nairobi. The purchase price on the package was Ksh. 34,000,000 ($4,533,333) with Ksh. 4,000,000 ($533,333) down and a bank loan to be repaid in four years (1981).[11] Officials in Kiharu Division, particularly the Chiefs and Assistant Chiefs, were instrumental in fostering and obtaining support for

WANGU.   In 1978 and 1979 no efforts were being spared
to encourage the citizens of Kiharu Division, which includes both Mbiri and Weithaga, to purchase shares in
the WANGU investment.   In fact, there was considerable
deception, as people were informed that the loan had to
be paid off by December, 1978.   This was a ruse to encourage them to buy more shares and to build up momentum for purchases.

Even the Locational Community Development Assistants were participating in the WANGU effort by talking
with the women's associations, explaining the investment procedures and encouraging the groups to support
WANGU.   In several instances, delegates from women's
associations were taken to visit the farm so that they
could report back to their membership about its benefits and value. In some cases the women's associations
assessed the advantages of making an investment in
WANGU, learned about the proposed returns on shares and
other pertinent information, and made a decision either
to purchase group shares or to limit their interest to
individual purchases on the part of group members.
However, this enlightened approach did not always
exist.

Of the women's groups interviewed in Weithaga and
Mbiri, the two groups which made the largest financial
commitment, on a per capita basis, were two of the
groups with the lowest literacy rates, the highest number of widows and elderly, and the clearest indications
of poverty.   Further, the officers of this group had
not visited the farm, had no idea about timing and rate
of return on the investment and were generally ill-
informed about its nature or purpose.   One summed up
the situation with the comment, "Many have given, so if
ours is lost, all have lost."[12]

In these two groups, many members were not young
and were leading a marginal existence.   It is clear
that they might have benefited more from immediate cash
return on a group effort than from projected return on
an investment some five or six years hence.   One may
conjecture about the reasons of these women for making
the investment.   The Community Development Assistant
suggested that the groups may not have wished to refuse
a request of the Chief who was a powerful person within
the Location and one whose requests or "wishes" were
not to be regarded lightly. Also, they undoubtedly did
not want to risk alienating a prominent politician and
potential patron for their group and community.[13]

As the women's associations improve their income-
generating and loan-sharing capabilities, their vulnerability to manipulation and to other forms of pressure
clearly increases. In Kenya's political environment
with its competitive jockeying for regional, class and
ethnic power, women's associations require strength and
political savvy in order to avoid being swept into the

political fray in ways which do not benefit their membership.

CONDITIONS FACILITATING EFFECTIVE WOMEN'S ASSOCIATIONS

What conditions foster local-level development activity through self-help groups such as the women's associations described here. A number are evident. Three external to the associations are important, and two internal to such groups are noteworthy.

Governmental Attitudes and Policies

A positive attitude toward women's associations on the part of the Government establishes a favorable setting in which they may function. The Government's support derives from the relevance of women's association activities to development objectives, from international interests related to women, from increased donor aid for women's activities, and the obvious public contribution which many women's groups make.

Examination of Kenya's development plans suggests that the women's groups conform to the thrust of national development strategies. The theme of the 1979-83 Development Plan was alleviation of poverty. Goals included improved medical care, nutrition, education and rural water supply, as well as diminishing the proportion of smallholders with incomes below Ksh. 2,400.[14] Underlying principles noted in the Plan included 1) wide-spread participation in shaping and implementing development programs; 2) a diversity of organizational forms for achieving these goals; and 3) mutual social responsibility such as the community initiatives found in Harambee.[15] Women's groups with their emphasis on food supply, water, shelter and education clearly deal with problems related to "alleviation of poverty." In this endeavor, they are wholeheartedly endorsed by the Government. This endorsement is official and public and permeates the entire bureaucracy. From the bureaucrat's point of view and the politician's as well, women's associations constitute a "safe" commitment, as long as they stay within the acceptable boundaries defined by an extension of traditional female roles. Moreover, they claim few public resources not earmarked for women and consequently are not yet competing in the public arena for the rewards of economic and political power.

Community Support

In addition to Government support, community support is a critical condition for sustaining effective
women's associations. Causation is, of course, circu-
lar. Women noted that their relatives approved of
their participation in a group because the group was
providing individual and community benefits. Contributions to various community services, such as dispensaries or nursery schools, have fostered favorable
attitudes toward groups within those communities. Income earning and sharing activities, as well as community donations, are recognized as beneficial to the individual families and to the community at large.

Widespread community support encourages enthusiasm
and high morale within a group reinforcing the members'
commitment to its activities. If a group is carrying
out its activities successfully, other women may seek
to join or to form similar groups. Kabanga Women's
Group in Mbiri had to turn away potential members suggesting that they form separate groups. In Kisiara
there are similar examples. Women have observed the
successful investments made by a few women's groups and
are becoming interested in organizing themselves within
their own community for similar purposes.

Resource-Base and Economic Opportunity

Economic opportunities on which a group may base
its activities do not exist in every location, but
where they do, they constitute an important means for
developing strong groups. They are most likely to
exist in resource rich areas. Moreover, as with other
local-level development efforts, the women's associations' activities do not stand alone. They must be
linked to a supportive infrastructure. A group making
pottery must have ways to transport the pots to market;
a group raising chickens must have access to feed and
to marketing opportunities. To provide resources in
the form of chickens or cloth or other inputs - as many
foreign donor agencies have discovered - is to waste
them unless a continuing support structure exists. In
this respect, the women's groups differ not at all from
a wide variety of other efforts at local-level development. Development does not take place in a vacuum;
communities must be linked into the wider socio-
economic system in ways permitting the effective execu-
tion of the specific projects and programs undertaken.

Leadership

Two conditions internal to the functioning of
women's associations are central to their effectiveness. The first is leadership. Among those interviewed, groups with effective income-generating and
loan-sharing activities generally exhibited strong
leadership. The chairman of the association had a
secure and prestigious place within the community, as
well as an outgoing, forceful personality. Sometimes
the leader's position was based on her own achievements, and sometimes it was more closely related to the
position of her male relatives.

In 80 per cent of the groups interviewed there had
been no change in the persons occupying the leadership
positions since the groups were formed. Despite elections, there was no accepted tradition of rotating the
responsibilities of leadership. A woman who was doing
a barely acceptable job would, in most instances, be
re-elected. Therefore, the personal characteristics,
community status and contacts of the individual leader
were particularly important in relation to the performance of the groups. A mediocre, lacklustre leader was
not likely to be replaced.

Procedures

Second, an effective group developed some systematic administrative procedures. Most important was the
bank account. If the group was earning money, that income had to be a public matter with full records open
to the entire membership. Of the groups interviewed,
more than half kept their money in a bank; 25 percent
distributed it upon receipt and did not require bank-
ing; several had special arrangements such as keeping
it in a church safe; and only three kept it at someone's home. This last category seems to be typified by
the woman who declared, "Oh, we keep our money in a pot
in the corner of the treasurer's house."16 The most
effective groups had managed to regularize and systema-
tize their functions, most particularly in regard to
money, and this was building confidence in the group
and loyalty to its activities and objectives.

WOMEN, TECHNOLOGY, AND RURAL TRANSFORMATION

Women have customarily worked as household agricultural labor undertaking major responsibility for
food supply using the simplest hand implements. When
improved methods for agricultural production, particularly in relation to cash crops have been introduced,
their control and use have gone to men. Women have

185

continued their work at subsistence agriculture using little more than the hoe.

By organizing themselves into women's groups working together as an agricultural labor force, women have altered the form, if not the substance, of female labor. They have assured themselves the benefits of more regular income-earning opportunities, and have made themselves less vulnerable to the whims of individual employers. Despite this change, they operate at the most basic level of untrained, unskilled workers in the labor force.

Group ownership and operation of maize mills is the only case in the five Locations where women are gaining control over a new technology. Control over maize mills is a direct departure from the customary relationship between changing technology and women. In those few instances where groups are operating mills, they have been successful, and women's groups in other localities are seizing upon this idea as a remunerative investment, relatively easy to manage, and highly beneficial to the women in the immediate community. This control over maize processing constitutes a structural change in economic and technological roles for women.

Women's groups are responding to other income-earning investment opportunities as well, and already some are moving in new directions, such as ownership of stores and production of cash crops. As owners and managers, rather than laborers, they will be in an entirely new relationship to the means of production, one which few rural Kenyan women have yet experienced. Changing the relationship of rural women to the means of production is, however, a long-term process. Moreover, it is occurring only in those areas with a rich resource base which provide an opportunity for women to expand their activities to include investment and ownership. Often these women do so on the basis of earnings derived from group agricultural labor. These activities are undertaken in the context of smallholder agriculture in a capitalist economy in which these women are struggling to win both individual and collective gains for their families and their communities.

The women's groups which have emerged throughout much of rural Kenya are a response to supportive public policy and perceived economic need and opportunity. They are particularly useful to low-income women in that they 1) provide some income-generating opportunities; 2) offer ways to save and invest; 3) provide some support mechanisms; and 4) enable people to work together to provide some of the community services they would not be able to obtain individually. In some cases groups serve as risk-diminishing, protective institutions; in others they may have new functions related to opportunities offered under changing rural conditions. They may, of course, simultaneously serve both functions.

Data from the two resource-poor Locations revealed that a disproportionally high number of women in the lowest income brackets belonged to women's groups.[17] Such groups, however, are not found solely among Kenya's poorest families. In the more affluent Locations where there are income-generating and investment opportunities, membership includes all socio-economic strata. The roles the groups play and the activities they are able to undertake clearly vary according to the resource base of the community.

By facilitating organization of women as unskilled laborers, by providing new opportunities for women to control technology and own investments, and by helping women to participate in the cash economy, women's groups are enabling women to respond with increasing effectiveness to changing socio-economic conditions within the context of family and community concerns. These concerns are perceived at the individual household and community level. There is not yet a broad political awareness among women in rural Kenya. Nor is there a political consciousness within the women's groups interviewed. Nowhere did anyone suggest that an association should join with others to achieve a common purpose or objective. The issues perceived are not the big ones such as rights to land ownership, inheritance laws, or even female education. They are immediate and pragmatic concerns - food, shelter, school fees, health care.

Given a favorable environment with public support and increasing economic opportunity, women's associations can continue to address the needs and interests of individual women, as well as families and communities. They can enable women to participate both individually and collectively in development projects. Perhaps they can contribute to the process of modifying key economic and social relationships in rural Kenya. Possibly, over time, they will link specific needs and opportunities to broad political issues shaping the future of Kenya's rural women.

NOTES

1. The Women's Bureau of the Ministry of Housing and Social Services in cooperation with the Central Bureau of Statistics, has gathered data on the activities of women's groups. A survey was conducted in 1978 and 1979.

2. These figures are drawn from the district files in Kericho, Embu, and Murang'a Community Development Offices, using the Annual Reports for each location for 1977 and 1978.

3. The rural groups differ substantially from

urban groups which may fit some of the stereotypes for urban women's associations.

4. Interview with Kabanga Women's Group, June, 1978.

5. This mutual aid system has a different name in each community. Among the Kikuyu it is called 'ngwatio.' Among the Kipsigis, it is 'kipagenge.'

6. Ministry of Housing and Social Services, Community Development Office, Murang'a District, Kiharu Division, Annual Reports for Weithaga Location and for Mbiri Location, 1977. Data collected was verified in interviews with women's groups in these locations.

7. Ibid.

8. Interview with Kaptebengwo Women's Group, Kisiara, March, 1979.

9. Government of Kenya, Central Bureau of Statistics, Social Perspectives, Vol. 3, No. 3, April, 1978, "Women in Kenya," p. 1.

10. Report on Inspection Visit to Women's Groups, 1976, SRDP Files, SRDP Office, Mbeere, Siakago.

11. Discussions with officers from WANGU Investment Corporation, Kirogo, Weithaga Location, May, 1978.

12. Interview with Chairman, Mujini Harambee Women's Group, Mbiri Location, June 7, 1979.

13. Locational Community Development Assistant, Mbiri Location, June, 1978.

14. Government of Kenya, Development Plan, 1979-1983 (Nairobi: Government Printer, 1979), p. iii.

15. Ibid.

16. Interview with Chairman, Mujini Harambee Women's Group, June, 1978.

17. Among all the female questionnaire respondents in Nthawa 11% belonged to women's organizations, whereas 37% of the women from households operating at subsistence levels belong to such organizations. In Mbiri 34% of all women interviewed belonged to women's organizations, where 62% of those from subsistence households belonged.

VIII
Development Dilemmas: The Politics of Participation in Self-Help

We have tried all we can with self-help projects and we have made progress, but I believe our problems will be greater in the future than they are now.

> Respondent
> Nthawa Location

Chapter I posed four questions concerning 1) the role of Harambee in Kenya's political process; 2) the impact of Harambee on local-level development; 3) the ways in which Harambee links national and locally-defined socio-economic objectives; and 4) the effectiveness of Harambee self-help as a mode of development. Chapters II through VII explored various facets of these questions. This chapter returns to the four questions in order to make some concluding observations about Harambee based on the research findings.

HARAMBEE IN THE POLITICAL PROCESS

As a political phenomenon, Harambee constitutes a dispersal of power and a minimal threat to those at the center. In this context, self-help in Kenya must be viewed as politicized but powerless. At the local level it can provide effective grassroots development; at the national level, it does not jeopardize the status quo.

Since Independent in 1963, Kenyan political power has been increasingly centralized both geographically, in Nairobi, and administratively, in the ministries of the Central Government. This process of centralization has constituted a pragmatic response by the Kikuyu elite to the age-old problem of aggregating sufficient power to govern. Gerald Heeger analyzes this problem in The Politics of Underdevelopment in which he suggests that the critical task of most new nations is one of political consolidation and acquiring the power to rule effectively. In many cases elites confront one another over who will control the government, yet no one group of elites can gather sufficient power to control it effectively.[1]

Politics in Kenya is indeed characterized by the shifting patterns of elite coalitions which Heeger describes. Yet Kenya has not fallen victim to the immobilism which is likely to result from these elusive, fragmented relationships among elite groups, no one of which is able to consolidate power. The reason is that the political leadership has made a conscious effort to counteract the fragmentation of power among elites and to aggregate it at the center. This policy has included action in 1969 to weaken local government by shifting some major responsibilities as well as sources of revenue to the Central Government. Similarly, local political parties have little power.

In the process of building the center, the Central Government has "tossed back" to the rural areas the responsibility for local development efforts. This policy has had several effects:

First, it has freed the Central Government from the need to initiate local development for a sensitized and mobilized rural public. The impetus for change must come from the local community, and resources for development must first be generated there.

Second, it has placed a premium on organizational capacity in the rural areas. Those who can organize their communities and take some initiative in development projects can gain access to whatever governmental or other external resources exist for rural development through Harambee mechanisms. Chambers points out that "the failures of local government and the weakness of the party in representing and giving meaning to local aspirations have coincided with the growth and vigor of self-help groups."[2]

Third, it has sharpened the inter-elite conflicts and intra-elite linkages, as politicians and other leaders at all levels strive to shape coalitions which will benefit themselves and their communities.

Fourth, these elite linkages and the resulting patron-client relationships, based as they are on ethnic and regional foundations, blur and diffuse class differences. Reliance on community or ethnic connections in the local development process has strengthened these loyalties and obscured identification with others in a similar socio-economic stratum.

Fifth, the policy has clearly linked successful self-help projects with political effectiveness on the part of leaders and joined development issues to political ones at the local level.

Harambee, as a key instrument whereby this policy has been implemented, has, above all, served to legitimize and justify the emerging political and economic systems to the Kenyan public. Harambee is used by elites to justify the accumulation of wealth in an economic system which permits great inequities. In addition it is used to legitimize the amassing of power because it serves as the instrument whereby those who are the most powerful can best aid their local communities.[3]

Harambee encourages a transfer of individual resources from the prosperous to the poor and from urbanites to rural residents. It provides a mechanism whereby some highly visible private wealth is put to public use in ways which are considered socially and ethically appropriate. Wealthy persons are supposed to distribute largesse, and Harambee provides a way to allow more than a few to benefit from the contributor's bounty while at the same time bringing a variety of returns to the donor. This obligation is intensified by ethnic and regional competition and loyalties, for one who prospers is expected to render some assistance, not only to family members, but to those of his own background who are less fortunate. The origins of Harambee largesse can be seen in the pre-colonial feasts and festivities organized by a community's prosperous residents for the benefit of the entire group.

While large sums of money may flow from affluent urbanites to rural communities and from the more prosperous local residents into community facilities and services, this transfer of funds does not signal a structural change in the overall patterns of wealth. In fact, it helps perpetuate the existing pattern. One must then ask if the Harambee approach to development primarily serves national elites because it mitigates the harshness of a political and economic system which does not address issues concerning great disparities of wealth and welfare as well as the need for structural reform? Does Harambee distort rural perceptions and perhaps distract attention from fundamental changes which would benefit Kenyans more broadly – changes in tax laws, pricing on agricultural commodities, or regulation of behavior of members of statutory boards?

Anything more than marginal improvement in productivity and welfare at the local level requires an integration of the program or activity, including self-help, with other kinds of development efforts and rests on political strategy and philosophy. These strategies and the underlying philosophy are shaped by political elites. As Huntington and Nelson have emphasized, elite choices as to "the relative priority of economic growth, socio-economic equity, political stability, and other goals shape the forms, bases and patterns of participation."[4]

In the case of Kenya, local government and political parties have been stripped of power, and development through self-help has been encouraged. Self-help

is nationwide in emphasis and in appeal, but it consists of myriads of independent groups. There is no
centralizing agency, no para-statal organization, no
Kenyan non-governmental organization which represents
the interests of self-help groups and committees. Instead they are represented by individual leaders, members of the Kenyan elite, in a complex form of vertical
mobilization through patron-client relationships. Has
Harambee broadened political participation? Clearly it
has, but it has done so primarily within the context of
inequitable relationships, reciprocity between unequals
and benefits and services to be rendered to individuals
or to specific communities. Rural communities have
welcomed the opportunity to "tap" the resources of the
center in ways provided by Harambee efforts, and in
many cases they have learned to do so with skill and
acumen. Nevertheless, this system of mutuality between
national leaders and local communities, while enhancing
some forms of participation and aiding some communities, does not alter fundamental power relationships
within the political and economic systems.

HARAMBEE AND LOCAL DEVELOPMENT

What has been Harambee's impact on local development and how effective has it been in enhancing local-
level productivity and welfare? This question has been
explored along three dimensions: self-help's impact on
building rural infrastructure; Harambee's influence on
equity issues; and its relation to local-level participation.

Rural Infrastructure

Within the communities investigated, self-help has
contributed in a variety of ways to building rural
infrastructure. Chapter V has explored the benefits in
increased productivity to be derived from cattle dips,
the potential benefits of water supply, the anticipated
returns on education, and the mediocre results of
health projects. In building rural infrastructure,
Harambee draws on local resources and provides management and organizational experience for rural residents.
Several important characteristics of rural infrastructure generated through self-help mechanisms have
emerged in the course of the study. First, as an
approach to development, it has been unsystematic and
uneven, favoring those communities most advantaged in
terms of resource base, organizational skills and leadership. Some locations and some sublocations are
active and successful; others are not. Second, evidence from the six locations suggests that projects

tend to cluster. One project serving the community well is likely to encourage the community to undertake another, and soon the primary school, which is usually the first project, is accompanied by a secondary school, local water project, cattle dip, a church or two and perhaps a health project or a nursery school. This phenomenon is related to a number of conditions including good leadership, adequacy of the resource base, management capability and a sense of solidarity within the community.

Third, in some communities, particularly those where a number of self-help projects are present, there is a growing social infrastructure which is supporting community concerns. Churches, for example, assist primary or secondary schools, and women's groups build nurseries. This sort of support structure is emerging particularly in the more affluent and developed areas. Economic development seems to be enhancing rather than diminishing this trend.

Finally, evidence from the six locations suggests that Harambee projects function most satisfactorily when supported by an integrated development infrastructure. For example, cattle dips were valuable projects in the context of improved veterinary services and marketing opportunities for an increased milk production. Without these two components of infrastructure related to upgrading livestock, the cattle dips were of very little use, as the situation in Nthawa revealed. When the dips in that location failed to operate, people did not really care; there was nothing to be gained by repairing them.

Rural economic growth and social change do not wing their way into a remote location. They are part of an overall pattern of change linking center and periphery, however tenuously, and moving some of the benefits, opportunities and problems of development to the rural areas. Growth and continued development stimulate new initiatives. The self-help project which is successful is likely to lead to other projects, to new action on the part of the community, and to new interaction with the Government and other entities outside the community. Self-help does not operate in a vacuum.

Equity

How has self-help affected equity issues within local communities? Evidence from the locations investigated suggests that local development through Harambee efforts is not characterized by an overall pattern of discrimination against the poor. Contribution levels are higher among more affluent socio-economic groups while benefits are enjoyed across socio-economic strata. Chapters V and VI provide evidence to show that local communities are capable of selecting projects with broadly based benefits, organizing the type and amount of contribution so that individual contributions are equitably determined, and insuring management of projects to minimize discrimination in their use. The types of projects undertaken have not been of a sort easily captured by local elites for the benefit of only a few. In particular, education, health and water services bring wide benefits. In some cases, economic projects have started with an orientation toward elite interests but the benefits have been perceived and gained by others.

Data from the six locations suggest that it is possible to foster a decentralized mode of self-help development which does not consistently favor the wealthier members of the local community. Funds, labor and material come from all socio-economic levels to community benefits in which the poorer strata partake as well as the higher income groups.

Looking specifically at self-help projects and equity issues in relation to gender reveals that both males and females benefit widely from some projects, particularly water, primary schools and medical facilities. Girls are not benefiting as much as boys from Harambee secondary schools. Female students in Harambee secondary schools constitute a small fraction of the student body. Evidence indicates that the more affluent the location, the higher the percentage of Harambee secondary school students who are female.[5]

Women contribute the greater portion of the labor required of each family for a project. In many cases they are called upon for regular contributions of labor for maintaining school buildings. Male contributions of labor are likely to be tied to a specific and limited task in the building process. In instances where separate cash contributions are required of men and women, the women's contribution is sometimes a token five or ten shillings. Should the contributions be scaled according to ability to pay, the women's scale is always substantially lower than the men's. The disparities are indicative of the limited access women have to resources other than their own labor as well as to income-generating forms of productivity.

Self-help groups have some impact on intra-community equity, particularly insofar as women are concerned. Those groups with labor-sharing and income-sharing mechanisms are particularly useful to low-income families. Where investment and income-earning opportunities exist, membership in such groups is likely to be drawn from across the socio-economic strata of the local community. Local residents perceive such groups as an economic opportunity and a way to increase the welfare of the family and community. The benefits

shared within a group cut across socio-economic lines,
thereby promoting intra-community equity.

Local-level Participation

Participation of communities in the political
system through Harambee has been evaluated earlier in
this chapter. Participation in self-help projects
themselves must be considered in terms of decision-
making, implementation of projects and group activities, receipt of benefits and evaluation of programs
and projects. In the six locations, self-help community projects mobilized widespread participation through
contributions of cash and labor. Further, these contributions were made on an equitable basis. Approximately three-fourths of individual project contributions made by respondents were benefiting the contributors of all socio-economic groups. In general, those
respondents who expressed dissatisfaction with benefits
from specific projects did not reject the self-help
model altogether. Dissatisfaction focused on incomplete projects, those projects which were not directed
specifically toward the local community, and committee
misuse of funds.
Participation in planning and decision-making, as
well as evaluation of projects, easily become the pre-
serve of elites unless communities adopt representa-
tional procedures for selection of committee members.
While committee membership may be skewed toward more
affluent local residents, the affluent do not have a
monopoly on committee positions. There is, however, a
network of committee members, and within a community an
interlocking committee structure customarily exists.
Local notables circulate among the various committees,
and the committee structures emphasize continuity and
stability with few changes in membership. In terms of
planning, decision-making and evaluation of community
projects, women participate far less than men. Some
committees have token female representation; nevertheless, there is a clear bias toward male involvement on
the self-help committees.
Self-help groups provide some opportunity for
rural people, especially women, to develop and exercise
group or organizational skills. In particular, these
groups are learning systematic processes of fundraising, of organizing group activity, and of accountability for group funds and functions. Participants in
these groups affirm the value of their group membership
in both economic and social terms. Sometimes these
organizations take a lead in stimulating and organizing
rural change, as in the case of the women's groups
which are purchasing maize mills. More often, they
provide a means for their members to respond to a

changing environment and to seize some opportunities more readily grasped by an organized group than by an individual family. The performance of these groups is highly dependent upon the energy, integrity and imagination of the group leaders, particularly the chairman.

LINKS BETWEEN NATIONAL AND LOCAL SOCIO-ECONOMIC OBJECTIVES

The broad strategies for socio-economic change which have been pursued by Kenya include an emphasis on economic growth and on perpetuation of the social and economic institutions established during the colonial period. This approach has led to a pervasive dualism in which standards of living, as indicated earlier, vary greatly between the top 10 percent of the population and the bottom 25 percent. This dualism has meant the co-existence of small modern groups of wealthy, largely urban elites and large numbers of primarily rural poor. Poverty, rural stagnation, inequities, increasing levels of unemployment and a growing balance of payments problem characterize the Kenyan economy despite an average annual growth rate between 1964 and 1977 of 5.8 percent.[6]

As Kenyans have become aware of the shape of political and social life in an independent Kenya, they have perceived the key role of education in determining, in Laswell's terms, "who gets what, when and how."[7] Therefore, it is not surprising that rural Kenya has focused more than half of its self-help effort on educational projects. The links between education and upward mobility are apparent. Rural Kenyans perceive the utility of self-help as a means of extending mobility opportunities and of enhancing a family's and a community's share of the nation's resources and opportunities. Evidence from the six locations supports these widespread rural perceptions. The more prosperous locations have more educational opportunities, have more links into the center, have more active patrons, have a larger group of educated residents, and have more vigorous self-help projects and groups. Causality may be obscure, but there is clearly a relationship between the community's resource base, educational facilities, self-help projects or groups, and mobility opportunities.

Given these perceptions of the role of self-help, particularly in the area of education, what are the respondents' views concerning the future of their communities? Consistently, the respondents in the poorer locations were more optimistic about the future than the respondents in the more affluent locations. In the poorer locations, respondents mentioned very specific kinds of improvements in the quality of their lives and

196

in opportunities for themselves and their children
which they anticipated having in the relatively near
future.   These improvements included better housing,
more   adequate schools,   grade cattle, more   cash crops
along with   improved agricultural   methods.   They en-
visioned specific changes relatively easily implemented
by themselves and the community.
    In   the richer   locations, there   was   concern and
fear over   what the future would bring.   Many respondents mentioned   land shortage as a serious   problem and
worried about landlessness and joblessness within their
communities.[8]   Many predicted   a large   group of   educated,   unemployed young   people.   A number   predicted
consequent lawlessness,   violence,   family   disruption,
social   disorder and   upheaval.   Some expressed their
concerns   in economic   class terms suggesting   that the
rich   were   getting richer   and the   poor   were getting
poorer.   A comparison of locations on a spectrum   from
poorer to   richer shows   that as   locations   become increasingly prosperous,   the percentage   of   people dis-
turbed about the future of their community and of their
family increases.   Table 8.1 shows these figures.

Table 8.1
Six locations: respondent views about the future[*]
(in percent)

| | Viewpoint | |
	Optimism: good rate of development, improved standard of living	Pessimism: land short- ages, unemployment, social malaise
Soin	82	18
Nthawa	62	38
Mbiri	49	51
Kisiara	35	65
Kyeni	34	66
Weithaga	15	85

* Locations: poorer ... richer
N = 500

    What   causes   these various   perspectives   on   the
future?   Perhaps as   people become   more educated   and
have more exposure to the outside world, their expectations rise,   and they are therefore more   vulnerable to
frustration and discouragement.   It is also true, however,   that   there are   more serious   problems   of land
shortage   and unemployment   in the more   affluent loca-

tions. People have hoped and expected that education would solve these problems and are now coming up sharply against the realization that educational opportunity must be accompanied by economic opportunity and growth. They see few easy or obvious solutions to these problems. In the poorer locations, for the most part, neither the presence of educated unemployed youth, nor the expectation of rapid social change and economic betterment are as widespread, and therefore disillusionment and concern for the future may be less.

EFFECTIVENESS OF HARAMBEE AS A MODEL OF DEVELOPMENT

In Kenya self-help is the primary method communities can employ to try to alter the distribution of goods, services and opportunities and to try to move themselves into the "modern" sector, thereby diminishing the dualism which characterizes the nation. Unfortunately, self-help exacerbates differences between rich and poor localities, regions and ethnic groups. As an instrument for promoting development, Harambee has fostered an ad hoc approach directed toward "the squeakiest wheel." That is, those self-help groups and those communities which collect the most money and have the most articulate and well-connected leadership can command the most attention from outside donors, including the Central Government. Those who are best able to organize themselves can draw on the loyalties of their members who have prospered beyond the immediate locale.

Communities vary widely in their ability to raise funds and implement projects. Investigation revealed substantial differences in rates of project completion, complexity of projects undertaken, and satisfactory management of projects between the affluent and poor locations in each of the districts investigated. The Government tries to be evenhanded in its distribution of funds through the District Development Committees or through the Community Development Office. In the case of the former, each District receives Ksh. 50,000. Projects choice in the three districts was skewed toward productive projects in resource-poor locations. The reality, however, is that these aided project represent a very small portion of Harambee activity.

Thus, self-help, operating as it does through a decentralized organizational structure and strong patron-client links, inevitably increases disparities between geographical areas. Among the Kikuyus of Central Province, fundraising and organizational skills are highly developed. The national figures show that Central Province, already politically and economically the most powerful of Kenya's seven provinces, receives nearly one-third of the value of Harambee resources generated. Murang'a District, which ranks 11th in

terms of district earnings from all sources, raised 2.4
million shillings ($320,000) for the Murang'a College
of Technology in early 1978, 2.3 million shillings in
May, 1978 for the Kahuti water project, and in 1979 was
well on its way to the estimated 2.5 million shillings
needed for a technical high school.[9] Few districts in
Kenya can match this level of fundraising at the
present time. Such figures would suggest that inequities deriving from Harambee development efforts will
remain; in fact, the gap may widen as more active communities are able to build on a broad base of accomplishments.

Self-help groups may exacerbate these disparities
between communities. Given that successful income-
earning and investment are related to the resource base
of the local community, those groups in more prosperous
locations are able to generate benefits more readily
than those in resource-poor locations. Thus both community projects and self-help groups contribute to
widening differences among communities, adding to the
regional/geographic/ethnic disparities found in Kenya.

Communal solidarity, as it is found at varying
levels of political and social organization, is a
potent force in the process of Kenyan institutional and
organizational change. At the national level the leadership makes considerable effort to achieve a delicate
balance of position, status and power among ethnic
groups. Within some ethnic groups, various sub-groups
or geographically-based factions must also be carefully
balanced. National policy de-emphasizes ethnic loyalties. Political ethnic associations are forbidden, and
ethnic loyalties in other organizations are discour-
aged. Public documents refer to provinces or regions
rather than to ethnic groups although they may be virtually synonymous. Despite governmental policy, ethnic
loyalties are strong. The Kikuyu ability to mobilize
on behalf of Harambee projects within their community
is a reminder of the power of these ethnic ties. The
Government, with its small grants to individual projects, does not provide a counter-weight to the informal
channels which have been developed for raising funds by
organizations such as the Murang'a Harambee Development
Fund.

Does the Harambee approach to local development
permit the Kikuyus to have the best of both worlds? As
key figures in the Central Government they are able to
take advantage of government policies which strengthen
the center. As the ethnic group best organized and
most able to take advantage of the informal opportunities for development through Harambee, they again benefit. At the time of Kenyatta's death his vice president, Daniel Arap Moi, became President. As a non-
Kikuyu and member of one of Kenya's smallest ethnic
groups, Moi has brought increased ethnic diversity to

the high ranks of government. Nevertheless, Kikuyus continues to dominate Kenya's structures of economic and political power.

Is there a convergence of class interests and ethnic interests, particularly insofar as the Kikuyus are concerned? It seems premature to draw such a conclusion, although signs may portend this possibility for the future. There are in Central Province many rural poor, despite the area's relative affluence. Central Province may have fewer households living under a poverty line than any other, but in the mid-1970's it still had 46 percent of its households with incomes of less than Ksh. 3,000 per year.[10] Is there increasing differentiation within the Kikuyu community which may polarize that community along class lines? Perhaps, though evidence from Murang'a suggests that there is an effort to incorporate everyone into the development process. WANGU investments are open to all persons living in Kiharu Division, for example, and the Murang'a Harambee Development Fund requires contributions from everyone according to ability to pay. Experience in Murang'a suggests that at the present time ethnic loyalties take precedence over class solidarity.

If elites, elite choices and elite behavior are short-term determinants of development patterns, including self-help, over time socio-economic conditions are the key determinants. These include inter-state conditions affecting Kenya, as well as internal socio-economic patterns. Increasingly Kenya is, at the beginning of the 1980s, caught up in a spiraling inflationary cycle with tremendous increases in prices of imports. The cost of oil imports alone rose between 1977-1980 from 150 million shillings to 400 million shillings.[11] The balance of payments is an increasing problem. Shortages of food related to unpredictable weather patterns are not uncommon. Planning in times of plenty has not necessarily prepared for times of lean. With the economy growing at an average rate of 5.8 percent, a population growth rate of 3.5 percent, and an inflation rate recently at 18 percent, the purchasing power of most Kenyans has declined.[12] Political unrest within and among Kenya's neighbors makes Kenya a relative oasis of peace and stability, but the nation is not immune to turmoil and frustration, as the coup attempt of August, 1982 indicates.

If economic conditions become less favorable, as appears to be the case for many nations in Africa in the mid-1980's, and if hopes for increased prosperity dwindle, what is likely to become of self-help? At the local level, enthusiasm for self-help is likely to continue. Rural people are after all among the poorest 25 percent of the population receiving 6.2 percent of the income, and Harambee is one way to release private funds for the benefit of a community.[13] In the rural

areas, self-help, where it is effective, takes the
sting from the diminishing value of the shilling. A
family which can make a Ksh. 50 contribution to a water
project and eventually have a water supply piped to a
communal tap near this home experiences a tangible
benefit worth far more to family convenience and well-
being than the original Ksh. 50 contribution. This is
true for other projects as well.

If the six locations are indicative, attitudes in
the rural areas are generally positive toward development through Harmabee. Among respondents to the survey, five percent held negative attitudes toward self-
help. An additional six percent were indifferent or
uninformed. Eighty-nine percent responded positively
to the presence of projects and the prospects of new
projects within their home communities. At the village
level, Harambee projects are a direct and logical outcome of perceived need and local effort.

From Kenyatta's early, post-Independence address
to the present, the wananchi, the ordinary citizens,
have been hearing from the Government that they are responsible for developing their communities. The media,
national and local leaders have carried their message.
It has been absorbed and local communities have responded accordingly. Rural Kenyans believe that they
both can and should act to help themselves and improve
their communities. This is not to suggest that a different way of releasing resources might not be more
just, particularly on an inter-community basis. It
does indicate, however, the high level of local interest in improving community infrastructure and services.

For the elites who have been contributing large
sums to Harambee, pressures of declining economic
opportunity may diminish their sources of largesse as
well as their enthusiasm for self-help. In this case,
the magnitude of self-help is likely to decrease. For
the urban middle class, employment pressures, inflation
and shortage of goods and services are certain to
diminish the willingness to contribute to self-help
projects. Already pinched by numerous demands for contributions, this group of middle management bureaucrats, secretaries, drivers, and office messengers may
increasingly find self-help contributions a heavy and
unwelcome burden.

In any polity choices have to be made. In a
polity which is short of resources and limited in its
economic and social infrastructure, decisions concerning development priorities will be particularly difficult. The current state of Kenya's economy suggests
that they will become more so. Self-help permits an
element of choice in development decisions for both
local communities and the Central Government. In this
way, it has been a politically defusing mechanism help-

ing to avoid a political confrontation between dissatisfied rural communities and the Government. In the
context of a deteriorating economy, it is likely that
the Government will continue to foster this role for
Harambee in the nation's political process.

Self-help can be an instrument whereby an energetic community can participate in development efforts.
It can also be an excuse for inactivity on the part of
Government officials and a justification for inappropriate programs. That is, since responsibility for
projects lies with rural communities, Government officials may fail to address local issues and needs crea-
tively. If communities do not prosper through Harambee
mechanisms, the Government can claim it is their
"fault" for failure to mobilize. Responsibility lies
at the grass roots. In effect, the idea is a variation
on William Ryan's Blaming The Victim - it is the fault
of the impoverished for being poor.[14]

Many communities have used self-help methods to
build rural infrastructure. They have addressed basic
needs in education, health, social welfare and increased economic opportunity. The self-help approach
has released private resources for community purposes
and generated opportunity for some rural citizens to
participate in project planning and management as well
as benefits. In the process, Harambee has also served
Kenyan politics, and Kenyan elites, increasing control
at the center, providing a buffer between rural residents and the Government, permitting elites to garner
resources and establish local power bases, and legiti-
mizing the political and economic system of post-
Independence Kenya. The rhetoric of Harambee stresses
cooperative effort for the benefit of all. The reality
of Harambee underscores a system in which some communities, some groups and some national-level elites benefit far more than others.

Harambee cannot be isolated from this broader context in which it operates. As an approach to development, Harambee will ultimately be judged not only on
its contribution to local-level improvements in productivity and welfare, equity and participation. It will
be judged on its role in developing a polity to which
all Kenyans feel loyal and in which all may prosper.
In the immediate post-Independence years, Harambee
served as a unifying ideology. Through the 1970s it
brought tangible benefits to many rural communities.
In the 1980s its divisive potential, separating rich
communities from poor and prospering ethnic groups from
impoverished ones, may become more apparent.

At the outset of this study we posed a fundamental
query: How can the rural poor organize themselves to
participate in economic and social development and to
assure themselves an equitable share of its benefits?

We then explored this question through an investigation of Harambee in Kenya.   Does Kenya's Harambee self-help offer a model useful to the rural poor in other coun- tries?   This analysis of six locations in rural Kenya demonstrates that communities which organize self-help projects and groups can enhance their well-being sig- nificantly, can increase their productivity, and can improve their access to national resources.   Neverthe- less, this model has led neither to long-term organiza- tional efforts nor to overall structural changes in the distribution of economic and political power within Kenya.   For organizational models which can accomplish these objectives and bring sustained structural change, the rural poor will have to look elsewhere.

NOTES

1.   Gerald A. Heeger, The Politics of Underdevel- opment (New York: St. Martin's Press, 1974), p. 135.
2.   Robert Chambers, Managing Rural Development (Uppsala: Scandinavian Institute of African Studies, 1974), p. 87.
3.   Government of Kenya, Development Plan, 1979- 1983, op. cit.   The Plan states that in 1976, the poor- est 25 percent of the population got 6.2 percent of income and the richest 10 percent got 37.7 percent. The share of the richest 10 percent has been reduced since 1969 from 56.3 percent, p. 5.   See also comments on the role of Harambee in diminishing inequities, p. 40.
4.   Samuel Huntington and Joan Nelson, No Easy Choice (Cambridge: Harvard University Press, 1976), pp. 169-171.
5.   In Weithaga, for example, several subloca- tions had put substantial effort and money into Haram- bee boarding schools for girls.
6.   Government of Kenya, Development Plan, 1979- 1983, op. cit., p. 2.
7.   Harold Lasswell, Politics, Who Gets What, When and How (New York: McGraw-Hill, 1936).
8.   The questionnaire elicited comments from re- spondents concerning personal problems, problems of their community, and what they thought their community would be like 20 years hence.
9.   The Daily Nation, November 13, 1978.
10.   Government of Kenya, Ministry of Finance and Planning, Central Bureau of Statistics, Integrated Rural Survey, 1974-1975 (Nairobi: Government Printer, 1977).   Data is adapted from pp. 44 and 52.
11.   David Lamb, "Bloom Fades from Kenya's Eco- nomy," The Los Angeles Times, April 17, 1980.
12.   Government of Kenya, Development Plan, 1979- 1983, op. cit., p. 2.   See also Lamb, op. cit.

1983, op. cit., p. 2. See also Lamb, op. cit.
    13. Government of Kenya, Development Plan, 1979-
1983, op. cit., p. 5 and p. 40.
    14. William Ryan, Blaming the Victim (New York:
Pantheon Books, 1971).

Epilogue
Harambee Revisited, 1985

        The opportunity for a researcher to return to the
scene of his or her investigations is always a welcome
one. In June, 1985, I visited Kenya and took advantage
of the opportunity to inquire into the continuing role
of self-help in Kenyan politics and in the nation's
development efforts.   I was interested in knowing in
what ways self-help in Kenya might have changed in response to the political and economic conditions of the
mid-1980's and whether or not insights and observations
made in the late 1970's continued to be valid. I found
that Harambee is indeed a focal point of administrative, political, and economic activity at all levels of
the Kenyan polity. Indeed, some of the issues raised in
this study are currently under consideration by the
Ministry of Finance and Planning.   Following are some
brief observations on the current context in which
Harambee functions, on several emerging trends in self-
help, and a key issue arising in regard to Harambee in
1985.

THE CONTEXT

        In recent years economic problems have dominated
public concern.   They have ranged from a large external
debt to diminished agricultural production caused by
severe drought.   Perhaps the most important event in
early 1985 was the arrival of the long rains, putting
an end to the drought of 1984. In that year failure of
the rains caused the maize and wheat harvest to fall
about 40 per cent below normal levels and precipitated
a 25 per cent depletion in livestock across the country.   In his presentation of the 1985-1986 budget to
Parliament, the Minister for Finance and Planning, Professor George Saitoti, noted that "the fall in total
agricultural production was largely responsible for the
virtual stagnation of Gross Domestic Product in 1984,
which grew by only 0.9 per cent.[1]

In spite of the adverse effects of the drought not only on agriculture and livestock, but also on related sectors such as fisheries or energy, Kenyans are optimistic as they approach the rest of the decade. Recently high export prices, particularly of tea and coffee, have helped to improve Kenya's foreign exchange position, and the Government's monetary policies have reduced the rate of inflation to 9.1 per cent compared with 14.6 per cent in 1983 and 22.3 per cent in 1982.[2] Agricultural production is expected to grow, and analysts anticipate that this growth will have valuable spin-off for the rest of the economy. People are confident that the Government moved swiftly and effectively in purchasing and distributing grain during the drought and that it is acting responsibly in terms of fiscal management. There is a widespread feeling that Kenyans have endured a difficult time and are successfully surmounting a variety of tough problems, giving cause for national pride.

What is happening politically? When President Moi succeeded Jomo Kenyatta in 1979, he took as his "philosophy" the Swahili term "Nyayo" which means "footsteps" and which, in this political context, suggested that he was following in Jomo Kenyatta's footsteps. In collaboration with Mwai Kibaki, then Vice President and Minister of Finance, and Charles Njonjo, his Minister for Constitutional and Home Affairs, two prominent and powerful Kenyan leaders from Central Province, Moi endeavored to secure his position as President. By mid-1982, however, this coalition was slipping midst widespread accusations of corruption at high levels and increasing dissatisfaction with the economy. Moreover, both Njonjo and Kibaki appeared to be bidding for broad political support among the "wananchi," the average Kenyan citizens.

The coup attempt of August 1, 1982, has been widely blamed on Luo dissidents. Whether or not this accusation is accurate, the event led to careful efforts by Moi to secure his control of the political system and his continued leadership. His position seems to have been consolidated with the fall of Charles Njonjo in 1983. Acting with great skill, Moi managed to render Njonjo politically ineffectual while preventing him from becoming a martyr or hero to the Kenyan public. Kibaki remains in a prominent but circumscribed position as Vice President and a Member of Parliament from Nyeri District. It appears that the crisis of legitimacy for Moi is over.

In early June, 1985, Moi unexpectedly announced that grass-roots party elections would be held later in the month and that national elections would follow three days later on July 1. The Weekly Review states that this announcement took most politicians completely by surprise denying them, by the short notice, the cus-

tomary time for electioneering and forging alliances.[3]
This action gave the President a large measure of control and suggested that he was "calling the shots" for
this election. The pre-election mood was described as
one in which "an unusual calm prevailed with hardly
anyone expressing a desire to challenge the incumbent
officials at branch level. At the national level, the
situation was even worse. Except for the incumbents
defending their positions, only a handful had declared
their interest in contesting a national seat."[4] As one
analyst put it, "Where is the fever of yesteryear?"[5]
Clearly Moi is in control.

KEY TRENDS IN SELF-HELP

The 1984-1988 Development Plan specifies that cooperative effort through self help "will be encouraged
and should be expanded during the Plan period."[6] This
viewpoint was recently reiterated by President Moi at
the Kenya Institute of Administration when he stated,

> Harambee is a basic Kenyan institution. . .
> Harambee initiatives are the grass-roots voice of
> the people, indicating what they want and
> what they are prepared to do to achieve it. The
> Harambee spirit is one that we must take seriously
> as the cornerstone for local resources mobiliza-
> tion. . ."[7]

The Minister for Finance and Planning emphasized
the importance of the private sector and of cooperative
effort in his presentation of the 1985-86 budget, stating, "The theme of my Budget message today is 'Mobilisation of domestic resources for renewed growth.' It is
my hope that as a result of the measures I shall
announce later today, Kenyans will seize the opportunity to save and utilize our scarce resources for economic recovery."[8]

What are the salient trends to be found in Harambee self help activities in the mid-1980's? Statistics
indicate that the total value of Harambee resource mobilization is increasing; cash labor and material contributions in 1981 had increased 60% over the value of the
contributions in 1977.[9]

Regional Variation

Data from 1981 reveal that the considerable regional variation in Harambee continues to follow the
patterns of the mid-1970's. (See Chapter IV.) Table
E.1 shows the value of Harambee projects in each province as a percentage of the total value of projects,

Table E.1
Value of Harambee projects in each province as a
percentage of the total value of projects in 1977
and 1981

Province	1977	1981
Central	29	42
Coast	6	4
Eastern	20	19
Northeastern	.5	.4
Nyanza	11	7
Rift Valley	18	11
Western	15	16

Source: Ministry of Housing and Social Services, Self-
Help Statistics, 1977 and "Harambee Resource Mobilisation Policy Issues" a background paper prepared for
policy issues review for the 1984-85 budget. Table
1.1, p. 5.

comparing 1971 and 1981.
     Provincial Levels. The Central Province increase
in share of total Harambee resource mobilization from
29 per cent in 1977 to 42 per cent in 1981 is notable.
Central Province is approaching half of the value of
all Harambee activity in that year.   Rift Valley and
Nyanza shares have declined; shares of other provinces
remain approximately the same as in 1977.   Thus, the
thrust of Harambee toward Central Province and, therefore, toward predominately Kikuyu communities seems to
have accelerated at the beginning of this decade.
     District levels. At the district level, 1981
figures for cash value of Harambee contributions are
available for 26 out of 40 districts. These statistics
reveal that 56 per cent of funds raised for Harambee in
1981 were for projects in the ten most affluent districts.   Although the data are not complete, they certainly indicate a continuing orientation of self help
activity toward the richest districts.   Two districts
in Central Province which are among the wealthiest
quartile in Central Province lead in total cash value
and in per capita contributions in 1981.   They are
Nyeri and Kiambu.   Murang'a, also a predominately
Kikuyu District in Central Province remains in third
place. In some measure the levels of Harambee activity
in Nyeri and Kiambu reflect the competitive politics of
Njonjo (Kiambu) and Kibaki (Nyeri) during the early
1980's. Nevertheless, the continued thrust toward the
more affluent districts and toward predominately Kikuyu
districts is apparent.

Community Fundraising Techniques

Increasingly communities are using Harambee as a technique to raise "seed money" from the community which can then be used as leverage to attract outside funding from the Government of Kenya or from other donors. What may have started as a process for raising local resources - which it indeed does - can, in the context of Kenya's political system, become a mechanism for generating new funds directed toward the local community. It also means that communities knowingly undertake large projects which they will be unable to complete without substantial outside support, then trying to put pressure on the Member of Parliament, government or donors to provide assistance. Many communities have entered into this process vigorously, negotiating the shoals of competition for resources with considerable and growing acumen and inserting their own priorities into the allocation of national resources. This phenomenon, described in detail in the course of this book, particularly in Chapter III, is becoming more widespread in the mid-1980's.

Composition of Community Contributions to Harambee

Contributions to Harambee projects continue to be in cash, labor and material donations. While there are some areas in which the labor contribution as a portion of the aggregate Harambee effort is increasing and some where material contributions are significant, overall there is a trend toward monetization of Harambee contributions.[10] Data from 1980 and 1981 suggest that increasingly, on a national scale, people are giving cash rather than labor or materials. Geographic variation, however, is substantial, as confirmed in the analysis of the six locations, and noted in Chapter IV. Such variation occurs on a location-by-location basis, for there are large differences within districts.

A KEY ISSUE: CHANGING RELATIONS BETWEEN RURAL COMMUNITIES AND THE STATE

In Kenya, self-help processes are central to the complex interaction between the state and rural communities. Local community initiative, local political savvy, and local capacity to generate resources have brought pressures on the state system, modified the allocation of national resources, and shaped the relationship between the state and locl communities in unanticipated ways. Holmquist's analysis is insightful:

. . . , it is important to note that the positive
shifts in peasant-state relations should be seen
as partial peasant victories - as products of
local struggle . . . peasants have altered every-
day relations with the state in a direction more
favorable to themselves; they have squeezed more
money out of the state for peasant-defined needs
than the state would otherwise have allocated; and
as political space self-help represents political
opportunity - for protest as well as for material
advantage.[11]

At the present time the Government is grappling
with ways to capture control over Harambee. This is no
small task for there are vested interests in the Harambee system as it currently functions. The Government
wants to continue using Harambee to mobilize local resources for development, but it wants to do so in ways
which neither increase managerial and budgetary burdens
of the state nor increase inequities across the nation.
It wants to harness local energy, initiative and drive.
To do so, of course, may dampen Harambee since much of
its vigor arises in the perception of community not
governmental needs.
What precisely is the Government trying to accomplish in regard to Harambee? It is trying to assure
appropriate planning, regulation and accountability.
First, it is attempting to incorporate Harambee resource mobilization more adequately into the planning
process. This involves a long-term effort to shift
Harambee away from a focus on basic needs and social
service infrastructure to production-oriented and
employment-generating projects. Many rural people
would concur with this objective and there need not be
conflict between local and national objectives in this
regard. Respondents interviewed for this study had
many innovative ideas about potential, economically
viable, production-oriented Harambee projects. (See
Chapter VI.)
Second, the Government intends to look carefully
at the mix of capital costs and recurrent expenditures,
sources of funds for each of these categories and relative contribution of state and local community. Of
particular importance to the Government is gaining control over the recurrent budget. One analyst notes,
"about 50 per cent of the Government of Kenya recurrent
budget is now tied to operations and maintenance of
facilities (primarily in terms of staffing) that were
built on Harambee basis. This cannot continue indefi-
itely, as it increasingly limits the Government's ability to make decisions about investments . . ."[12] Indeed, Kenya's fiscal crisis and policies of the IMF and
the World Bank have put new pressures on the Government
to regulate Harambee and to limit recurrent costs re-

lated to social services.

Given the decentralized and ad hoc process of Harambee project development, the Government has clearly had relatively little control over the planning and design stages of self-help activity. To achieve this control and to maximize effective planning not only in regard to Harambee but also in regard to other public sector activities, the Government is in a process of decentralizing planning to the district level. In so doing, it hopes to bring about "the progressive rationalization of harambee initiatives, reducing waste and avoiding unsupportable recurrent burdens, without seriously curtailing the harambee spirit."[13] Initially there will be a detailed roster of harambee project activity which will be developed mid-1985 in order to incorporate Harambee activities into the district plan annexes for 1985-1986. Guidelines for Harambee resource mobilization are to be prepared, and a study of the types, trends, and viability of projects, as well as the viability of Harambee as an alternative form of taxation" is to be completed by the end of 1985.[14]

The central issue in this process is whether or not the Government can both control and encourage self help. Can it provide incentives while will channel new Harambee efforts into productive activities particularly in less affluent areas without oppressive and deadening regulatory mechanisms? Can it permit initiative and innovation to flourish at the local level while at the same time harnessing it to more comprehensive planning efforts? In short, can Harambee survive as a way to address locally perceived needs and still conform to the long-range interests of the state? Efforts to harness Harambee will require sensitivity and gradual implementation lest its value be diminished. That Harambee is an issue at all, that it is perceived by the government as a phenomenon bearing closer supervision, attests to the lively and controversial role which it has played not only in local resource mobilization, but also in national-level resource allocation.

To some extent Harambee has thrived on a competitive, confrontational style, and the consequence is that some communities have prospered and others have not. If the process is coopted by the Government perhaps the inequities resulting from differential access to resources through self-help can be addressed. Perhaps the "irrationalities" in this approach to development can be eliminated. These are worthwhile objectives. Worthwhile also are the many improvements in rural infrastructure and the numerous benefits from Harambee projects. The organizational and managerial capacities which the Harambee process has fostered within local communities, and the growing capabilities of rural people in speaking out and acting on their own behalf through cooperative, self-help efforts are valuable too. These benefits must not be lost in the process of rationalizing Harambee. There are many key issues in Kenya's political economy which remain untouched by a self-help approach to local development, but self-help as a method for mobilizing local energy and resources has moved the nation in new directions to the benefit of many rural communities. Kenya, and rural Kenyans in particular, should be proud of these accomplishments.

NOTES

1. The Weekly Review (Nairobi: The Weekly Review, Ltd.), June 21, 1985, p. 5.
2. Government of Kenya, Ministry of Finance and Planning and the Central Bureau of Statistics, Economic Survey, 1985 (Nairobi: Government of Kenya), 1985, p. 1.
3. The Weekly Review, (Nairobi: The Weekly Review, Limited), Jun 21, 1985, p. 4.
4. Ibid.
5. Ibid., p. 7.
6. Government of Kenya, Ministry of Finance and Planning, Development Plan, 1984-1988, (Nairobi: Government of Kenya), p. 45.
7. Daniel Arap Moi, "The Role of Harambee in District Development," speech at a KIA seminar, 1985, undated, p. 1.
8. The Weekly Review, (Nairobi: The Weekly Review Limited), June 21, 1985, p. 2.
9. Judith Geist, "Harambee Resource Mobilisation Policy Issue," a background paper for policy issues review for the 1984-85 budget, 1984, p. 5.
10. Ministry of Finance and Planning, "Harambee Resource Mobilisation and Basic Needs," prepared by J. Geist, background paper prepared for a National Seminar on Employment and Basic Needs Planning in Kenya," sponsored by the ILU, May, 1984, p. 10.
11. Frank Holmquist, "Self-Help: The State and Peasant Leverage in Kenya," Africa 54 (3), 1984, pp. 84 and 88.
12. Geist, correspondence, June 2, 1985.
13. Geist, "Harambee Resource Mobilisation Policy Issues", a background paper for policy issues review for the 1984-85 budget. p. 20.
14. Geist, op. cit., p. 23.

Bibliography

Books, Papers, Reports

Adelman, Irma and Morris, Cynthia. Economic Growth and
    Social Equity in Developing Countries. Palo Alto:
    Stanford University Press, 1973.
Almond, Gabriel and G. Bingham Powell. Comparative
    Politics: A Developmental Approach. Boston:
    Little, Brown and Company, 1966.
Anderson, J.E. "The Harambee Schools: The Impact of
    Self-Help," in Jolly, Richard (ed.). Education in
    Africa. Nairobi: East African Publishing House,
    1969.
Banfield, Edward C. The Moral Basis of a Backward
    Society. New York: The Free Press of Glencoe,
    1958.
Barkan, Joel, Frank Holmquist, David and Migot-Adholla
    Shem. "Is Small Beautiful, The Organizational
    Conditions for Effective Small Scale Self-Help
    Development PRojects in Rural Kenya," paper de-
    livered at the African Studies Association,
    November, 1979.
Bentley, A.F. The Process of Government. Bloomington,
    Indiana: Principia Press, 1949.
Black, C.E. Dynamics of Modernization. New York:
    Harper Torchbooks, 1966.
Bodenheimer, Susanne. "Dependency and Imperialism," in
    Fann, K.T. and Donald C. Hodges (eds.). Readings
    in U.S. Imperialism. Boston: P. Sargent, 1971.
Bolnick, B.R. Comparative Harambee: History and
    Theory of Voluntary Collective Behavior. Working
    Paper, #139. Nairobi: Institute for Development
    Studies, University of Nairobi, 1974.
Brokensha, David and E.H.N. Njeru. Some Consequences
    of Land Adjudication in Mbeere Division, Embu.
    Working Paper, #320. Nairobi: Institute for
    Development Studies, University of Nairobi, 1977.
CARE. Report on CARE Assistance to Development Proj-
    ects during Fiscal Year, 1976-1977. Nairobi: Un-
    published document, 1977.
CARE. Report on CARE Assistance to Minor Rural Water
    Schemes during Fiscal Year, 1976-1977. Nairobi:
    Unpublished document, 1977.
Chambers, Robert. Managing Rural Development, Ideas
    and Experience from East Africa. Uppsala: Scan-
    dinavian Institute of African Studies, 1974.
Chen, M. "Organizing the Poor in Bangladesh: Evolu-
    tion of an Approach to Rural Development," Paper
    prepared for the Rural Development Seminar, Har-
    vard Institute of International Development, Cam-
    bridge, Mass., March, 1981, p. 13.

Cohen, John M. and Norman T. Uphoff. Rural Development
    Participation: Concepts and Measures for Project
    Design, Implementation and Evaluation. Monograph
    Series #2. Ithaca: Cornell University, Rural
    Development Committee, 1977.
Coleman, James S. and Carl Rosberg. Political Parties
    and National Integration in Tropical Africa.
    Berkeley: University of California Press, 1966.
Collins, Randall. "A Comparative Approach to Political
    Sociology," in Bendix, Reinhard (ed.). State and
    Society. Boston: Little, Brown and Company,
    1968.
Deutsch, Karl W. "Social Mobilization and Political
    Development," in Eckstein, Harry and David E.
    Apter. Comparative Politics. New York: The Free
    Press, 1963.
Development Alternatives, Inc. Strategies for Small
    Farmer Development: An Empirical Study of Rural
    Development Projects. A report prepared for the
    Agency for International Development, Washington,
    D.C., 1975.
Devitt, Paul. Notes on Poverty-Oriented Rural Develop-
    ment. Report prepared for ODM, 1977.
Geertz, Clifford. "The Integrative Revolution: Pri-
    mordial Sentiments and Civil Politics in the New
    States," In Finkle and Gable. Political Develop-
    ment and Social Change. New York: John Wiley and
    Sons, 1971.
Geist, Judith. Correspondence with author. June,
    1985.
Gerth, H.H. and C. Wright Mills. From Max Weber:
    Essays in Sociology. Translated and edited with
    an introduction by Gerth and Mills. New York:
    Oxford University Press, 1946.
Gertzel, Cherry, Maure Goldschmidt and Donald Rothchild
    (eds.). Government and Politics in Kenya.
    Nairobi: East African Publishing House, 1972.
Heeger, Gerald. The Politics of Underdevelopment. New
    York: St. Martin's Press, 1974.
Heyer, D., Ireri and J. Morris. Rural Development in
    Kenya. Nairobi: East Africa Publishing House,
    1971.
Hill, Martin. Self-Help in Education and Development:
    A Social Anthropological Study in Kitui, Kenya.
    Unpublished paper, University of Nairobi, 1974.
Holmquist, Frank. "Implementing Rural Development
    Projects," in Hyden, Goran, Robert Jackson and
    John Okumu (eds.). Development Administration,
    The Kenyan Experience. Nairobi: Oxford Univer-
    sity Press, 1970.
Hunter, Guy. Modernizing Peasant Societies. London:
    Oxford University Press, 1969.
Hunter, Guy and Janice Jiggins. Farmer and Community
    Groups. Agricultural Administration Unit: Local

214

Diagnosis, Farmer Groups and Coordination of Ser-
vices Network; Paper IV, Overseas Development
Institute, London, 1976.
Huntington, Samuel P. Political Order in Changing
Societies. New Haven: Yale University Press,
1968.
Huntington, Samuel P. and Joan Nelson. No Easy Choice.
Cambridge: Harvard University Press, 1976.
Hyden, Goran, Robert Jackson and John Okumu (eds.).
Development Administration, The Kenyan Experience.
Nairobi: Oxford University Press, 1970.
Hyden, Goran. Beyond Ujamaa in Tanzania, Undevelopment
and an Uncaptured Peasantry. London: Heinemann,
1980.
Institute for Development Studies, University of
Nairobi. An Overall Evaluation of the Special
Rural Development Programme. Unpublished docu-
ment, Nairobi, 1972.
Institute for Development Studies, University of
Nairobi. Second Overall Evaluation of the Special
Rural Development Programme. Unpublished docu-
ment, Nairobi, 1972.
International Bank for Reconstruction and Development,
The World Bank, World Development Report, 1983
(New York: Oxford University Press, 1983),
p. 2.
Kenyatta, Jomo. Facing Mt. Kenya. New York: Random
House, 1965.
Kenyatta, Jomo. Harambee! The Prime Minister of
Kenya's Speeches, 1963-65. Nairobi: Oxford Uni-
versity Press, 1964.
Killick, A. Strengthening Kenya's Development Stra-
tegy: Opportunities and Constraints. Discussion
Paper, #239, Institute for Development Studies,
University of Nairobi, 1976.
Kuper, Leo and M.G. Smith (eds.). Pluralism in Africa.
Berkeley: University of California Press, 1969.
Lamb, Geoff. Peasant Politics. Dorset: Davison Pub-
lishing Limited, 1975.
Lambert, H.E. Kikuyu Social and Political Institu-
tions. London: Oxford University Press, 1956.
Lasswell, Harold. Politics, Who Gets What, When and
How. New York: P. Smith, 1936.
Lele, Uma. The Design of Rural Development, Lessons
from Africa. Baltimore: Johns Hopkins University
Press, 1975.
Lerner, Daniel. The Passing of Traditional Society.
New York: The Free Press, 1958.
Leys, Colin. Underdevelopment in Kenya. London:
Heinemann, 1975.
Lipton, Michael. Why Poor People Stay Poor: Urban
Bias in World Development. London: Temple Smith,
1977.

Little, Kenneth. West African Urbanization: A Study
     of Voluntary Associations in Social Change. Cam-
     bridge: Cambridge University Press, 1965.
Manners, Robert A. "The Kipsigis of Kenya: Culture
     Change in a 'Model' East African Tribe," in
     Steward, Julian H. Three African Tribes in Trans-
     ition, vol. 1 of Contemporary Change in Tradi-
     tional Societies. Urbana: University of Illinois
     Press, 1967.
Mbithi, P. and C. Barnes. A Conceptual Analysis of
     Approaches to Rural Development. Discussion
     Paper, #204. Institute for Development Studies,
     University of Nairobi, 1974.
Mbithi, Philip. Rural Sociology and Rural Development.
     Nairobi: East African Literature Bureau, 1974.
Mbithi, Philip M. and R. Rasmusson. The Structure of
     Grassroots Harambee within the Context of National
     Planning. Nairobi: University of Nairobi, De-
     partment of Sociology, Unpublished paper, 1974.
Mbithi, Philip and R. Rasmusson. Self-Reliance in
     Kenya, The Case of Harambee. Uppsala: Scandi-
     navian Institute of African Studies, 1977.
McClelland, David C. The Achieving Society. Prince-
     ton: Van Nostrand, 1961.
Migdal, Joel S. Peasants, Politics and Revolution.
     Princeton: Princeton University Press, 1974.
Migot-Adholla, S.E. "Traditional Society and Coopera-
     tives," in Widstrand, Carl Gosta (ed.). Coopera-
     tives and Rural Development in East Africa. Upp-
     sala: Scandinavian Institute of African Studies,
     1970.
Moi, Daniel Arap. "The Role of Harambee in District
     Development," Speech given at KIA seminar, 1984.
Muriuki, Godfrey. A History of the Kikuyu, 1500-1900.
     London: Oxford University Press, 1974.
Musyoki, Rachel Ndulu. Socio-Economic Status of
     Families and Social Participation: A Multi-
     Dimensional Analysis of Commitment and Alienation
     in Rural Kenya. Nairobi: University of Nairobi,
     Department of Sociology, thesis, 1976.
Mutiso, G.C.M. Harambee and Employment. Kenya Employ-
     ment Mission, Unpublished paper, 1972.
Mwaniki, H.S.K. The Living History of Embu and Mbeere.
     Nairobi: East African Literature Bureau, 1973.
Mwanzi, Henry A. A History of the Kipsigis. Nairobi:
     East African Literature Bureau, 1977.
Nelson, Courtney. Administration and Economic Planning
     in Eastern Africa. A Ford Foundation Program
     Evaluation, internal Ford Foundation paper, 1977.
Ng'ethe, Njuguna, H.W.O. Okoth-Ogendo, S. Schonherr and
     P.W. Wyeth. Reaching the Rural Poor: Lessons
     from the Kenya Special Rural Development Program.
     Working Paper, #295. Institute for Development
     Studies, University of Nairobi, 1977.

Ng'ethe, Njuguna. Harambee and Rural Development in
    Kenya, Towards a Political Administrative Re-
    Interpretation, Working Paper, #302. Institute
    for Development Studies, University of Nairobi,
    March 1977.
Orchardson, Ian Q. The Kipsigis. Nairobi: East Afri-
    can Literature Bureau, 1961.
Oyugi, W. Ouma. Participation in Development Planning
    at the Local Level. Discussion Paper, #163.
    Institute for Development Studies, University of
    Nairobi.
Oyugi, W. Ouma. Local Government and Development in
    Kenya since Independence. Staff Seminar Paper,
    #14, Department of History, University of Nairobi,
    1976-1977.
Peristiany, J.G. The Social Institutions of the Kip-
    sigis. London: George Routledge and Sons, 1939.
Popkin, Samuel L. The Rational Peasant. Berkeley:
    University of California Press, 1979.
Powell, John D. "Peasant Society and Clientelist Poli-
    tics," in Finkle and Gable, Political Development
    and Social Change. New York: John Wiley and
    Sons, 1966.
Reynolds, J. Eric and M.A.H. Wallis. Self-Help and
    Rural Development in Kenya. Discussion Paper,
    #241. Institute for Development Studies, Univer-
    sity of Nairobi, 1976.
Rosberg, Carl and John Nottingham. The Myth of Mau
    Mau: Nationalism in Kenya. New York: Praeger,
    1966.
Rudengren, Jan. Peasants By Preference? Socio-
    Economic and Environmental Aspects of Rural Devel-
    opment in Tanzania. The Economic Research Insti-
    tute, Stockholm School of Economics, 1981.
Runciman, W.G. and E. Matthews. Max Weber, Selections
    in Translation. Cambridge: Cambridge University
    Press, 1978.
Scott, James C. The Moral Economy of the Peasant. New
    Haven: Yale University Press, 1976.
Schermerhorn, Richard. Comparative Ethnic Relations.
    New York: Random House, 1970.
Sorrenson, M.P.K. Land Reform in the Kikuyu Country.
    Nairobi: Oxford University Press, 1967.
Sutton, F.X. "Social Theory and Comparative Politics,"
    in Eckstein, Harry and David Apter (eds.). Com-
    parative Politics. New York: The Free Press,
    1963.
Tendler, Judith. Inter-Country Evaluation of Small
    Farmer Organizations. Final Report for Office of
    Development Programs of the Latin America Bureau
    of AID (Program Evaluation Studies on Ecuador and
    Honduras), 1976.
Tilly, Charles. "Western State-Making and Theories of
    Political Transformation," in Tilly, Charles

(ed.). The Formation of National States in
Western Europe. Princeton: Princeton University
Press, 1975.

Truman, David. The Governmental Process. New York:
Knopf, 1951.

Uphoff, Norman. Analyzing Options for Local Institu-
tional Development, a report prepared by the Rural
Development Committee, Cornell University, for the
Office of Rural and Institutional Development,
Bureau of Science and Technology, U.S. Agency for
International Development, May, 1984, p. 19.

Uphoff, Norman T., John M. Cohen and Arthur A. Gold-
smith. Feasibility and Application of Rural
Development Participation: A State-of-the-Art
Paper. Ithaca: Cornell University Rural Development Committee, Monograph Series, #3, 1979.

Uphoff, Norman T. and Milton Esman. Local Organization
for Rural Development: Analysis of Asian Experience. Special Series on Rural Local Government
Committee, 1974.

Wallis, Malcolm. The Community Development Assistant
in Kenya: A Study of the Administration of Personnel and Rural Development. Discussion Paper,
#231. Institute for Development Studies, Univer-
sity of Nairobi, 1976.

Warwick, Donald P. and Charles A. Lininger. The Sample
Survey: Theory and Practice. New York: McGraw-
Hill Book Company, 1975.

Weaver, James and Jameson, Kenneth. Economic Development, Competing Paradigms. Washington, D.C.:
University Press of America, 1981.

Weisskopf, Thomas E. "Capitalism, Underdevelopment and
the Future of the Poor Countries," in Bhagwati,
Jagdish N. (ed.). Economics and World Order from
the 1970's to the 1990's. New York: Macmillan,
1972.

Wisner, Benjamin G. The Human Ecology of Drought in
Eastern Kenya. Unpublished dissertation, 1978.

Wolf, Eric. Peasants. Englewood Cliffs, New Jersey:
Prentice-Hall, 1966.

Young, Pauline V. Scientific Social Surveys and Research. Englewood Cliffs, New Jersey: Prentice-
Hall, 1966.

Periodicals and Newspapers

Ahluwalia, Montek S. "Inequality, Poverty and Development," Development Digest, vol. 16, no. 2, April,
1978.

Anderson, Robert. "Rotating Credit Associations in
India," Economic Development and Cultural Change,
vol. 14, no. 3, 1966.

218

Anderson, Robert. Voluntary Associations in History,"
    American Anthropologist, vol. 73, no. 1, February,
    1971.
Bendix, R. "Concepts and Generalizations in Compara-
    tive Sociological Studies," American Sociological
    Review, August, 1963.
Bolnick, Barry. "Collective Goods Provision through
    Community Development," Economic Development and
    Cultural Change, vol. 25, no. 1, 1976.
Bouman, F.J.A. "Indigenous Savings and Credit Socie-
    ties in the Third World," Development Digest, vol.
    16, no. 3, 1978.
Brokensha, David and j. Glazier. "Land Reform Among
    the Mbeere of Central Kenya," Africa, vol. 43, no.
    3, July, 1973.
Ciparisse, Gerard. "Anthropological Approach to Socio-
    economic Factors of Development: The Case of
    Zaire," Current Anthropology, vol. 19, no. 1,
    March-June, 1978.
Cornell University, Rural Development Committee. Rural
    Development Participation Review, vol. 1, nos. 1 &
    2, 1979-1980.
Daily Nation. Nairobi, issues for 1977, 1978, and
    1979.
DeWalt, Billie. "Alternative Adaptive Strategies in
    Mexican Ejido: A New Perspective on Modernization
    and Development," Human Organization, vol. 38,
    1979.
Frank, Charles R. and Richard Webb. "Policy Choices
    and Income Distribution in Less Development Coun-
    tries," Development Digest, vol. 16, no. 3, 1978.
Geertz, Clifford. "The Rotating Credit Association: A
    'Middle Rung' in Development," Economic
    Development and Cultural Change, vol. 10, 1962.
Godfrey, E.M. and G.C.M. Mutiso. "The Political
    Economy of Self-Help: Kenya's Harambee Institutes
    of Technology," Canadian Journal of African
    Studies, vol. 8, no. 1, 1974.
Hamer, John. "Voluntary Associations as Structures of
    Change Among the Sidamo of Southwestern
    Ethiopia," Anthropological Quarterly, vol. 40, no.
    2, 1967.
Hamilton, Gary. "Regional Associations and the Chinese
    City: A Comparative Perspective," Comparative
    Studies in Society and History, vol. 21, no. 3,
    July, 1979.
Holmquist, Frank W. "Self Help: The State and Peasant
    Leverage in Kenya," Africa, vol. 54, no. 3, 1984.
Holmquist, Frank W. "Toward a Political Theory of
    Rural Self-Help Development in Africa," Rural
    Africana, no. 18, 1972.
Keller, Edmond J. "Harambee! Educational Policy,
    Inequality, and the Political Economy of Rural

Community Self-Help in Kenya," Journal of African Studies, vol. 4, no. 1, 1977.

Kurtz, Donald. "The Rotating Credit Association: An Adaptation to Poverty," Human Organization, 32, 1973.

Lande, Carl. "Networks and Groups in Southeast Asia: Some Observations on the Group Theory of Politics,:" American Political Science Review, vol. 66, no. 1, 1972.

Lefeber, Louis. "On the Paradigm for Economic Development," World Development, vol. 2, no. 1, January, 1974.

Mbithi, Philip. "Harambee Self-Help: The Kenyan Approach," The African Review, vol. 2, no. 1, 1972.

Mbithi, Philip. "Issues in Rural Development in Kenya," East Africa Journal, vol. 9, no. 3, March, 1972.

Nayar, Baldev Raj. "Political Mainsprings of Economic Planning in the New Nations," Comparative Politics, vol. 6, no. 3, 1974.

Ollawa, Patrick E. "On a Dynamic Model for Rural Development in Africa," The Journal of Modern African Studies, vol. 15, no. 3, 1977.

Schluter, Michael. "Constraints on Kenya's Food and Beverage Exports," IFPRI Abstract, Washington, D.C. International Food Policy Research Institute, #44, April, 1984.

Scott, James C. "Patron-Client Politics and Political Change in Southeast Asia," American Political Science Review, vol. 66, no. 1, 1972.

Streeten, Paul. "Distinctive Features of a Basic Needs Approach to Development," Development Digest, vol. 16, no. 1, 1978.

Sunkel, Osvaldo. "National Development Policy and External Dependence in Latin America," Journal of Development Studies, 6, October, 1969.

Tipps, Dean C. "Modernization Theory and the Comparative Study of Societies: A Critical Perspective," Comparative Studies in Society and History, vol. 15, no. 2, March, 1973.

Walker, Malcolm and Jim Hanson. "The Voluntary Associations of Villalta: Failure with a Purpose," Human Organization, vol. 37, no. 1, 1978.

Weekly Review. Nairobi: Stellascope Ltd. Issues for 1977-1979.

Weekly Review. Nairobi: The Weekly Review, LImited. Issues for 1985.

Weingrod, Alex. "Patrons, Patronage, and Political Parties," Comparative Studies in Society and History, vol. 10, no. 4, 1968.

Wilkie, Mary. "Colonials, Marginals and Immigrants: Contributions to a Theory of Ethnic Stratifica-

tion," Comparative Studies in Society and History,
    vol. 19, no. 1, January, 1977.
Winans, Edgar V. and Angelique Haugerud. "Rural Self-
    Help in Kenya: The Harambee Movement," Human
    Organization, vol. 35, 1976.

Documents

Government of Kenya:

Ministry of Cooperatives and Social Services/Ministry
    of Housing and Social Services. Self-Help
    Schemes - 1968: A Statistical Analysis. Nairobi:
    Government cyclostyled report, 1969.
Ministry of Cooperatives and Social Services/Ministry
    of Housing and Social Services. A Statistical
    Analysis of Self-Help Projects, 1967-1971.
    Nairobi: Government cyclostyled report, 1972.
Ministry for Economic Planning and Community Affairs.
    Development Plan, 1979-1983, Part I & II.
    Nairobi: Government Printer, 1979.
Ministry of Economic Planning and Community Affairs,
    Central Bureau of Statistics. Statistical Ab-
    stract, 1978. Nairobi: Government Printer, 1978.
Ministry for Economic Planning and Community Affairs.
    Central Bureau of Statistics. Economic Survey,
    1979. Nairobi: Government Printer, 1979.
Ministry for Economic Planning and Community Affairs.
    Report of a University of Nairobi team in prepara-
    tion of the 4th Development Plan, 1979-1983.
    Towards Strategies for Intensified Social Develop-
    ment. Nairobi: Unpublished report, December,
    1977.
Ministry of Economic Planning and Development, Central
    Bureau of Statistics, The Integrated Rural Survey
    1976-1979, Basic Report, 1982.
Ministry of Finance and Planning. Central Bureau of
    Statistics. Economic Survey, 1977. Nairobi:
    Government Printer, 1977.
Ministry of Finance and Planning. Central Bureau of
    Statistics. Economic Survey, 1985. Nairobi:
    Government Printer, 1985.
Ministry of Finance and Planning. Development Plan,
    1974-1978. Nairobi: Government Printer, 1974.
Ministry of Finance and Planning. Development Plan,
    1984-1985. Nairobi: Government Printer, 1984.
Ministry of Finance and Planning. "Harambee Resource
    Mobilization and Policy Issues," background paper
    prepared by J. Geist for policy issue review for
    1984-85 budget, 1984.
Ministry of Finance and Planning. "Harambee Resource
    Mobilization and Basic Needs," background paper

prepared by J. Geist for National Seminar on Employment and Basic Needs Planning in Kenya, 1984.

Ministry of Finance and Planning. Central Bureau of Statistics. Integrated Rural Survey, 1974-1975. Nairobi: Government Printer, 1977.

Ministry of Finance and Planning. Central Bureau of Statistics. Social Perspectives. Vols. 2, 3, and 4 for 1977, 1978 and 1979.

Ministry of Finance and Planning. Statistical Abstract, 1976. Nairobi: Government Printer, 1978.

Ministry of Finance and Planning. Central Bureau of Statistics. 1969 Census of the Republic of Kenya. Nairobi: Government Printer, 1970.

Ministry of Housing and Social Services. Department of Social Services, Community Development Division. Self-Help Statistics. Vols. 1974, 1975, 1976 and 1977. Nairobi: Unpublished reports.

Colonial Reports

Embu District Documents:

Annual Reports, 1930-1961. Microfilm, Reels 14 & 15. Government of Kenya Archives, microfilm library.

Handing Over Reports. Reel 85, HOR/278-296. Government of Kenya Archives, microfilm library.

Political Record Book 24-30. Reels 68 & 69. Government of Kenya Archives, microfilm library. Including Embu Land Tenure System; History of Embu; Notes on the Embu Division and People; a Study of Kabare Village.

Missions and Churches, 1931-1957. File DC/EBU.9.1. Government of Kenya Archives.

Fazan, S.H. An Economic Survey of 'Kikuyu Proper', Kiambu, Fort Hall and Nyeri. A paper for the Commission on Native Lands to be used for developing a policy suitable for the Reserves, 1932. Government of Kenya Archives.

Fisher, J.M. Reports on the Kikuyu. Material collected from August, 1950 to July, 1952 under the auspices of the Colonial Social Science Research Council. Government of Kenya Archives.

Kericho District Documents:

Agricultural Gazetter, 1956. Written by the District Agricultural Officer, February, 1955. Government of Kenya Archives.

Annual Reports, 1920-1960. Sec. 1, Reels 35 & 36. Government of Kenya Archives, microfilm library.

Handing Over Reports, 1930-1938. Reel 2. Government of Kenya Archives, microfilm library.

Political Record Book. Sec. 2, Reel 4. Government of
     Kenya Archives, microfilm library.
Maher, Colin. Soil Erosion and Land Utilisation in
     the Embu Reserve. Part I, April, 1938. Govern-
     ment of Kenya Archives, Unpublished document.

Murang'a District Documents:

Annual Reports, 1920-1961. AR342-384, Reels 12 & 13
          (AR 1920 to 1930, Reel 11). Government of
          Kenya Archives, microfilm library.
Handing Over Reports. HOR/297-338. Government of
          Kenya Archives, microfilm library.
Labour Section of Document Section. Communal Labour
          File. Govenment of Kenya Archives.
Political Record Book. PRB/31/38. History of Ft.
          Hall, 1888-1944. Government of Kenya Archives,
          microfilm library.

Government of Kenya District Documents:

Embu District Development Plan, 1974-1978. Nairobi:
     Government mimeographed document, 1974.
Embu District Development Plan, 1984-88. Nairobi:
     Government mimeographed document, 1984.
Kericho District Development Plan, 1974-1978. Nairobi:
     Government mimeographed document, January, 1976.
Kericho District Development Plan, 1984-88. Nairobi:
     Governent mimeographed document, 1984. Ministry of
     Housing and Social Services, Community Development
     Office, Embu District, Annual Reports and files
     for 1963-1978, as available.
Ministry of Housing and Social Services, Community
     Development Office, Kericho District, Annual
     Reports and files for 1963-1978, as available.
Ministry of Housing and Social Services, Community
     Development Office, Murang'a District, Annual
     Reports and files for 1963-1978, as available.
Murang'a District Development Plan, 1974-1978.
     Nairobi: Government mimeographed document, May,
     1976.
Murang'a District Development Plan, 1984-88. Nairobi:
     Government mimeographed document, 1984.
Nyasime, D.O. "Final Report on Mbeere SRDP," May 1977.
     From the SRDP files in Siakago, headquarters for
     the Mbeere SRDP.

Index

224